Language As Disclosure

Carolyn Norman Slaughter

To Charles,
   without whom none of this; he enabled every turn of the screw.

Eternal love and gratitude to Elliott,
who rescued and revived this project when it had foundered,
who conceived and invented the means of producing the book,
tutored, guided, managed its production,
and published it himself

Contents

Preface

In university English Departments in the 1980's when I was writing *Language As Disclosure*, "theory" was the order of the day. Deconstruction was that theory, and Jacques Derrida (Irvine, Paris), who had introduced and developed it, was Principal Theorist. I was a Ph.D. student in Critical Theory at the University of Arizona, reading major works of Western thinkers from the ancients to the postmoderns—including the works of Martin Heidegger. Derrida had been a student of Heidegger's. Indeed, his "Deconstruction" was his appropriation of Heidegger's *Destruktion*—the task Heidegger had set for himself, to rethink the history of ontology (*Being and Time* 44).

Even before I had read the works of Derrida I had become accustomed to the literary climate that issued from Deconstruction. I had developed an antipathy to the "program" (as I considered it) of searching out a literary text's sources and instances of power, effect, in order to "stamp them out"—a process called "demystification." It was part of the general reification and/or psychologizing of "knowledge" underway at that time (and since) as science-technology settled over (dimmed down or snuffed out) our historical sense of it.

This was an exciting period in university literary studies. Perhaps there had never been more intense, rigorous intellectual activity than during this moment at the pinnacle of the postmodern movement when literary works were reapproached, reexamined, and reappropriated or dismembered or dissolved under the acid edge of the ruthless scrutiny of the new theoretical apparatus. Derrida defined the objective (to *deconstruct* the Western philosophical tradition); demonstrated the procedure (by way of his own lectures, articles, books); rallied (awakened, aroused, inspired) the willing, the capable; and set the pace.

At the heart of the postmodern project lay the deconstruction of language itself. Derrida's "*différance*" presented the dilemma: language differs in kind, he said, and in time from whatever it might "say." Indeed, it was a postmodern mantra: language is a system of signifiers signifying merely other signifiers; language tropes other language, is cut off ineluctably from the world of things it intends to "say."

I watched the "best and brightest" academic intellectuals set about the tedious, towering task of achieving not what they intended but what has since transpired: the undermining of English Departments, the concomitant unraveling of Humanities programs, and—more serious and pervasive—the levelling or dissolving of the purpose of the university itself and the meaning of *knowledge*.

Language for Heidegger, meanwhile, operates inevitably at the core of realities, for better or worse. It is language itself that opens—dis-closes—the world, wrests it from chaotic disorder.

My dissertation, *Language As Disclosure*—which argues that Derrida's strongest concepts were dependent on Heidegger's original notions even as they sought to displace them, that Derrida was mistaken about Heidegger's thought and had led current Western thinking astray—was not accepted for publication, though it received a little flurry of attention at the time.

Today I am offering the book *Language As Disclosure* again, again at a moment when Heidegger's standing is at issue after publication of his *Black Notebooks*. I have revised the book a little and wish to make it available to the idle Heidegger reader.

The burden of my book is not argumentative, not even "theoretical," but "disclosive." I.e., it presents Heideggerian readings on the nature of language as I show it "working" in works of five American modernist authors. I contend that these authors were "seeing" what Heidegger was "seeing," and it is that rich insight into the more-than-ever-essential working of language that I hope to "disclose."

Language As Disclosure

After Nietzsche: Heidegger

Nietzsche (chaste syphilitic) was father of the moderns, precursor of a future man—proclaiming that he (that Zarathustra) was not that (over-) man but was sent to bear witness of that man.

Of course Nietzsche was not father of the moderns and not even precursor of the future (though Zarathustra perhaps was), but father-murderer. He murdered not God (God was dead) but Plato. Nietzsche made us orphans. After Nietzsche we had to father ourselves.

Heidegger's response to the rupture in the paradigm was not to forge ahead, but to go back to the beginning. Among the ruins of Western philosophy he found the Phoenix embers of a pre-Socratic order and breathed them back to life. The decision was whether (1) to submit to the onrushing currents of so-called history or time, of technology, of a scientistic "progress" negligent-to-contemptuous of its human way (i.e., the choosing-shaping of leading questions), of perhaps the fatal abandonment of human destiny; or (2) to take hold: resolutely and with human violence to break open new paths, guided, however, not by arbitrary or capricious whim or by appetite, drive; not by principle nor by formal or logical systems; but by the Event of Being. The apprehension of such an event required nothing less than the re-viewing, -thinking, -saying of every thing. Thus the works of Heidegger open up a new "way," based and guided and historically going-on outside or prior to the history of transcendental metaphysics, and they at the same time recover by re-vision the discredited Western philosophic tradition (Gadamer 229-30; Caputo 259-60).

Some of the habits of thinking that Heidegger's thinking super-sedes are: (1) analysis as cutting-up, -apart, things that never exist in such compartmentalization, things that are always with- or toward-each other—e.g., mind and body, subject and object, human and world; (2) categorization according to genus-species; (3) concepts of time and space as discrete, linear, and objective; (4) atomistic or organic grounding concepts; (5) formula or formalization as methods of understanding (form-content, process); (6) language as represen-tation: grasping, capturing—and reducing and dominating the entity inscribed, described; and of course (7) an entire metaphysical tradi-tion—Being as presence, as essence, as totality, as unity (Heidegger reuses all of these words but their former meanings are rejected or erased), truth as *adaeguatio, correspondentia, convenientia*; (8) in short: rationality as the nature, the way, and the limit of thinking-toward-truth.

The complaint brought most often against Heidegger is that he did *not* escape transcendental metaphysics (that his Being is the old metaphysical Be-All in a new arrangement of terms), that he occupied himself with philosophy and, of all things, ontology, when the possibility of both had passed below the horizon. The problem in reading Heidegger is that one must go with him, follow him, into his thinking. One cannot draw his thinking or its insights back into the framework of the past or present day. Every thing and its site and its ground must be addressed in a new way; afterwards it is not that one must find new language (all languaging language is new) but that "language" too has been changed; it is re-charged with new "meaning" (and "meaning," of course, means something new). Much opposition to Heidegger's thinking is not opposition at all (it has never stood before it), but a declining to follow.

I shall address here, briefly, two aspects of the opposition of one of his most formidable critics, Jacques Derrida, addressing thereby some problems of reading Heidegger and some central issues in his thinking.

The opposition of Derrida is essential, for Derrida's thinking comes through, by way of, Heidegger's thinking to stand, as he says, on the horizon of Heidegger's ontico-ontological difference.[1] Since Derrida's radical deconstruction of all historico-ontological "meaning" wields a dominating influence on the positions and the direction and tone of institutional thinking today, a brief preview and comparison of his thinking and Heidegger's may clarify the position and the direction and the tone of the work I am offering below in my readings of modern novels.

Derrida takes as the ground of his thinking the subverted Western metaphysical paradigm, for there is no other ground today; "ground" is a matter of fact for us, not choice. All the language and the systems of thinking extant in the West belong to, partake of, carry in them, this now untenable founding logocentrism. It was Nietzsche who undermined the base, and it was Heidegger who uncovered, for Derrida, the nexus of the predicament.

The path of deconstruction makes its way into the interior of a thinking-work, seeking its very foundations (*Of Grammatology* 60). Each work of deconstruction is another exposure of the inner and inter- structures of Western logocentrism and the void that functions as its center. Perhaps never before has rational thinking been given such a rigorous rational examination. Powerful Western thinking and thinkers are exposed in Derrida's readings as inconsistent or contradictory, as forgetful or disingenuous.

Derrida uses the kinds of thinking he finds ready-to-hand, not systematically, yet with unrelenting logic; he is something like his version of Levi-Strauss' *bricoleur* dreaming toward an engineering (*Of Grammatology* 138-9; "Structure, Sign, and Play" 256). In many respects his way is a quasi-Heideggerian scouting around on the

---

[1] Ref. this moment in *Kant and the Problem of Metaphysics* 118, 128, and *Being and Time* 32-35.

chance that something will show up;[2] something does. The contorted shapes his thinking takes are experimental and difficult and arresting: he goes where he may not go; he makes new paths as he goes (61). This going, making, too is a Heideggerian wresting of being from nonbeing[3] (compare his view of the futility of desire's desire to wrest meaning from language, below). He thinks in such shapes as shadows: "as-though … ," but not. He thinks under erasure (as Heidegger did), in parentheses, hoping to exhaust the faulty paradigm (60), hoping to force (like rabbits in the brush) the future.

Since Derrida takes as his point of departure the ontico-ontological difference of Heidegger, above, I will first compare their elaboration of this point, with particular reference to passages in Derrida's *Of Grammatology* and Heidegger's *Kant and the Problem of Metaphysics*, works that examine *a priori* structures of human understanding, preconditions for experience.

In *Of Grammatology* the moment of *différance* is the movement of the trace, a *production* of difference.

> It is not the question of a constituted difference here, but rather, before all determination of the content, of the *pure* movement which produces difference. *The (pure) trace is* différance. (63)

Différance does not belong to the constitution or the content of different entities. The trace is not an event in clock time. It is a pre-"experience" process producing the possibility, the precondition of, the predisposition toward, language—which can afterwards produce for itself a (non-) origin (the trace as trace).

> … its [the trace's] possibility is by rights anterior to all that one calls sign … , concept or operation, motor or

---

[2] Or "announce itself in the filigree of some margin" (*Margins* 61).

[3] Compare Heidegger, *An Introduction to Metaphysics*, trans. Ralph Manheim (New Haven: Yale UP, 1959) 110.

> sensory. This *différance* is therefore not more sensible
> than intelligible and it permits the articulation of signs
> among themselves within the same abstract order ... or
> between two orders of expression.... . (62-63)

The trace, not sensible, founds sensibility, makes possible the sensible plenitude of presence; not intelligible, founds intelligibility, makes possible the conceptual (metaphysical) oppositions of, for example, "the sensible and the intelligible, ... signifier and signified, expression and content, etc." (63), the articulation of differences: writing (60). The trace as the movement of an arche-writing, arche-synthesis, is the *a priori* production and constitution of human understanding.

The trace marks the mind with an imprint, *engramme*, that is not physiological, that does not exist in time or space, "neither *in* the world nor in 'another world,' which is not more sonorous than luminous, not more *in* time than *in* space, ..." (65). The mark is an effect, a change, a producing of a differ-ing/ence. An evolution occurs, not physical, in a worldless "zone," an event which is the "temporalization of a *lived experience*." Out of nowhere, in the movement of a temporalizing process we can not follow, "differences appear ... produce elements" as such, which are the elements of the writing of differences that will constitute forms—"the *texts*, the chains, and the systems." "*The trace is the differance* [sic] which opens appearance [*l'apparaître*] and signification." All forms are founded in the non-stuff of the trace/*engramme*. This movement is "*the absolute origin of sense in general. Which amounts to saying once again that there is no absolute origin of sense in general.*" This moment or movement or trace of differing differentiates "the 'world' [appearing] and 'lived experience' [appearance]."

This point of *différance*, the very prerequisite and precondition for human experience, is under erasure.

> [*Différance*] can ... be thought of in the closest prox-
> imity to itself only on one condition: that one begins

by determining it as the ontico-ontological difference before erasing that determination. The necessity of passing through that erased determination, the necessity of that *trick of writing* is irreducible.... (23-24)

This "trick of erasure" is in one sense the trick of making deliberate (aware, careful) use of a fiction.[4] There is no possibility of discovering or determining an "origin"—but it is necessary to posit one as a functional point of departure, as a means of setting-forth, beginning or going on. In a second sense, this "trick of erasure" may be the trick of wriggling out of an old skin. It is something of a new birth, a moment of evolution, determined in this case by human will. Perhaps *différance* eventually is the difference between Zarathustra and the over-man. We pass from an era of parousia, receptivity-reading, into a new day of pure writing. This notion is not new with Derrida. Heidegger reading Kant states that it is divine creation that does not receive or perceive (read) ob-jects but e-jects (writes) them (30f.). Heidegger joined with Nietzsche in his annunciation of an over-man who in overcoming himself "comes into his own full nature" so that he becomes capable of assuming dominion over the earth (*What is Called Thinking* 57f.).

We compare a similar moment in Heidegger's reading of Kant's explication of the *a priori* in *Critique of Pure Reason*. Heidegger-Kant describes a pre-ontological structure. It too founds all differences; it too is elaborated as a pre-experience activity which provides the

---

[4]Joseph N. Riddel describes Derrida's use of the term "erasure" in a footnote to his article "Metaphoric Staging": "To put a concept 'under erasure' means to submit it to a rigorous questioning in a manner that reveals the figuration of the concept, that it is grounded in a reference that is no less metaphorical, and so on. The erasure of a concept (or crossing it out) nevertheless leaves an imprint or trace of it, so that far from simply negating or vanquishing the notion to the status of a fiction or false idea, erasure reemploys the concept as a problematic or illogical notion, a functional nonconcept, a splitting or pluralizing of its illusory univocity or its singular, referential meaning..." (355).

preconditions and the pre-structures for the sensibilization and the articulation of essents. It too describes something of a process—though it is not so much an economic notion as a structural. But the dissimilarities are essential. The *a priori* structuration is not a prior event, for it is always already occurring. It is not a structure under erasure afterwards. Bringing the structure to light is not the artificial invention of an origin necessitated by a guilty error of perspective that we are not free yet to free ourselves of, and not a track by which we track our history out of a dark metaphysical forest. The "genesis" of pure reason that Heidegger traces in Kant's work is an originating (not an origin, not a non-origin) of the *a priori* ontological structures that ground human orientation toward entities. It is a radical re-vision of human being, not a strategic re-creation.

Heidegger characterizes this reading as " 'analytic' in the broadest sense of the term" (*Kant and the Problem of Metaphysics* 45).

> The term "analytic" as it appears here does not signify a dissolution in the sense of a reduction, i.e., as if it were a matter of reducing pure finite reason to its elements. Rather, the term signifies a "dissolution" which loosens and lays bare the seed [*Keime*] of ontology. It reveals those conditions from which springs an ontology as a whole according to its intrinsic possibility. In Kant's own words, such an analytic "is brought to light by reason itself;" it is that which "reason produces entirely out of itself." This analytic, then, lets us see the genesis of finite pure reason from its proper ground. (46)

Analysis in this sense does not dissolve a thing into elements. It sets free and brings to light the founding structures (seeds) of, in this instance, pure reason—the preconditions which determine its "intrinsic possibility." In Western metaphysics the core of entities (as presence), their essence, is grounded and articulated in pure reason. Heidegger in this reading, however, delves through essences, past reason, beneath metaphysics, to a ground of a different kind. (Ground is not cause, is not organic mother.)

The ontological structures of human understanding are delineated in terms of Kant's analytic of pure reason. Heidegger critiques and completes Kant's *Critique*, meanwhile developing his own analytic of structures and forestructures proposed previously in *Being and Time*. (According to Walter Biemel, *Kant and the Problem of Metaphysics* is a part of the work originally outlined but never published as the second division of *Being and Time*.) He is examining the very pre-ontological structures that Derrida takes as his point of departure, the moment of *différance* that differentiates, in Derrida's terms, "lived experience" from "the world."

For Heidegger-Kant, human understanding (for Kant an "act of representation of unity," *Kant and the Problem of Metaphysics* 78) is indeed a secondary, finite horizon already predetermined in its structures and its modes by a primary pure horizon projected by the pure imagination. The original ground of the conditions and possibilities of, first, pure understanding and, second, finite understanding is temporality. Time in the modes of its temporalization underlies and shapes the pre-ontological unifying structures of human understanding; provides the site of ob-jectivity—the site for the meeting, the inter-encounter, inter-course of human understanding and essents of whatever kinds; determines the possibilities in the structures of beings and of experience. Time (not Kant's series of *now*'s) is a primordial pure horizon of existence. All beings "are" and may be "known" in and according to temporality. (The categories express modes of temporalization, 110.) Heidegger has opened up beneath the metaphysics of reason a ground fertile enough to support more or other forms of specularity. The pure pre-ontological and the finite ontological structures delineated here show the character of unifying-synthesizing the manifold of intuited objects, betray a necessary predisposition for rules, for conceptual regulating (thinking), and bring their own *a priori* horizons and modes of experience. Now for Kant, as for Derrida, these structures which mediate between human being and entities-in-themselves also separate them. Beyond human understancing Kant conceptualizes an unknowable something, a unity beyond the manifold intuited sensibly. Kant designates this projected entity as "X." But Heidegger reappropriates this X as the nothing, as "pure horizon" (127-8), the very condition for the possibility for the rising "appearing" of the object in the first place (Derrida's passivity of sensibility) and for its apprehension (Derrida's writing). Beyond or in the phenomenon is not an unknowable essent, but an ontological horizon against or upon which the essent may come into view and into purview. The ontological structures which for Kant and Derrida mean exile from reality constitute the ground for the possibilities of reality for Heidegger. The turning-from (differing, deferring) in Derrida's différance is Heidegger's turning-toward, which provides the horizon for the experience of ob-jects (74ff.). The *difference* between the ontic and the ontological, between entity and being (*Of Grammatology* 22) is Derrida's point of departure from Heidegger's ontico-ontological *unity*.

There are important points of agreement. The *a priori* structures in the Heidegger-Kant study resemble Derrida's: (1) in their site: the non-site of a no-place in pure (thematically undifferentiated) temporality and non-space; (2) in their activity: the constitution and production of essents/elements, of all texts, chains, and systems, and (3) in their prior grounding function: "The unheard difference between the appearing and the appearance ... is the condition of all other differences ... [and, as *trace*, is] 'anterior' to all *physiological* ... or *metaphysical* problematics ..." (Derrida, *Of Grammatology* 65). These structures provide the preconditions for and the intrinsic possibilities of sensibility and intelligibility—for human experience and for a world.

There are other interesting points of comparison. Compare, for example, the motivating and structuring function of temporalization; compare Derrida's originary (ontological) passivity (of language, of sensibility) with Heidegger-Kant's originary (pre-ontological) intuitivity, receptivity; compare Derrida's arche-synthesis that underlies so as to permit differences with the primary synthesis in Heidegger-Kant that underlies and mediates between intuition and thinking; compare Derrida's spacing, the other-than-experience, the dead time interrupting what could otherwise be taken for presence, with Heidegger-Kant's X, nothing, pure horizon, where essents can appear; and compare the secondary appearance or production of subjectivity or apperception in both.

There is some surprising (but not essential) agreement in their accounts of pre-ontological structures, the point of ontic-ontological difference (prewriting). There is (essential) agreement as to the fact that an epoch is passing, is now being defined, totalled, and negated, and that a new one is emerging in such works as theirs; as to the necessity of the "trick" of erasing an epoch from the inside.

In a later discussion of the founding difference between what can and what cannot be "known" ("On the Origin of the Work of Art"[5]), Heidegger describes this point which Derrida will articulate as *différance*—where what we know and what we do not know meet, where understanding abuts the "unknowable" other or the nothing—as a "world"-"earth" confrontation. The world is the light*ing* where b*eings* are appear*ing*.

> The world is not the mere collection of the countable or uncountable, familiar and unfamiliar things that are just there. But neither is it a merely imagined framework added by our representation to the sum of such given things. The *world worlds*, and is more fully in being than the tangible and perceptible realm in which we believe ourselves to be at home. World is never an object that stands before us and can be seen. World is the ever-nonobjective to which we are subject as long as the paths of birth and death, blessing and curse keep us transported into Being. Wherever those decisions of

---

[5] See also Part 4, "*Aletheia* (Heraclitus, Fragment B 16)" 102-123.

our history that relate to our very being are made, are taken up and abandoned by us, go unrecognized and are rediscovered by new inquiry, there the world worlds. (44-5)

Earth belongs to a chaotic "emerging and rising in itself and in all things" (*phusis*) as "that on which and in which man bases his dwelling."

> We call this ground the *earth*. What this word says is not to be associated with the idea of a mass of matter deposited somewhere, or with the merely astronomi- cal idea of a planet. Earth is that whence the arising brings back and shelters everything that arises without violation. In the things that arise, earth is present as the sheltering agent. (42)

All beings have the earth-thing character of remaining in conceal- ment, sheltering-over, hiding. There is a continuous power struggle going on between being and not being (and between originating ap- pearing and false or dissembling appearance) in and among all beings that inhabit and constitute the world. Beings are appearing when human beings (essentially poets and thinkers) are seeing them in such a way as to set them free as the things they are and are appro- priating language (essentially works of art)—or vice versa—to hold open the space where they are appearing. In such a space appears the primordial conflict between earth and world, between chaos and law (law as Nature or as form). Never and nowhere is the conflict resolved. Each combatant is as original, as necessary, as the other. The burden of the human, world, word, art, is to wrest mastery over not the earth but the yoke that binds the concealed and the unconcealed together in their striving. In *Nietzsche, Volume I; The Will to Power as Art*, Heidegger describes this essential opposition between earth and world as it occurs in classical art (Nietzsche's "grand style"):

> But the fundamental condition is an equally original
> freedom with regard to the extreme opposites, chaos
> and law; not the mere subjection of chaos to a form,
> but that mastery which enables the primal wilderness of
> chaos and the primordiality of law to advance under the
> same yoke, invariably bound to one another with equal
> necessity. Such mastery is unconstrained disposition
> over that yoke, which is as equally removed from the
> paralysis of form in what is dogmatic and formalistic as
> from sheer rapturous tumult. Wherever unconstrained
> disposition over that yoke is an event's self-imposed law,
> there is the grand style; wherever the grand style prevails,
> there art in the purity of its essential plenitude is actual.
> *Nietzsche* 1: 128.

Concealment is the condition of the possibility of unconcealment; the "jointure" ("*Aletheia*" 115) of this mutual necessary opposition delineates again the Heideggerian site of Derrida's *différance*.

According to Heidegger's earth-world schematic, beings come into and remain in historical Being when and as human understanding lets entities be and holds them (and is thereby held) in Being. The way whereby human being makes way for Being, and vice versa, is the way of Saying.

Language is a problem for moderns and postmoderns: (1) thematically as to its nature and its function and (2) systematically as its problem infects the thinking of every other problem—all systems have become forms of language, signifiers cut off from signifieds. The idea of representation undermined, the Nietzschean-Derridean world of pure play threatens pure relativity. And whatever the intrinsic character of language, there is the problem of origin, originality, genealogy, the suspicion of repetition, secondariness, the Don Quixote principle of multiple-mirror distortions of reality, entanglement in the labyrinth. Yet Heidegger sets up his "abode" in language.

To compare the language theory of Derrida and of Heidegger, we consider in detail a summary passage, a pair of images from *Of Grammatology*, and contrast to it a brief synopsis of Heidegger's thinking.

It has become necessary, Derrida writes, to characterize the total field of the disappearing historico-metaphysical epoch as "language" in order that it be deconstructed, in order that it may eventually come to be taken as a "writing," a writing capable of moving beyond the limits of so-called language via pure play which is—and has always been—its element. Derrida posits, as we have seen above, the notion of a pre-writing (precondition of writing, predisposition to write) that founds what has been taken for a "primary writing" (7), for a primary signified (an original text of God's or Nature's to be deciphered, interpreted). All instances and accounts of human being are and have always been inscriptions, writings, subject only to the "law" of pure play, have been and shall remain free writing: signifiers signifying signifiers.

In the beginning of his book he sketches the problem:

> [The epoch "must determine as language the totality of its problematic horizon," he has written.] It must do so not only because all that desire had wished to wrest from the play of language finds itself recaptured within that play but also because, for the same reason, language itself is menaced in its very life, helpless, adrift in the threat of limitlessness, brought back to its own finitude at the very moment when its limits seem to disappear, when it ceases to be self-assured, contained, and *guaranteed* by the infinite signified which seemed to exceed it. (6)

In this image is posited a first-order human "desire." Desire desires to "wrest" from language its object, desires to wrest its object from and by way of the "play" of language. But the object, "all that desire had wished to wrest ..." (reappropriation of presence, as Derrida often puts it; the signified), "finds itself" a prisoner of the very play of language it has taken for its source and its instrument, finds itself to be bound to, restricted to, mean-*ing*, signify-*ing*—playing (writing).

We examine the characters in this drama. "Desire" is separate from and precedes all encounter with or use of language; desire is groundless here—it simply is—but not object-less; the play of language holds something that desire has attempted to wrest from it. In transcendental metaphysics this object is "meaning." Desire-for-meaning wrestles with language. The ground of meaning is the play of language. Since play as play is ungrounded, meaning too is groundless. Language is the ground of the play of language, is the source of and the means by which human desire seeks meaning. Language too is groundless here. It just is, is where desire can reach it and use it. Perhaps it belongs to desire, perhaps to itself or to something else.

In a second image "living" language is undergoing an identity crisis. On one side it is threatened by finitude; gone or disappearing are the "real" signifieds that used to seem to secure and guarantee the identity and the integrity of functional elements of language. On the other side it is threatened by limitlessness, this revelation like the revelation of finitude grounded in Saussure's setting signifiers free from signifieds, setting them against each other instead, in boundless play of differences. (The ontic-ontological difference occurs here as a desire-language distinction and alienation.)

Thus in two images the predicament of our epoch is depicted and its cause hinted—a conceptual error, delusion by over-hasty, self-absorbed desire. In the event narrated—psychological or historical—an unmotivated transformation occurs. Desire, which searches and uses language to find and enjoy its object, seems to engender or to become its own object—meaning, meaninglessness; for what else in this drama but desire could "find itself"? That is, we know that meaning does not "find itself," for meaning does not exist in itself (there are no signifieds; that is the realization achieved here), and since only desire preceded language (and language is a source, instrument, and snare), it must be desire-become-illusion or -paranoia that awakens, correctly aware (strangely enough, since Hegel should be erased here) that it is a prisoner of language, and that language is in trouble, adrift .... Paranoid selfconsciousness recognizes its "true" condition or position as captive to the play of language. Meanwhile the "true" nature of language appears—whether to desire or to itself somewise in some absolute realm is not clear: play, essentially incapable of producing the desired signified.

The moment of crisis identified, named as such, and articulated in its structure and its event (and in its portent, meaning, significance) here is the movement of *différance*, discussed above. Desire-for-meaning has engendered or become meaning, has become selfconscious, and is becoming aware of its (true) meaning: meaninglessness. The image resembles the psychoanalytic unconscious-conscious difference, especially Julia Kristeva's more recent representation of a translinguistic material process in which subjectivity is secondary to instinctual drives (which belong to a material negativity) and in which language has a similarly useful function without "real" relationship to "real" signifieds.

The entities that I claim, above, are "groundless"— desire, language, the transformation of one to the other, the validity of the thematic issuing from this groundless consciousness in and by means of groundless language—are grounded in this work, I suppose, in the man Derrida's "desire" (he posits them) or in some unessential desire of some unessential spirit of the episteme (the kind of ghost that irrupts into, disrupts, history for Nietzsche and Foucault). Of course they all belong to modernist Western theorizing. Desire is post-Freudian psychoanalytic theory; language theory has developed from Saussure's linguistics; the transformation of one to the other has been given a structure in psychoanalysis. Derrida starts with or uses these ready-to-hand products of thought. He claims repeatedly the same—that we begin in the middle on ungrounded ground, and that there is no alternative. It is a popular theme now. (It is a Heideggerian theme.)

The problem is that the image above reveals an unmotivated sui-cide. The "meaning" it conveys is destroyed by the meaning it conveys. The fundamental question is the validity of the self-revelation of this paranoid desire. And it is that "revelation" that declares the meaning paranoid. The undermining is only as good as the underpinning; it is good only if the underpinning is good. Foothold? On a tar-baby.[6]

Meaninglessness and limitlessness themselves are in fact the empty paranoid. These "meanings" take their meanings from "mean-ing" and "limit." In themselves they assert nothing positive; they simply negate the meanings of "meaning" and "limit." They depend on the meanings of these lost or absent entities for any significance of their own. Inherent contradictions, they are suicide words.

It was Saussure's linguistics that unhinged language, that set it adrift. But language is adrift only as it appears in relation to old discounted signifieds. If those signifieds—things-in-themselves, the "truth" of things, of a world of actuality—are set free too, then this free language is the very, the only, language that could "say" such things, such a world, reality. Language is no longer adrift *from* reality, but is freed *to* it. Everything is "adrift"—unfixed, not static, not truth or being or presence. Not only language but life is a writing. Both are boundless and finite.

But neither has disappeared. Neither is nothing. Reality is an ac-tual writing of actual living. And all has not become abstract relativity. In and among the immediate upsurging, things are; essents emerge into being and are held in the open (or not) by the human word. Things are things. Not the former present essences, but temporally

---

[6]In a characteristic "trick" of thinking, Derrida claims that his "*designation*" of the "impossibility" of metaphysical contraries has eluded "the language of metaphysics only by a hairsbreadth"; he continues, "For the rest, it must borrow its resources from the logic it deconstructs. And by doing so, find its very foothold there" (*Of Grammatology* 314).

finite be*ing* and presenc*ing* things—"manifold validity" (*Nietzsche, Volume I* 148)—and, at least for the length of the epoch of history,[7] they are being and presencing in human writing.

What if meaninglessness and limitlessness—those seeming-abysses into which meaning and limit fall—are pseudo notions that conceal the very abyss from which meaning and limit spring. In Heidegger's thinking "nothing" is the horizon of Being; Being—what-is—is projected in opposition to it. Meaning is not an illusory answer to a paranoid riddle. Language is not a substitute (supplement) for nothing. Being *negates nothing*—opposes, "differs from," and "arises" from the nothing ("What is Metaphysics?" 353). "Meaning" does not rely upon something beyond things; language does not imply signifieds standing behind things—there is nothing transcendent or metaphysical in the old sense (Heidegger invests these words with new, finite significance).

In his account of language—and his work as a whole is this account—Heidegger describes the fundamental originating function of language, the function of a Saying, which includes (1) a thinking-questioning (Kant's orientation-toward), setting things free in their own being; and (2) a language/word/poetry-making Saying—by which essents are disclosed in the world and by which or by lack or forgetting of which they do not appear. In such a questioning and Saying, not only are beings established in being, but human being too is established in being as language/world/history-maker (poet).

In Heidegger's early thinking beings come into being on the pre-ontological (pure) horizon of human orientation-toward Being, as we briefly noted above. But a being is not an entity-as-presence whose essence must be brought to light. It is the event of an appearing, which appears according to the relationship occurring between (and beneath

---

[7]One urgent Heideggerian theme is the challenge of modern technology as enframing, especially as the essence of human being is asserted or is subsumed. See esp., "The Question Concerning Technology" and *What is Called Thinking*.

and around and in) it and human being—and this relationship exists in and according to language.

> … we added that here the relation between thing and word comes to light, and further that thing here means anything that in any way has being, any being as such. About the 'word' we also said that it not only stands in a relation to the thing, but that the word is what first brings that given thing, as the being that is, into this 'is'; that the word is what holds the thing there and relates it and so to speak provides its maintenance with which to be a thing. Accordingly, we said, the word not only stands in a relation to the thing, but this 'may be' itself is what holds, relates, and keeps the thing as thing; that the 'may be,' as such keeper, is the relation itself. "The Nature of Language" 82-3

Is not the word itself a "thing"? No, nor is it a nothing:

> Neither the 'is' nor the word attain to thinghood, to Being, nor does the relation between 'is' and the word, the word whose task it is to give an 'is' in each given instance. But even so, neither the 'is' nor the word and its Saying can be cast out into the void of mere nothingness. What, then, does the poetic experience with the word show as our thinking pursues it? … (87)

We say not that the word "is," but that it "gives": gives Being:

> The word, too, belongs to what is there—perhaps not merely 'too' but first of all, and even in such a way such [*sic*] that the word, the nature of the word, conceals within itself that which gives being. If our thinking does

> justice to the matter, then we may never say of the word
> that it is, but rather that it gives—not in the sense that
> words are given by an 'it,' but that the word itself gives.
> The word itself is the giver. What does it give? To go by
> the poetic experience and by the most ancient tradition
> of thinking, the word gives Being.... (87-8)

"Word" is displacing Kant's "Reason" as the pre-ontological rule (schematism) that governs aspect.

> The word's rule springs to light as that which makes
> the thing be a thing. The word begins to shine as the
> gathering which first brings what presences to its presence.

> The oldest word for the rule of the word thus thought,
> for Saying, is *logos*: Saying which, in showing, lets beings
> appear in their 'it is.' "Words" 155

Words, language, brings beings into Being. Entities thus disclosed appear in the lighting, belong to world, though their being is always in every way in dispute from the concealing-sheltering earth.

Such a concept of Being can be conceived as non-metaphysical only if the fecund possibilities in Being are granted in (1) the human imagination (as Blake had it) or in (2) a concept of being-in-the-world freed from traditional essential and substantial limitations. The latter is Heidegger's way. The world and things in it, as appearing that lingers, endures, is such a realm as poets explore best. This is Heidegger's (poetic) account of the realm of concealing/unconcealing, as he discovers it in early Greek thinking (Heraclitus):

> ... It is the abode wherein every possible 'whither' of
> a belonging-to rests. Thus the realm, in the sense of

μη δυνον ποτε is unique by virtue of the extent of its gathering reach. Everything that belongs in the event of a rightly experienced revealing grows upward and together (*concrescit*) in this realm. It is the absolutely concrete. But how can this realm be represented as concrete on the basis of the foregoing abstract expositions? This question appears justified only as long as we fail to see that we must not precipitously assault Heraclitus' thought with distinctions like 'concrete' and 'abstract,' 'sensuous' and 'nonsensuous,' 'perceptible' and 'imperceptible.' That they are and have long been current among us does not guarantee their supposedly unlimited importance. It could very well happen that Heraclitus, precisely when he utters a word which names something perceptible is just then thinking what is absolutely imperceptible. Thus it becomes obvious how little we profit from such distinctions. "*Aletheia*" 115

The world, the "event of lighting," is described:

> ... we have seen that never entering into concealment is the enduring rising out of self-concealing. In this way does the world fire glow and shine and meditate. If we think it as lighting, this includes not only the brilliance, but also the openness wherein everything, especially the reciprocally related, comes into shining. Lighting is therefore more than illuminating, and also more than laying bare. Lighting is the meditatively gathering bringing-before into the open. It is the bestowal of presencing. (118)

Heidegger's first question (*Being and Time*), ultimately the question of the nature of Being in general, addresses the structures of human being. Throughout his life Heidegger's thinking moves ever closer to the ever more compelling question of the being—and the Saying and finally the Event—of Being. Dasein's resoluteness and domination give way to the greater initiative of Being. The language of Being (and past Being *Ereignis*, Appropriation, "The Way to Language"[8]) more and more initiates and dominates the Saying. Being is not God. This strangest upsurgence is the very life we stand-toward; and the most irreal of joyful-tragic possibilities are as-yet-possible ways of human being.

Derrida and others object to a "fundamentality" (*Of Grammatology* 19, for example) in Heidegger's thinking. "Ground" is an onto-theological notion, Derrida warns. There is indeed a "founding," "grounding," in Heidegger's thinking, but ground is not first cause, not prime mover; ground is *topos*, field, region—where things are, and are together, not randomly or arbitrarily. Here things (not present-in-their-essence) are brought-into-*presencing*, into appearing, into Being, in reciprocal perspectival-perceptual relationship with human seeing, thinking, saying. "Ground" is something like "relationship"; it is Heidegger's way of thinking Derrida's (the age's) "differences," estrangements.

But ground itself is groundless. In, especially, "On the Essence of Truth"[9] the nothing from which being arises is described as "freedom" (cf. Nietzsche's "*jouissance*" and Derrida's "free play"). If ground is "fundamental" the abyss underneath it swallows all hopes (or charges) of fundamentalism.[10] If "ground" is taken in the rational sense as basis, foundation, cause, reason, then there is no ground grounding Heidegger's Being, and Derrida's claim is refuted. If ground is thought outside metaphysical notions, distrust of fundamentalism becomes moot.

---

[8]See also *On Time and Being.*

[9]"On the Essence of Truth." *Existence and Being.* Trans. W. B. Barton, Jr., and Vera Deutsch. A Gateway Edition. Chicago: Henry Regnery Company, Fifth Printing, 1967. 305.

[10]John D. Caputo presents a powerful, dark synopsis of this groundlessness, which he calls "the danger of Heidegger's path" (245-54).

The latter is the appropriate thinking. Heidegger's "world" is not conceived according to nor does it attain to any model; it is disclosed, searched-out, found—seen, thought, said. The disclosure is not the old totality, Truth, and it is not disclosed once for all. This thinking, saying, seeing is *way*. Concealment remains prior to unconcealment and is always contesting it, while unconcealment is not fixed or final. Seeing is multiple-levelled polyvision.

> A dialogue of Plato ... can be interpreted in totally differ-
> ent spheres and respects, according to totally different
> implications and problematics. This multiplicity of pos-
> sible interpretations does not discredit the strictness of
> the thought content. For all true thought remains open
> to more than one interpretation—and this by reason of
> its nature. Nor is this multiplicity of possible interpre-
> tations merely the residue of a still unachieved formal-
> logical univocity which we properly ought to strive for
> but did not attain. Rather, multiplicity of meanings is
> the element in which all thought must move in order to
> be strict thought. To use an image: to a fish, the depths
> and expanses of its waters, the currents and quiet pools,
> warm and cold layers are the element of its multiple mo-
> bility. If the fish is deprived of the fullness of its element,
> if it is dragged on the dry sand, then it can only wrig-
> gle, twitch, and die. Therefore, we always must seek out
> thinking, and its burden of thought, in the element of its
> multiple meanings, else everything will remain closed
> to us. *What is Called Thinking* 71

The ways to see, think, say, are, as Derrida has it, boundless and finite.

What Derrida, Heidegger, and the rest of us desire of language is some genuine issue. With Derrida and the age, Heidegger finds most language to be dead and deadening language—language as representation. Representational language stands for entities, stands between human seeing and entities (not entities-as-presence, but as being), blocking and distorting their appearing. All language taken as representation is already containing and controlling, inscribing, circumscribing, the entities it represents, not setting them free as they are. All assertions or propositions have by the taking of a position, perspective, dimmed-down the appearing of the entity they purport to disclose.

And language, even living language, dies if it is not lived in. It endures in works of art, which hold open the space where a world-earth conflict is taking place. But it endures in works of art only when we continue to stand in the space they open up. If we fail to do so, the space closes and the being is lost to Being ("On the Origin of the Work of Art" 74-5; "Holderlin and the Essence of Poetry" 282-3).

To follow Heidegger's thinking is to change the traditional meaning of reality, but not our "sense" of reality. It is this elusive unsaid sensing-experience that opens itself to our thinking as we follow his way. Works of art—without philosophical or scientific respectability—have been our most direct route to these unthematized realities, our most effectual saying of what there is to say. Modernist literature discloses the historical experience (Heidegger's historical having-been) of the moderns, primarily their confrontation with the spectre of meaninglessness, their task of creating worlds on crumbling foundations. In the readings below, guided by the thinking of Heidegger, I shall investigate especially the nature of language, the function/power of language to write the world, and the effects of writing the world in terms of a subject-object dichotomy (the Cartesian-Kantian paradigm). These subjects are not dissociable. I will attempt to follow each work as and where it leads, with special regard to these issues.

Rethinking Williams Thinking

The following essay is a Heideggerian reading of William Carlos Williams' *In the American Grain*. In Appendix A I point out explicitly some of Heidegger's insights that I am finding among Williams' insights here.

Of course Williams was anti-intellectual.

> But who [he baited the critics], if he chose, could not touch the bottom of thought? The poet does not, however, permit himself to go beyond the thought to be discovered in the context of that with which he is dealing: no ideas but in things. The poet thinks with his poem.... (Williams, *The Autobiography*[1])

But from the beginning most scholars, among them distinguished intellectuals,[2] remarked Williams' failure of intellect. That failure is

---

[1] William Carlos Williams, *Autobiography*, quoted in note before *Paterson* (New York: New Directions, 1963).

[2] R. P. Blackmur, for example, "John Wheelwright and Dr. Williams," *Language as Gesture; Essays in Poetry*, 1935 (New York: Harcourt, Brace, 1952); and Kenneth Burke, "Heaven's First Law," rev. of *Sour Grapes*, *The Dial* 72 (1922): 197-200; "Subjective History," rev. of *In the American Grain*; *New York Herald Tribune Books* (14 March 1926); "William Carlos Williams, 1883-1963," *The New York Review of Books* 1.2 (1963): 45-47.

part of the portrait the century has produced of him. Authors even as they point out complexities of Williams' thought disparage his careless or clumsy intellection. At worst: " 'No ideas but in things' ... reveals a pompous, bigoted mind, not merely anti-intellectual in attitude, but dedicated to the principle of non-intelligence."[3] But I submit that the conflict may be semantic and historic, involving the meanings of "intellect" and "thinking." If we carry these terms with their traditional meanings as measuring instruments into Williams' work, his intellect and his thinking will fall short or long. His intellect is contaminated with esthetic and moral influences, and his thinking is not strictly or essentially rational. Yet I shall read Williams' *In the American Grain*[4] as an experiment in radical thinking, a reading more readily granted to his poetry; see, for example, J. Hillis Miller's general assessment of Williams in *Poets of Reality*, as going farther than any other twentieth century poet past the boundaries of the tradition. (See also Miller's reading of *IAG* in his "Presidential Address 1986," with which my study is in general accord,[5] and Joseph N. Riddel's Heideggerian-to-Derridean reading of Williams in *The Inverted Bell*.[6]) My thesis is not that writing poetry and thinking are the same, though I do urge Heidegger's contention (and Williams' Poe's in *IAG*, below) that each involves the other essentially, but I claim that Williams writes these essays, as they have been called, for the purpose of proving (in the sense of "proving" in the Poe chapter, 230) a thesis, that art serves thinking in this work and not the other

---

[3] Joseph Bennett, "The Lyre and the Sledgehammer," *Hudson Review*, 5 (1952): 300.

[4] *In the American Grain* (New York: New Directions, 1933).

[5] "Presidential Address 1986. The Triumph of Theory, the Resistance to Reading, and the Question of the Material Base," *PMLA* 102.3 (May 1987): 281-91.

[6] *The Inverted Bell: Modernism and the Counterpoetics of William Carlos Williams* (Baton Rouge: Louisiana State UP, 1974). Compare especially Chapter 1, the most Heideggerian section of the book, in which Riddel discusses beginnings, the self, descent, the local, play or dance, and art as preservation of opposition, in Williams' work as a whole, as I have discussed them above in *IAG*, which Riddel did not treat in detail.

way around, and that he proves ("shows") himself as thinker as he proves ("shows") not his conclusions but his "method" of thinking.

It is true that "thought" conceived as a purely logical, purely mental activity was never the end of Williams' work. Such thought not only evinced no positive value in terms of the thinking he preferred, but it was immoral—in its source, its activity, and its effect. His concept of thinking was larger, more inclusive, involving more, indeed all, of the human faculties and more still. He quotes, for example, Poe's argument that "the calculating faculties" and "the ideal" [the "poetical" faculties] "are never to be found in perfection apart. The highest order of the imaginative intellect is always preeminently mathematical; and the converse" (218). But it is more than that for Williams, more particular and plural than two categories, than even these two, can express. Two categories Williams prefers in *IAG* are the moral and the aesthetic, both fleshed out in characterizations that enlarge and invigorate their traditional definitions. His moral and aesthetic admonition and challenge issue not from ideological ground, but from the ground of the very ground, an actual and particular place (America, here), solid and yet impermanent, "frail," losable, a place to which one may, indeed must, give oneself (Rasles, Boone), in which one must submerge, bury oneself (Houston), declare, risk, lose oneself (Burr), in order to arise "from under," "through a dead layer," to proceed "from the center out" in an originating ("fresh") thrust toward: method (Poe section). Such a dense formulation requires elaboration.

To locate Williams' and our post-Williams entry into the argument, in a phrase: philosophically (after Aristotle) we in the West called man the thinking (rational) animal until we learned to assign "thinking" to subjectivity, subjectivity to consciousness, and consciousness to the insensible but traceable tyranny of the unconscious, namely desire; in these (rational) transformations thinking loses its authority without surrendering its office. Now Williams, ignoring or deriding ideas in themselves, chose rather to see, sense, touch, "marry," than to think or know; driving ignorantly, critics agree, over or past or through whatever subjectivity or consciousness might be, in a sort of blazing immediacy. "This is writing that by a Jacob's wrestle with words *gets down what happens*," writes Hugh Kenner.[7] Yet these *IAG* essays delineate not only thinking and desire, but a hierarchy within each and a relationship of necessity that holds them together and commands them.

Desire, associated with the unconscious as a pre- or non-linguistic impulse or energy, resists linguistic definition, lends itself, unsuccessfully as yet, to the logic of physics (this temptation to pure objectivity is moderated in Lacan) or to the self-erasing, privative language of Derrida and others. We may say that something like Freudian desire appears to be the grounding, driving force in *IAG*, citing the sensuous, murderous, voluptuous Cain element that drives the lusty conquerors in the early sections, and the driving, playful, flaming forcing that forces onto love in the Poe section (see above). But in order to write this list of Freudian characteristics I have had to cut apart, cut up, cut parts out of the *IAG* ground and force (to analyze rationally, to select parts and order them rationally), while ignoring the seeing-knowing character of these same elements and performing the inhuman, immoral denial of what is here before me that the author rejects in, for example, the Puritans.

For in Williams' work this force, this forcing, does not (as we have detailed above) precede the sensible, seeing, recognizing faculty that belongs to the linguistic; nor is it independent of or at variance with it; nor does language satisfy, supplement or complement the driving energy. Indeed, the business of being human involves at every point a complexity of features deprived of their essence and function (a brutalizing and dehumanizing bereavement) when they are separated from each other analytically. We may be accustomed to distinguish and separate out "that obscene flesh" from "the sensitive mind" or "the spirit"; but they and perhaps other discernible but undiscerned aspects of being human are inseparable, undissociable, here. "That

---

[7]*Poetry* (Aug. 1952): 276.

obscene flesh," mass of undifferentiated "life," is not physical drive or
negativity (and not Sartre's nauseous objectivity), but is that "in which
we dig for all our good, man and woman alike" (207). The actual world
that the author urges upon the senses feeds the spirit as well as the
flesh: "The world is made to eat, not leave, that the spirit may be full,
not empty" (205). We may fault Williams, as we usually fault poets
(and they reciprocate; we enjoy an ancient antagonistic symbiosis) for
his incapacity to distinguish and isolate the elements in the mass, or
we must entertain the possibility of a credible non-analytical thinking
("conception," "[study]," "heed," "intelligent investigation," 109): the
"method" which is the study and the exercise of this work.

In fact, the relationship of particle to mass, represented in an
unconventional and provocative way, is a salient point in Williams'
argument and will serve to launch us into the text. The Puritans'
"magnificent logic" is "[disproportionate]" to the "flamboyant mass
of savagery" about them. Applying the parts-to-whole principle, we
may say that the problem is misappropriation: the Protestant colony's
thinking belongs to Europe and is inappropriate in America. The
theme is basic, as we know, to Williams' argument. Or the problem
may be analyzed as the inadequacy of language (logic) to fulfill its
purpose; it falls short, is not sufficient to account for "savagery." Or
perhaps the correlation between language and life is flawed from the
outset, logic and reality essentially estranged. But the discrepancy,
disagreement, that the author describes is not rational but moral. The
particle and the mass are not analyzed in terms of their common
essence or structural unity, but they are evaluated in terms of original
relationship. Puritanism, the particle, is incapable of "recognizing"
the too-large "mass," the Indian and his world. The discrepancy is
not lack of recogni*tion*, but lack of recogni*zing*; morality is not an
abstraction but a relation;[8] and not due to the weakness of logic

---

[8]Relation is fundamental to existence in Heidegger's thought. From the contex-
tuality and directionality of Being-in-the-world and Care, to the notions of neighborhood and region on to the Open and the oneness of the fourfold, Dasein and
the rest "are" in and according to relation. In fact, what "relation" entails outstrips

but to the abuse of it. The problem does not inhere in the form of the logic but in the form*ing*; that is, the formal aspect is flawed in two ways. (1) This logic developed in Europe, not America—not that the logic applied to Europe but that it was grounded there. A logic belongs actively to its own ground. The Puritans have moved to a new ground retaining the logic of the old. (2) This logic is no longer forming; it is a hardened, rigid, dry form. The very purity of its form occasions its "[blindness] to every contingency, mashing Indian, child and matron into one *safe* mold" (112). The problem is moral and it inheres in a source, i.e., "their religion," an "immoral concept," and in its "brutalizing" effect, which is to isolate each individual in a separate religious experience and to blind him to the world and to his ground. (This isolation reappears in the end as the Puritans' legacy to the milieu that Poe contended against, inside and out, their contribution to his tragedy, 232-3.) Further, the immorality of the immoral concept lies in its conception—not in conceptualizing per se, but in *this* conception: this "thinking," we offer tentatively; this "method," we may say with assurance after the Poe chapter.

The author articulates the problem: the Puritans did not dare to think as they did not dare to see ("All that they saw they lived by but denied," 112). Their "magnificent logic," dwarfed by "the flamboyant mass of savagery" that surrounded them, served them as a hard, dry protective covering, its rigidity their strength and sharp cutting edge, weapon and pathfinder. Holding fast to the form ("fixed … formula") of their dogma, they held at bay the terror. Meanwhile this concept, which postponed "blossoming" to Eternity, emptied the world of not merely significance or reality, but of the Indian, his existence, his actual ground. ("The *immorality* of such a concept,

---

existence (Being-toward death, e.g., the trace of the unthinkable in presencing, etc.). Relation per se is discussed in "The Nature of Language" where the word, bringing an entity into existence and holding it there, "is the relation itself" (83, "*das Wort stünde nicht nur in einem Verhältnis zum Ding, sondern das Wort 'sei' selber dasjenige, was das Ding als Ding hält und verhält, sei als dieses Verhaltende: das Verhältnis selber*") and in *What Is Called Thinking?* in terms of thinking and facing, *vorstellen* (79f., 85f., 97f., e.g.).

the inhumanity, the brutalizing effect upon their own minds, on their SPIRITS ...'" 113; Williams is rewriting Nietzsche's *Genealogy of Morals*.) The Puritan religion which provided that concept is "an IMMORAL source" (113) and its "flower," Cotton Mather's books, repeats its "brutality, inhumanity, cruel amputations" (111). The charge, in short, is that notwithstanding the ground "all blossoming about them—under their noses" the Puritans systematically denied, opposed, and destroyed the Indian and his world and implanted the (Elizabethan) seed of the puritanism that infects America today, "an immorality that IS America" (114), an immorality which the author will attempt to extricate from the New World, from history, from himself, and to isolate: in order to annihilate.

The thematic is reiterated, this time positively. Against the Puritans' insular, rigid, confrontational method of dealing with the New World the author sets for contrast Pere Rasles' "recognition": "It is a living flame compared to their dead ash" (120). Instead of "[stating]" to the Indians "the chief articles of the Christian religion," as the English Protestants would do (and from some distance; the minister "would not suffer the contrite Indians to lay their hands upon him," 119), Rasles "lived thirty-four years, ... with his beloved savages, drawing their sweet like honey, TOUCHING them every day" (120). Where is this Jesuit priest's "logic"? In heaven, or in Rome, where the author is only relatively pleased that the Catholics have placed it, with the advantage at least that the priest's hands are freed for embraces (120, 128-9). Instead of Mather's chilling accounts of witch trials we have the letters Rasles wrote, "a moral source not reckoned with, peculiarly sensitive and daring in its close embrace of native things" (121). The language in this passage entangles what we have traditionally separated as the physical and the mental: "His sensitive mind. For everything his fine sense, blossoming, thriving, opening, reviving—not shutting out—was tuned...." (121).

Shall we conclude that "logic," that particle, is an evil in itself? The Poe chapter will clarify the issue. In the Rasles example, as in the Puritans, the major issue is ground—not as an idea or a principle, but as an original (moral) source. The Puritans refuse to touch the ground of the New World; Rasles is "absorbed" into it. The human condition is grounded and local for Williams. Culture is cultivation (224-5). Morality originates from the ground; that is, what issues from the ground is moral. As we shall see in the Poe chapter, "method" itself emerges from a lostness in massiness. There is no alternative to going under.[9]

It is the Indian that Rasles loves, touches, marries, and "releases" into "emergence." "He exists, he is—it is an AFFIRMATION, it is alive" (121). "It," the affirming sensitive attunement ("For everything his fine sense ... was tuned" 121) of Rasles' recognition, which grants to the Indian in his world his very ontological ground, "is alive." The *living* of the affirmation admits no rational or biological explanation. But we note that just as in the case of the Indian, and in the case of morality, of particles and mass, of ground, so in the case of history, above, of fact and words, eventually of method; in the case also of what transpires from and through these, and of the unfixed, unformed "open" into which they issue; in all cases where the actuality of things is indicated, this living "freshness" may be descried. Note also that Williams' "ignoring" of philosophy in order to "recognize" what is under his nose, his "recognizing" which "releases into existence," is radical ontology.[10] As Rasles releases the Indian into existence, Poe will release the American ground, and the author will release Poe (226).

The principle of originality is delineated further in the Franklin essay. Briefly, Franklin was imbued with two qualities of the New

---

[9]Bernhard Radloff offers a Heideggerian "poetics of the local" drawn from or applied to four Williams poems, more faithful to Heidegger than to Williams, perhaps, which describes not the ground that I am finding in Williams but something like the Heideggerian ground from which I myself approach Williams' "design." "Name and Site: A Heideggerian Approach to the Local in the Poetry of William Carlos Williams." *Texas Studies in Literature and Language* 28.2 (1986): 140-63.

[10]Compare Heidegger's notion of the participation of Dasein in the appearing of beings and world; compare the importance of letting-be. His early works are especially resonant here.

World: "[1] a bulky, crude energy, something in proportion to the continent, and [2] a colossal restraint equalizing it" (153-4). He played the two against each other. "Franklin is the full development of the timidity, the strength that denies itself" (155). His relationship to his ground registers on our continuum somewhere between the Puritans' and Rasles'; he neither ignores it nor marries it, but uses it, handles it, "in a 'practical' way."[11]

> The character they had (our pioneer statesmen, etc.) was that of giving their fine energy, as they must have done, to the smaller, narrower, protective thing and not to the great New World. Yet they cannot quite leave hands off it but must TOUCH it, in a "practical" way, that is a joking, shy, nasty way, using "science" etc., not with the generosity of the savage or scientist but in a shameful manner. The sweep of the force was too horrible to them; it would have swept them into chaos. They HAD to do as they *could* but it can be no offense that their quality should be *named*. They could have been inspired by the new QUALITY about them to yield to loveliness in a fresh spirit.

> It is the placing of his enthusiasm that characterizes the man. (157)

Franklin placed his enthusiasm in "his wits."

> Do something, anything, to keep the fingers busy—not to realize—the lightning. Be industrious, let money and comfort increase; ....

---

[11] Compare Heidegger's discussion of "handling," his distinction between "proper use [*eigentliche Brauchen*]" and "mere utilizing [*bloßes Benützen*]" in *What Is Called Thinking?* 186-87.

> His mighty answer to the New World's offer of a great
> embrace was THRIFT. Work night and day, build up,
> penny by penny, a wall against that which is threatening,
> the terror of life, poverty. Make a fort to be secure in.
> (156)

The issue is immorality, deliberately or shyly or slyly not looking
at, not seeing, and touching in a "nasty" way what is about; blinding oneself, cutting oneself off to protect oneself by means of the
(mis-)appropriation of logic—dogma or practical axiom—as fortress
or palliative against actuality. The positive aspect of the issue is the
disclosure (releasement) of morality: "recognition," in a word. Of
interest for our rumination on Williams' thinking is the interasso-
ciation of seeing and knowing, and their subsumption of thinking.
Ignorance—of the Indian, of the ground, of loveliness, of history—is
ignoring. Ignoring "denies," and denying denies existence. In this
schema the mind or the mental is often invoked, never precluded,
but thinking per se as logic or adage enters into the equation only as
a temptation to delay, defer, the impact of experience. But we have as
yet only a preliminary sketch of Williams' project.

The essay is more than a history lesson. Williams in the persona
of himself is looking at, seeing, penetrating, his own ground. America
"IS" "an immorality" (114) because …

> Because the fools do not believe that they have sprung
> from anything: bone, thought and action. They will not
> see that what they are is growing on these roots. They
> will not look. They float without question. Their history
> is to them an enigma. (113)

"Because …. They will not see …. They will not look," this time
not at the ground as the Indian's world but at the ground as their own
history. Seeing, looking at, the Indian's ground means living with the
Indian, at his side like Rasles, on the trail, on the warpath. Seeing,

looking at, their own ground means reading records, questioning the enigma of their own history. But though the second looking looks to books and even to Europe, to nothing under the feet and palpable, it nevertheless looks for something present and living. Here not merely "facts" of history but the meaning of "history" is being rewritten. Just as Burr will be spoken of later as belonging to history and history as belonging "in me" (the author of the history), "and so I dig through lies to resurrect him" (197), so in this case this "puritanism" is a living, breathing " 'thing' " that "sallies" out from the books of Mather from time to time "to strike terror through the land" (115); it is a stench "all about you" in America; indeed Larbaud observes that the author himself is "brimming" with that and other similarly historical influences. Seeing history, looking at it, "understanding [it] aright" means "to make it SHOW itself" (116). To understand means again to release into appearing, to see, and to see means nothing passive or static or ocular.

Meanwhile the particle to mass relationship is rearranging itself. The author smells the stench of the puritanism which is part of the character of Americans now and attempts to extricate it and to "isolate" it in order to "annihilate" it. We discovered isolation as an anti-life principle in the doctrine of the Puritans, above. Isolation means disconnectedness from ground, means non-originality, immorality. Life lives in massiness. But massiness is what recognition frees things from: for annihilation or for disclosure. In the account of the event which we are following here we can expose a double image: annihilation is working at least twice.

The author is tracking the source of the offensive smell, searching through history. Meanwhile he is looking at, seeing, history—releasing it into existence. One effect of this facing, releasing, is that the concept of history as the bound content of books is "annihilated." The brash young American angrily casts aside "history, that lie" for "what is in [the books]"—a "freshness; if it exist" (109). His interest in history is not Valery Larbaud's "taste for books," the first indication of "a civilized interest in the world," but an urgent salvage operation to recoup history "as a living thing, something moving, undecided, swaying" (192), which "lives in us practically day by day" (187).

> That of the dead which exists in our imaginations has as much fact as have we ourselves. The premise that serves to fix us fixes also that part of them which we remember. (189)

And so on. Annihilation of puritanism will occur in a similar looking, seeing; annihilation of the unoriginal and releasement of the original. And this must not be the end of the annihilation. There must be a total sweeping out.

> However hopeless it may seem, we have no other choice: we must go back to the beginning; it must all be done over; everything that is must be destroyed. (215)

The author's gesture anticipates Poe's: "a movement first and last to clear the GROUND" (216)—to clear the ground for "a *beginning*" (217).[12]

I think we can agree that this tracking, this looking, seeing, is or involves thinking if not analysis. The particle to mass ratio is, in the author's figure, a blossom to ground, water to spring, relationship.

---

[12]From his call for the destruction of the "hardened...traditional content of ancient ontology" (*Being and Time* 44), the problem of beginnings is treated in all of Heidegger's works. A couple of passages will indicate the Williams resonance: "A beginning ... always contains the undisclosed abundance of the unfamiliar and extraordinary [*die unerschlossene Fülle des Ungeheuren*], which means that it also contains strife with the familiar and ordinary [*des Streites mit dem Geheuren*]" ("The Origin" 76); "A beginning [*Der Anfang*] can never directly preserve its full momentum; the only possible way to preserve its force is to repeat, to draw once again more deeply than ever from its source [*daß es in seiner Ursprünglichkeit ursprünglicher wieder-holt wird*]. And it is only by repetitive thinking [*denkende Wieder-holung*] that we can deal appropriately with the beginning and the breakdown of the truth" (*An Introduction* 191).

The terms are not literal and not rational, with objective entities objectively analyzable as to components or elements and to physical cause. The terms, freshly defined, are moral and esthetic and derive from a new definition of "origin": what is true or legitimate is original; what is false is not original, is "copied" or imported. The point is essential in the working of this work, essential also to our inquiry into Williams' thinking. A related point is that we usually take thinking to involve the martialing of evidence; these essays present an obliging procession of figures and events from American history. But we note that in the annihilation of "history," "fact" becomes a doubtful, detached, elementary particle, all that remains of "truth" (189-90). With the annihilation of "history," evidential, inductive "thinking" is decimated (transformed) as well. We have seen above what "props" Williams' (Poe's) "deductive" logic will admit. We have seen also how his "method" works to reconstruct history from such elementary particles as these "facts."

In the "annihilation" of "history" we see the moral-esthetic way (method) to address "*things* non-metaphysical" (222), beginning with a descent into the ground and then from that "basis," "from under" or "from the center out," touching-marrying-releasing original things into existence or isolating-annihilating things not-original—puritanism, e.g., "history": everything that is no longer beginning. The Indian or history is released into actuality by recognition; by recognition American puritanism is annihilated. The disclosure of original ground and the annihilation of non-original "impedimenta" seem to be two functions of the same "recognition," at the same time a sensible and a mental activity, at the same time the essence of the esthetical and the moral (109).

"Recognition" seems to be an activity of the understanding in large, the seeing made possible by looking, the releasing by giving that allows things to declare themselves. There is no separate organ or instrument of understanding. Thinking as mental activity and as reason is a particle to the mass of gross flesh/fine mind human character, if particles are participant and integral, not elements or components.

In the Poe chapter we find "method" described explicitly. We have read in the sequential stories of conquerors, explorers, and national fathers one continuing story of outsiders, Europeans, resisting and opposing or accepting and penetrating the ground of America. Poe's is a different story; it begins *on* that "flamboyant mass" of American ground; yet he too must "go down and wrestle with [local] conditions" (225). "His greatness is in that he turned his back and faced inland, to originality, with the identical gesture of a Boone" (226).

> ... insistence upon primary distinctions, that seems coldly academic, was in this case no more than evidence of a strong impulse to begin at the beginning. (217)

In the earlier chapters we were spectators to the "emerging" of Puritans, Indians, into existence; we watched alongside Rasles and the author as they released them; but in Poe's section we follow the emerging from the inside out. This birth that wills itself an immaculate conception is a birth of a self; we may compare it to (if we are willing to risk the annihilation of) self-consciousness. In this chapter the author too is facing inward; the text enacts and in its language mirrors and repeats the experience of Poe.

But we must clear some ground ourselves. Is not this compulsion to destroy everything a puritanic motive, or worse—not ignoring or fending off, but annihilating "blossoms" underfoot? The very notion of immaculate conception is theological, and the impulse "to detach a 'method' from the smear of common usage" (221) is contemptuous of the local, and isolationist in principle. Add the self-serving use of logic "to hold the ["hated"] loose-strung mass off." Recall Rasles' absorption and compare Poe's "standing off to SEE instead of forcing himself too close" (229), his "refusing" to "handle" "the contamination of the UNFORMED LUMP" (228) which Hawthorne faithfully represented.

Riposte: Poe does not violate the principles established earlier, but refines them while he completes or continues the author's project of revealing the function of original, originating ground. Poe's impulse to clear the ground for a beginning is the essence of morality in this work: relatedness to ground. The notion of immaculate conception is a fresh one here, replacing as it annihilates puritanical idealism. "Conception" is cleansed of idea, of content, released into a purity of "intent," the intention of original genius: of self ("to find a way to tell his soul"), of ground (to "express" itself). The Puritans appropriated logic as a closed system, not as method. The immorality of their logic obtained not in its artificiality but in its camouflage, not in its opposition to the mass but in its inappropriateness, disproportion, to *this* mass. Poe's holding off the mass, standing back to see, his approach from above, "adopting a more elevated mien" (229), does not contradict the necessity of going under; it follows it, follows after his "facing inland," is the continuing trajectory of his emergence from the center out. (The possibility of seeing originally and of forging an original method follows after grounded self-conception.)[13] Now Poe appears as the first original American author, expressing, not representing, the original thrust of the "re-awakened genius" of the New World (216). As for Hawthorne, Poe faults him, as the author has faulted Franklin, for "handling" what he was refusing to "touch, marry," for "copying" the American "scene" in the European style instead of rebuilding it from the American ground.

The paradigm or, better, "method" that "emerges" in the Poe chapter can be sketched as follows. The first and dominant character of *IAG* is the ground. Although the ground has the character that we have called the "massy" ("the generous bulk of its animal crudity"), yet the mass, as we have seen, has a genius of its own, "genius of place," the "sullen, volcanic inevitability of the *place*." It may be sardonic, hot, angry; it smiles; "in its lusts' eye" is a "purpose" (213). This

---

[13]Compare Heidegger's discussion of Zarathustra's "downgoing [*Untergang*]" as Nietzsche's "Moment [*der Augenblick*]" in *Nietzsche, Vol. II: The Eternal Recurrence of the Same*, trans. David Farrell Krell (San Francisco: Harper and Row, 1984) 59ff, 67. See Dasein's authentic Being-towards-death and resoluteness in *Being and Time*, Division Two, I and II, as well as the "moment of vision [*Augenblick*]," H. 328, 338.

ground as a peculiar mass with a peculiar genius is something like the man this work recommends (Burr): "Burr knew what a democracy must liberate…. Men intact—with all their senses waking" (206), a combination of what the author calls the esthetic and the moral: waking senses and original genius in one self-asserting sensibility. Indeed the flesh and the ground seem to be the same thing: the "physical," informed like the Greeks' *phusis* with the psychic as well:[14] the very event of the emerging of what is living.

This genius of ground rises through the genius of the poet, Poe, as the felt need to clear the ground, an impetus to beginning. Now a second local factor impresses itself upon and into the poet's "emerging"—in Poe's case the ostracizing, embittering opposition of the sentimental, loveless public. This second local influence is not secondary, it seems, though in this case it is not original, since it is disconnected from and opposing the ground. Local environment, one's historical time and place (in Williams' sense, as living, moving)—"the mass of impedimenta which is the world"—infiltrates a poet's self and expression, supports or thwarts it, assists to determine and shape it.[15] In spite of the difficulty of his passage Poe "emerges"

---

[14] "We oppose the psychic, the animated [*das Seelische*], the living, to the 'physical.' But for the Greeks all this belonged to *physis* and continued to do so even after Aristotle" (Heidegger, *An Introduction* 16).

[15] Compare Heidegger's notion of Dasein's intrinsic entanglement in the everyday "they," *Being and Time* 435: "The authentic existentiell understanding is so far from extricating itself from the way of interpreting Dasein which has come down to us, that in each case it is in terms of this interpretation, against it, and yet again for it [*je aus ihr und gegen sie und doch wieder für sie*], that any possibility one has chosen is seized upon in one's resolution." In *Nietzsche, Vol. II*, discussing Nietzsche's attempt to prevent philosophy from humanizing its objects: "the *Da* is the sole possible site for the necessary location of [Dasein's] Being at any given time [*der mögliche Ort für den je notwendigen Standort seines Seins*]. From this essential connection we also derive the insight that humanization becomes proportionately less destructive of truth as human beings relate themselves more originally to the location of their essential corner [*den Standort einer wesentlichen Ecke*], that is to say, as they recognize and ground Da-sein as such." But, again, the "location" of this "corner" is ontological, not geographical: "Yet the essentiality of the corner is defined by the originality and the breadth in which being as a whole is experienced

as the first original American author, this author claims, and his work founds a genuinely American literature (226). "[Poe] had the sense within him of a locality of his own, capable of cultivation":

> …Culture is still the effect of cultivation, to work with a thing until it be rare; as a golden dome among the mustard fields. It implies a solidity capable of cultivation. Its effects are marble blocks that lie perfectly fitted and aligned to express by isolate distinction the rising lusts which threw them off, regulated, in moving through the mass of impedimenta which is the world.

> This is culture; in mastering them, to burst through the peculiarities of an environment. (224-5)

The gold dome and the regular marble blocks are not natural organic outgrowths or products of the ground. They are thrown off by the power of lusts moving against local impedimenta. There seems to be a tendency in freshness to become stale, to harden; freshness depends upon fresh rising—of lusts from the ground. The fresh lusts break up the accumulating impedimenta. Regular marble blocks are altogether different from a mass of impedimenta. Like gold domes they have been made rare through work, the work of cultivators—selves, poets. The origin of the works of culture is the ground, its lusts rising, but the works of cultivating—artificial, of enduring substance, regular—belong to selves, poets; like Poe's perfect *Gold Bug*, or *Murders in the Rue Morgue*, they seem to be monuments to moments of equilibrium achieved between the rising and the working. (They do not "betray" the "deeper intent" that drove them from the beginning and could drive them over the edge, as less successful works do, the "lesser Tales," 229).

---

and grasped—with a view to its sole decisive aspect, that of Being [*nach der allein entscheidenden Hinsicht, nämlich der des Seins*]" (119).

We note that this image of gold dome and marble slabs, reminiscent of the Laocoön, the Grecian urn, Byzantium, refers in *IAG* not to the work of art but to the work of culture, as though the work of art were first of all the work of culture, cultivation of ground.[16] When the poet clears the ground for a new beginning, he does not enter into a nature-culture opposition but submerges in, becomes one with (marries), a ground which is a "basis" for "satisfaction." Nature per se is not a consideration at all. What cultivation opposes is not nature but the local mass of impedimenta. "In all he says there is a sense of him *surrounded* by his time, tearing at it, ever with more rancor, but always at battle, taking hold" (226).

In sum, the genius of place rising through the genius of the poet rises through the impedimenta of the local, expressing the peculiarities of the local as it works its way up through them. In the Poe section this impulse driving through the poet or the self is described at length and in detail. The impulse ("desire") in the poet, in Poe's case the necessity to begin, requires opposition: differing from, separating from, fighting against, the local milieu through which it ascends. The process is a self-defining, self-insisting "method" of "composition." It is, as we have noted, the birth of a self, an immaculate conception of two original parents: its mother is the ground, the New World; it fathers itself (216-22).[17] The sometimes religious terminology recalls the traditional (European) drive to truth, but compared to either religious or secular tradition Williams' truth and the drive that conceives

---

[16]Though Heidegger usually disparages "culture [*Kultur*]" (e.g., *An Introduction* 47-8), he describes an essential, essentially poetic reciprocity between the human and the earth comparable to Williams' in, e.g., "Building Dwelling Thinking" 325ff. and in "... Poetically Man Dwells ...," *Poetry, Language, Thought* 211-29. For "cultivating [*Pflegen*]" as "genuine building [*eigentliche Bauen*]" see "Building" 147ff. and "... Poetically" 217ff. For discussion of art as founding and preserving and of its relationship with history, see "The Origin."

[17]"Self" in Heidegger, not an "I [*ein 'Ich'*]," not a "we [*ein 'Wir'*]" (*An Introduction* 143-44), can be differentiated from the "they" by a decision for authentic resoluteness (*Being and Time*, Section IV). The primary and ineluctable opposition of the "they-self" is comparable to Williams' "impedimenta" here; compare, e.g, *Being and Time* 167-68.

and delivers it is essentially different: it is neither ideal nor ideological; it is actual, historical, contingent (on ground and local conditions). Nor is the method "natural"; its necessity precedes any concept of physical law. The originality of the method is active; origin means originat*ing*; the ground is actual and active in and throughout the emerging of the poet's genius. The end of original method is its own composition, which is not an ending but a performing; thus method declares, proves, itself, or, as in Poe's case, it does not; it collapses. The original intention is to tell the soul, to express itself; in its "telling," i.e., "building" (trying to find a way to tell) itself, the New World and the period emerge too, express themselves too (231, 233). The end of the tale is truth only if truth means free self-expressing; it proves not its conclusions but its actuality, its potency.

The nature and function of language is new here commensurate with the original nature and function of composition and telling. Language is comprised of "authentic particles" (231); the unit is original "names" (226), or words:

> With Poe, words were not hung by usage with associ-
> ations, the pleasing wraiths of former masteries, this
> is the sentimental trap-door to beginnings. With Poe
> words were figures; an old language truly, but one from
> which he carried over only the most elemental quali-
> ties to his new purpose; which was, to find a way to tell
> his soul. Sometimes he used words so playfully his sen-
> tences seem to fly away from sense, the destructive! with
> the conserving abandon, foreshadowed, of a Gertrude
> Stein. The particles of language must be clear as sand.
> (See *Diddling*.) (221)

The originality of language springs from the originality of the poet or the self, "originality that presupposes an intrinsic WORTH in the reasoner ...." The poet or the self is grounded: "Unwilling to concede the necessity for any prop to his logical constructions, save the locality upon which originality is rested" (224).

We may consider this linguistic method of self-conception and self-expression in terms of the particle-mass relation. The one thing that Poe detaches from the mass of "common usage" is already something; logic is not a thing that Poe creates. In fact, he does not even choose it but is forced by the conditions of his place into that field. Thus, as we have seen, the method is the outcropping of a genius of *place* in the genius of the poet, emerging into and ascending through a locality. It begins, continues, and supports itself throughout as one part of a schism within the mass, an internal self-contradiction undertaken not for the sake of isolation and annihilation of the "crude" portion of itself but for mastery, and mastery not to oppress but to express: the genius of self, the genius of place, the impulse rising, driving; to express not as stating or achieving an anterior "meaning" but as performing itself.

The original impulse appears in Poe's case to be the driving force of his critical theory, the impulse "to sweep all worthless chaff aside.... to clear the GROUND (116). This point gives priority to thinking or the intent to think over art, as though the desire for purity, cleanness, for method (for language) were a primary reaction against the undifferentiated—a primordial human desire to differentiate. It is interesting too that the method that will detach the one thing from the mass is not analytical and not representational; it will not sort out the elements that compose the mass so that the mass is now discovered in its essential organization. It detaches one thing in order to oppose the rest, thereby declaring itself. Method is a mode of assertion, not proposition but self-assertion, working according to a principle of opposition. And there is an implication that there is no one generally correct or true method, but that there is in each case a particular, needed (forced), available one. Poe's use of "cold logic" is not necessary to "method" but only necessary to the particular opposition demanded here, against the "gluey imagination" of the public.

But in this notion of method, is there no conflict between the possibility of play and pure self-assertion on the one hand and the possibility of understanding and of grounded "authentic particles" that are the "fibre" of the method (229) on the other? "Understanding" has traditionally implied thematic truth; "ground" and "authenticity" some original or final cause, authority. The difficulty here is in suspending these meanings long enough to get a sense of Williams' fresh meanings. Understanding and authenticity have been transferred in this work from truth and authority to ground—the original, originating genius of place and of self. Self-assertion too has derived from that active source. But what of "play"? Here play is not unrelatedness or arbitrariness, but freedom and *jouissance*. Both play and ground operate in the method of Poe, and we may examine them in an explicit description.

"The significance and the secret" of the method as it operates in the tales is, the author explains: "the *method*" itself (231), i.e., the way it does what it does:

> ...authentic particles, a thousand of which spring to the mind for quotation, taken apart and reknit with a view to emphasize, enforce and make evident, the *method*. Their quality of skill in observation, their heat, local verity, being *overshadowed* only by the detached, the abstract, the cold philosophy of their joining together; a method springing so freshly from the local conditions which determine it, by their emphasis of firm crudity and lack of coordinated structure, as to be worthy of most painstaking study— The whole period, America 1840, could be rebuilt, psychologically (phrenologically) from Poe's "method." (231)

The "authentic particles," which the method takes apart and rejoins for its own sake, seem to belong to the mass the method opposes. The "quality of skill in observation" seems to inhere in these particles, not in the method or in Poe. Their "heat, local verity" seem to indicate their lively, essential participation in their actual locality. Again, in the stuff of this method, the things it takes up to its purpose, we find the same animated mass, a non-metaphysical thingness; the *virtu* that stands in metaphysics *behind* or *beyond* entities is incorporated *in* them here. Everywhere we find the living, active ground. But what of freedom? We find freedom in the method of the poet or the self, which reorders or composes these particles for its own purpose, i.e., to conceive and to express itself, the method springing, however, like the particles, from the locality. Freedom is the "preposterous" "extreme" of the play of Poe's inventions predicted, to be sure, by "a [deeper], logical enjoyment, in keeping with his own seriousness," but limited only by the limit of his power to "[make] them WORK" (230). "And by the very extreme of their play, by so much the more do they hold up the actuality of that which he conceives": his self.

Everywhere in this work, but especially in the last climactic pages, the "method" is presented in psychological terms or figures. The author deconstructs Poe's texts, selecting for his purpose the less serious, less polished tales, in which "numerous illuminating faults" betray "what Poe is driving at in his tales," the underlying "original fibre" which is their motivation. In the context of current post-Nietzschean and post-Freudian notions of play and of desire, Williams' thematic is provocative.[18] The "authentic particles" ("words," "logical constructions") have been disassembled from their traditional assembly and reassembled in "extreme," fantastic, new assemblies, designed to "go," "[to] prove him potent." The new linguistic inventions (the tales) assert no truths except the actuality of what they "show": method, in and by way of which the poet or the self emerges and asserts and sustains itself, a show of will to power, "mastery" by "understanding" (232), Nietzschean even in its psychological aspect, i.e., the "prop" of an originality in "its legitimate sense of solidity which goes back

---

[18] The tragedy of language exceeding itself in the Poe chapter is the very dramatization of Kristeva's linguistic theory in *Revolution in Poetic Language* except in the essential nature of the characters in the drama, particularly in the nature of ground.

to the ground, a conviction that he [Poe] *can* judge within himself" (216). This solidity, this conviction, like the "satisfaction" that is the motivation of the self, the poet, is the author's anti-metaphysical ground for an actuality which is simply the human performance of free invention—the "expression" of the genius of a place and a self or poet; "expression" not as thematic statement but as psychological building, arranging, holding in arrangement (232).

There is a density of Freudian elements at play in the author's method here. The name of massiness when it is recognized in its blinding, terror-striking radiance, as that against which Poe's method contends, into which it dissolves when it can no longer hold onto itself, its "arrangement," is "love." The "desire" which impelled the poet, the "enjoyment" and the for-the-sake-of-satisfaction that drives him, seem to be all of a piece: this mass, love. It was touching, marrying, we recall, that rendered Rasles' esthetic-moral recognition of the Indians, for example; Burr's trust of "that gross flesh" that engendered his authenticity. Williams seems to be writing a Freudian interpretation not only of Poe's texts but of the artist, of the period, of all that is, the world. When he writes that Poe's desire bursts through the poem that would master it and finds itself revealed to itself as this nonlinguistic, overpowering love, he seems to reinvent or appropriate the essence of the Freudian paradigm—except that in Williams the desire, the lust, is the very locus or essence of "genius," something we generally think apart from "gross flesh." Here is the genius of America: the "shy and wild and frail, the loveliest, to be cherished only by the most keen, courageous and sensitive" (214); the genius of Burr: "His profound refinement, his sense of the deeper forces working in his world that demanded freedom" (195).

And Williams' "satisfaction" cannot be reduced to something physical or to a principle of contradiction, must leave behind or open up and multiply our notion of sexuality: "A poet is one related to a basis of material, aesthetic, spiritual, hypothetical, abnormal—satisfaction …."(213-14). Further, Williams takes desire too far and informs the universe with it. The "love" which emerges under the pressure of "desire" in the Poe section is the very "freshness" that has informed everything that has emerged in the entire work: the ground, the local, history, things anti-metaphysical. It does not seem sufficient to name this massiness "desire" in a Freudian sense (though Lacan has given that potentiality a complexity beyond a physical or material impulse). It contains after all that imbedded fineness. If "desire" is a human quality, then everything in *IAG*, even chaotic massiness, is human; since that suggestion makes the term "human" meaningless, we must say instead that desire seems to be a quality of the chaotic, the undifferentiated, and pertains to the world as to man. What is significant, it seems to me, is Williams' "mastering" (understanding) of this potentiality, not by rational reduction or by representation, but by his "method," which in its driven play proves the actuality of what emerges thereby into existence, mass and particles. Williams is something of a deconstructionist in unraveling ("seeing," looking at") linguistic inventions that have dominated what is not invented, in annihilating closed logical systems, and also in setting free the stuff against which invention contends—the mass of the ground and the human. (There is much grist for a Marxist mill in this text, but again Williams goes too far. The ground [original basis, not fact but place and self], the local [milieu of time and place], and the human or artist—all have the undifferentiable sense-sensibility character. A material principle cannot be dissociated.)

There is a prophetic aspect to the notions in *IAG*: the suggestion that a method that must work in opposition to the local is always a circumstance of history—one marble slab—and that the cultivation of a locality could render it more receptive to inevitable "love." There is a vision of "careless truth" free *of* system, free *to* design (206) "in the open." Such freedom is already possible in a democracy, already manifest in "the directness of 'common people' " (206)—but harder "to maintain ... up through the scale," impossible so far in an aristocracy or among "the great rulers of the world" (206). This possibility is expressed in the accusations against the locality which in its lack of originality and of love isolated, embittered, and destroyed Poe:

"Had he lived in a world where love throve, his poems might have grown differently" (233). The notion of "method" illustrated in the work offers new possibilities of invention via language, "arrangement" versus "mass," in which living things might be released from old interpretations. Indeed, it is the announced intention of *IAG*: "to re-name the things seen, now lost in chaos of borrowed titles, many of them inappropriate, under which the true character lies hid" (note before text, paperbook edition).

It is this element of positive potentiality that leads some critics to call Williams sentimental or romantic or Platonic[19] in spite of his aversion to "gluey imagination" and to metaphysics. But if Williams is nostalgic, his revised sense of history redirects the meaning of nostalgia, for in *IAG* the past is present ("[history] lives in us practically day by day") and futural ("our greatest well of inspiration, our greatest hope of freedom," 189). I am claiming that hope which originates from such a ground as this work declares and manifests—ground-*breaking* for the intellect and for thinking—may be worthy of reexamination for what "strange phosphorus" it may release into existence.

Finally a caveat: Though I find what I have called a radical ontology expressed emphatically here in this text, yet I "recognize" in the text no explicit break with traditional ontology as such. Williams' intellectual terminology is conventional and does not contend against the conventional. Williams escapes the tradition by for the most part avoiding intellectual terminology, writing about what professed, professional intellectuals write about, but "directly," i.e., in everyday or in poetic terms and figures. But though he has not argued philosophy "in the smart language" (215), and thus has not unseated it, has not submerged in it in order to rise through and against it, re-originating it or annihilating it (the project of Nietzsche and Heidegger), he has subverted it nevertheless—and by virtue of his thinking.

---

[19] For example, Carl Rapp, "William Carlos Williams and the Modern Myth of the Fall," *Southern Review* 20.1 (1984): 82-90.

Appendix A: Heideggerian Insights

There is no such thing as an empty word [*ein leeres Wort*]; at most a word is worn out [*ein vernutztes*], though still filled with meaning [*das ein erfülltes bleibt*]. The name "being" retains its appellative force [*behält seine Nennkraft*]. "Away from this empty word 'being'; go to the particular essents" proves to be not only a hasty but also a highly questionable counsel.

(Martin Heidegger, *An Introduction to Metaphysics* 79)

The misinterpretation of thought and the abuse to which it leads can be overcome only by authentic thinking that goes back to the roots [*ein echtes und ursprüngliches Denken*]—and *by nothing else....* To surpass the traditional logic does not mean elimination of thought and the domination of sheer feeling; it means more radical, stricter thinking, a thinking that is part and parcel of being [*ursprünglicheres, strengeres, dem Sein zugehöriges Denken*].

(Martin Heidegger, *An Introduction to Metaphysics* 122)

Williams' turn to "things themselves"—"no ideas but in things"—appears to be hasty counsel. There is a seeming naivety in Williams' impatient immediacy. For example, in *In the American Grain* Williams' avatars practice a "recognition" of things that "releases" them into their *actual, essential* existence. Here "essentiality" removes from its Platonic superstructure, its Aristotelian substrata, casts off all pretension to truth as well as objectivity, and becomes an open question. The thing itself must answer. It does. It breaks in to experience with such immediacy and essentiality that there is little need for, room for, the mediation of a "word"—unless we count in "phosphorus."

Williams' turn to "things themselves" returns to them their "strange phosphorus," their essential character ("being") all but buried under a history of linguistic uses and abuses.[20] Let us count in "phosphorus," and also Williams' word *IAG*, as intercessors. We must do so. In such language Williams stakes his claims to "things themselves."

Heidegger's "language" makes a similar claim. The word as "it gives" gives not itself but Being/being. And Heidegger also remarked the tendency for language to lose or withdraw its efficacy, as he too prescribed and commenced the task of discounting received language, of opening thinking up to "what calls for thinking," i.e., letting things be in their Being, and of establishing Being in the word that will hold a place for it (Being) to happen.

When Williams resituates "essence" in things as they are, essentiality retains a kind of integrity, but its purity is compromised. On the whole it appears the richer—and more disturbing. There is a comparable transformation when Heidegger *destructs* and recovers the same word. We find it from the first page of *Being and Time*, where Heidegger is already evoking the work as a whole. In his description of one "existentiale" of Dasein, for example, he is (but not explicitly) surrounding it with and imbedding it in all the others, not yet described "in themselves." The *ontic* is never absent from the *ontological*, for example, nor *mood* from *understanding*, nor *falling* from *authenticity*. Here as elsewhere we find that Nietzsche's unsettling inclination *not* to cut asunder whatever always appears or occurs together is fundamental in Heidegger's thought. And it is fundamental in Williams' study of American history above. Whether it be Red Eric or blossoms underfoot, the character of the Indian or the character of morality or of history, the facts, factors, and concepts Williams assembles prove themselves to be living entities—else they are exposed as imposters and ousted from the work. As living entities they are inscribed as they appear or occur, without regard for rational justification.

---

[20]Note before text, *IAG*.

Another fundamental concern Williams shares with Heidegger is what Heidegger calls, for example, "being-in-the-world" and "dwelling." These words connect being and dwelling (and building and preserving)—not just etymologically, Heidegger insists, but in language essentially and in history. (Both Heidegger and Williams reinscribe the life-giving event of language and the meaning of historicity.[21]) We can compare Williams' notions of "ground" and of "culture" as "cultivation," though of course there are profound differences in the temper, the emphases, and the effects, as well as the magnitude and scope of the thinking in each case. Another comparison of interest is the sense of ground as particular, regional. In Williams the ground itself in its particular and local genius provides the "moral" ground of human character and action and history; indeed, this grounding gives "morality" its meaning in *IAG*. Contrariwise, for Heidegger a *locale* receives its character in relation to human building and dwelling.[22] While "historical destiny" is a prominent Heideggerian theme, the redefinition of both "history" and "destiny" (see, e.g., *Being and Time*, Section V, esp. H. 382-87) relieves the phrase of its former metaphysical freight and brings human choice to the fore (resoluteness), as well as human being in its character of care and in its historicity and temporality.

Neither is Williams' "ground" Heidegger's "it gives" (in language, poetry, art), giving whatever-is; for this giving given is not "ground," even less "earth," is no thing, and it is not regionally differentiated.[23]

---

[21] See "Building Dwelling Thinking" 355-359 and *Being and Time* H. 53-4, e.g. For discussion of historicity as "authentic resoluteness [*eigentlichen Entschlossenheit*] ... in which Dasein *hands* itself *down* to itself, free for death, in a possibility which it has inherited and yet has chosen" (435), see *Being and Time* H. 382-87.

[22] It is difficult or impossible to read Heidegger's language, given its own historical context, according to his own transformed "meanings," ignoring the common interpretations of such terms as "fate," "destiny," and "historical destiny," or to grant him immunity from the moral, political, and historical implications and effects of using such language as he did over the next few years, but that is an issue outside the scope of this study that cannot be addressed in parenthesis.

[23] In *Schelling's Treatise*, written at the period and in the language of the Rectorship Address, Heidegger writes that the mechanical thinking of the Western countries

Language is the free (groundless) establish*ing* of ground. The most important comparison in the two thinkers' conceptions is their non-metaphysical reconceptualization of ground: this very ground for Williams (though something essential inhabits and emanates from it), the groundless grounding of language for Heidegger.

Williams makes much of "relation" as the arbiter of morality. Relation is fundamental in Heidegger as well: the Being-in-the-world structures of Dasein, the creative strife of world/earth, the nature of language—i.e., of the open itself, of Saying, of the word as gathering and as giving—and of the oneness of the fourfold.[24] Heidegger's violent, mutually belonging-to "relation" (language) also compares (and contrasts) in its operation with Williams' oppositional self-conception (a "method" of "composition") in the Poe section.

Like the other American authors in this study, Williams is "Heideggerian" in his assumption and elaboration of a radical ontology. Like the others, Williams brings a renewal of a Heideggerian sense of *phusis* in the actuality of things and of relationship in human experience; of complexity, multiplexity, and contradiction inhering in such "actuality," such "relationship." Williams alone, however, dramatizes a particularly Heideggerian change-of-point-of-view: the vantage of the (tautological) circle. For nineteen chapters Williams presents figures from American history, redefining and reinforming that history, those figures; the presentation is situated as from the sideline of

---

should be opposed not by a German thinking but by a tougher, more rigorous, "more primordial and correct thinking." He quotes Schelling: " 'Truly universal philosophy cannot possibly be the property of a single nation [*das Eigenthum einer einzelnen Nation*]. As long as a philosophy does not go beyond the limits of an individual people [*eines einzelnen Volks*], one can confidently assume that it is not yet the true philosophy although it may be on its way' " (90). The question of Heidegger's nationalism remains outstanding, of course. His statements regarding German destiny deserve special study. See for example "Remembrance of the Poet," trans. Douglas Scott, *Existence and Being* 233-69.

[24]See for example "The Nature of Language": "Language is, as world-moving Saying, the relation of all relations [*als die Welt-bewëgende Sage das Verhältnis aller Verhältnisse*]" (107). For the oppositional nature of language see for example "The Origin" 168ff.; *An Introduction* 167ff.

history or in the aftermath. But in the twentieth chapter the perspective shifts, and Poe is presented as from the inside of history; that is, the narrator follows Poe's "emergence" from the center/ground out. His "way" can be described as: self-assertion via contradiction. This shift of perspective enacts, it seems to me, something like Heidegger's shift of philosophy from the site of spectator to that of participant, not solving the problem of the blindness of insight (or the anxiety of influence) but accepting the dilemma as one's place, looking out from it, through it. Everything from that view is changed.

As I Lay Dying:
Demise of Vision

The following essay is a Heideggerian reading of William Faulkner's novel. In Appendix B, I point out explicitly some of Heidegger's insights that I am finding among Faulkner's insights here.

The criticism of William Faulkner's *As I Lay Dying*[1] manifests the heterogeneity, the ambivalence, and the outright contradiction that characterize Faulkner criticism in general. Meanwhile the work continues to provoke ever more provocative commentary. Among traditional interpretations that even yet attempt to find meaning as statement, nontraditional readings have begun to let the meaning lie while they follow Faulkner's strange experiments with time and space, with memory and imagination, with consciousness and unconsciousness.[2] Still, whatever the reading, it is usually expressed in terms of rationalist thinking, i.e., in negative terms, as disruption, disjunction, vacancy, and absence, as distortion and loss. The only novelty I hope

---

[1] New York: Random House, 1964.
An early version of this essay was published in *American Literature* 61:1 (March, 1989): 16-30. Republished in *Twentieth-Century Literary Criticism* 141, 86-92.

[2] Notably, for example, John T. Irwin, *Doubling and Incest/ Repetition and Revenge: A Speculative Reading of Faulkner* (Baltimore: Johns Hopkins, 1975).

to offer is that my interest is to describe what shows up or what happens where old meanings have disappeared without merely speaking in reverse. Exploring the novel's explicit treatment of language, my study will make its way literally along, searching the bare bones of the narrative, attempting not to repeat or to archaeologically reconstitute the work, but to follow alongside it in a thinking.

It is Addie who gives emphasis to (raises the spectre of) language as such. Words, she claims, are ineffectual.

> And so when Cora Tull would tell me I was not a true mother, I would think how words go straight up in a thin line, quick and harmless, and how terribly doing goes along the earth, clinging to it, so that after a while the two lines are too far apart for the same person to straddle from one to the other; and that sin and love and fear are just sounds that people who never sinned nor loved nor feared have for what they never had and cannot have until they forget the words. (165-66)

Not words but "doing"—something terrible that belongs to the earth—is what matters. Addie's essential disagreement with Anse turns on precisely this point of doing versus not-doing, a horizontal-vertical earth-space set of contraries. Things God meant to stay in one place, says Anse—such as trees, men—He set in an upright, vertical position; things devoted to moving—roads, snakes—He made horizontal. Anse cordially loathes movement. Living in Addie's terms is evil in his (34-35).[3]

Living in her terms is evil in the terms of her culture, too: Mississippi Bible-belt terms which counsel to suffer the little children,

---

[3] Compare Faulkner's remarks in an interview for *Paris Review* in 1956, in which he equates life with motion and motion with motivation, claiming that the intention of the artist is "to arrest motion, which is life, by artificial means and hold it fixed so that a hundred years later, when a stranger looks at it, it moves again since it is life." Quoted in *Lion in the Garden*, eds. James B. Meriwether and Michael Millgate (New York: Random House, 1968) 253.

not to relish whipping them; to honor father and mother, not to hate the father for "planting" one; to submit to the husband, not to deny unequivocally his significance; to bring up a child in the way he should go, not to reject him (Darl), not to worship him (Jewel); not to commit adultery; not to refuse to confess or repent; not, above all, stubbornly to choose one's own terms. In Addie's culture, natural instinct is fallen nature; desire is lust; will is willfulness; initiative is disobedience; independence is pride.

But when Addie insists on choosing her own "terms," does she escape the function or the necessity of words? And can we ignore the tautology in the denial of the validity and utility of words by the character whose words provide the title of the novel and the central chapter? Setting these doubts aside for the moment, we commence our exploration after Addie's example, with a story, with Addie's story, taking her literal statement as our first subject of inquiry. The "Addie" chapter gives an account of Addie's lifetime of interpreting and rein-terpreting (1) the nature of the words of her culture, their emptiness and inadequacy, and (2) the nature of living—a "doing," separate and different from those words.

Addie's first interpretation is partial and instinctual, derived as a young teacher, a lonely, educated woman in a Mississippi country community, profoundly frustrated, all the more for the lack of a direct cause or a direct object. The opening sentence in her chapter sets the tone: "In the afternoon when school was out and the last one had left with his little dirty snuffling nose, instead of going home I would go down the hill to the spring where I could be quiet and hate them." At night, as she recalls, "Sometimes I thought that I could not bear it, lying in bed ... with the wild geese going north and their honking coming faint and high and wild out of the wild darkness," and during the day, "it would seem as though I couldn't wait for the last one to go so I could go down to the spring." She interprets her hate in terms of the "secret and selfish" thoughts and lives of the children, each with his own "strange" blood. Thus she whips them till the skin welts and bleeds, till she has "marked" their blood with her own in a cruel empathic (sado-masochistic) catharsis.

In a later reinterpretation Addie expressly attributes this early frustration to the problem of words. Whipping the children was a futile attempt to mitigate the condition of aloneness—aloneness, she later understands, by reason of their dependence upon words for touching. She and the children "had had to use one another by words like spiders dangling by their mouths from a beam, swinging and twisting and never touching, and ... only through the blows of the switch could [her] blood and their blood flow as one stream" (164). In this image, the beam is a part of an apparently stationary structure. Hanging from the beam at intervals are spiders that dangle and twist without touching each other. Each spider is connected to the beam by its own thread, but the connection of spider to spider is contingent on the beam, whose essential function is not related to spiders'. Like the given beam, preestablished language does not originate in Addie and the children or in their essential function: doing. In this image, as in the vertical-horizontal image above (and the geese image below), language is a high, separate, separating non-mediator.

Addie and the children "use" each other "by words" as the spiders hang onto the beam "by" their mouths. Words are like the spider threads; their origin is essential but their function is artificial and mechanical, routed through the non- and dis-connecting beam: dysfunctional language. When words do not mediate, cannot penetrate, interpenetrate, then human intercourse requires something more, more essential: doing. "Doing" for Addie incorporates a principle of violation—a violation not merely physical, but a violation of *aloneness*. Whipping the children is an attempt to make-them-aware-of-me; and it fails (164).

"And so I took Anse." The word "so" (162-63) indicates an essential relationship between Addie's frustration and her "taking" of Anse (not her being-taken-*by* Anse; "doing" is her modus operandi, not his). The same implication is given by the same word a few paragraphs later. Addie tells Anse that she has never known any kind of people, living or dead, who were not "hard to talk to"; the next paragraph begins, "So I took Anse." Again the "so" implies a relationship between frustration and taking Anse, but this time the problem is indirectly identified with ineffectual language in her first—implicit—critique of language.

Marrying Anse means a violation-of-virginity, the oldest remedy in the world for the oldest frustration; but marriage fails to satisfy Addie's violation-principle. The violation which satisfies her demand occurs with the birth of Cash. This "doing" brings the more-than-physical violating and restoring of aloneness which provides at last a wholeness (of aloneness),[4] a "circle" exclusive of "time, Anse, love, what you will"—but not of Cash or of lov*ing*, the deed displaced by the word "love." (This insular self-inclusiveness is characteristic of Faulknerian women, an often bitter, hard, wise insensitivity, principle of female endurance, enduring.) A second violation, a second pregnancy—a "trick" of Anse's word "love"—will motivate the rest of the story, but to our purpose here, the "doing" of "having" the children is, Addie discovers, the "answer" to "terrible" living; and it includes, involves, the earth: "Sometimes I would lie by [Anse] in the dark, hearing the land that was now of my blood and flesh" (165). If we analyze Addie's condition, if we sort her answers and terror and blood into mental, emotional, and physical categories, or if we attempt to define her state in terms of objective reality or subjective interpretation, we sacrifice their "flooding," "boiling" actuality, and enact the very process of abstraction that she has discovered and denounced.[5]

---

[4]The authenticity and the her-ownness that Addie demands are compatible thematically with some of Heidegger's discussion of authenticity, *Being and Time* H. 294, e.g.

[5]Heidegger resists Nietzsche's emphasis on the body, physiology (*Nietzsche*, Vol. IV 133-35), as he shares Nietzsche's resistance to rational analysis (noted in the Williams chapter above), on the basis of the primordial unity of the ontical-ontological structures of Dasein (not presence or totality; only death can provide totalization). See *Being and Time* H. 47-48, 52ff., 180ff., 235ff.

Compare Addie's former frustration, lying at night alone listening to the geese cries overhead. Now, after she has "had" Cash and Darl, when she has achieved some essential potentiality, she lies awake,

> ... hearing the dark land talking of God's love and His
> beauty and His sin; hearing the dark voicelessness in
> which the words are the deeds, and the other words that
> are not deeds, that are just the gaps in peoples' lacks,
> coming down like the cries of the geese out of the wild
> darkness in the old terrible nights, fumbling at the deeds
> like orphans to whom are pointed out in a crowd two
> faces and told, That is your father, your mother. (166)

"Other words" are orphans, though their parents are living: words as deeds, which belong to the "dark voicelessness" of the "dark land talking." "Other words" are all the words she knows, we assume, since she denounces words per se, denies and contradicts their meanings. "Other words" are alienated words, dissociated from and without effect upon real—i.e., doing—living. "Other words" are inert and must be forgotten in order to deal directly with living, doing.[6]

She thinks about the function of words:

> ... I would think: Anse. Why Anse. Why are you Anse.
> I would think about his name until after a while I could
> see the word as a shape, a vessel, and I would watch him
> liquefy and flow into it like cold molasses flowing out
> of the darkness into the vessel, until the jar stood full

---

[6]Compare Heidegger's account of fallen words: "Naming does not come afterward, providing an already manifest essent with a designation and a hallmark known as a word; it is the other way around: originally an act of violence that discloses being, the word sinks from this height to become a mere sign [*das Wort sinkt aus der Höhe seiner ursprünglichen Gewalt-tat als Eröffnung des Seins zum bloßen Zeichen herab*], and this sign proceeds to thrust [*schiebt*] itself before the essent," *An Introduction* 172.

and motionless: a significant shape profoundly without
life like an empty door frame; and then I would find
that I had forgotten the name of the jar. I would think:
The shape of my body where I used to be a virgin is
in the shape of a/ /and I couldn't think *Anse*, couldn't
remember *Anse*. It was not that I could think of myself
as no longer unvirgin, because I was three now. And
when I would think *Cash* and *Darl* that way until their
names would die and solidify into a shape and then fade
away, I would say, All right. It doesn't matter. It doesn't
matter what they call them. (165)

In Addie's analogy a name is like a jar that has a shape, a prefab-
ricated form—with contours, definition, limitation (a name already
belongs to language). Into this jar the strangely adapting Anse flows.
Since the form is already made, shaped, limited, the transforming
Anse fills that form, takes that shape, admits that limit. The jar is not
Anse, is not an image of him, not a representation, but a shape (a form,
signifier) lent to Anse (a doing, signified), a shape which accommo-
dates Anse himself. The adaptation of Anse to the jar is reminiscent
of what we usually call "concept," meaning a psychological construct
of Anse in the mind of Addie. But if we resist the temptation to call it
"concept," we may obtain a new view of the phenomenon appearing
here. In Addie's description the jar is not the same phenomenon as
Anse himself, sleeping beside her as she thinks about the function
of his name; yet to install a third entity in the scheme, an idea in the
mind of Addie, does not answer to the phenomenon either, since
the jar is only temporary. The jar-name dissolves and leaves Anse
behind—or it leaves nothing, since Anse is "dead." What remains is
not the jar but what flows into the jar and is released.

And what is the nature of what the jar "Anse" receives and releases?
Anse himself, strangely (unaccountably) adapting to the transference,
is present to Addie through the function of the word, and outside it.
This being-present-to is perhaps another mode of the same miracle

by which Anse sleeping would be present to her if she turned her attention to him. The notion of a recurring or cumulative Anse who has been and may be present to her ignores or dismisses the metaphysical concept of Anse-in-himself. Thus we object that this Anse is, or is altered by, Addie's subjective perception. But in this text it is not possible to locate any entities-in-themselves, and so the point is moot. At any rate, to return to the function of the word, the jar does not so much contain Anse as it maintains him. That is, Addie recalls the name "Anse" first, separately, then recalls Anse—flowing into, filling the word-jar. The name serves to bear or carry Anse, to bring or call him to presence. But once the name has performed this function, the name itself is displaced by Anse and in itself is forgotten.[7]

Addie would forget the name of the jar; to recall it she would think of Anse himself. If a name stood in a reciprocal or a necessary relationship with a person, then the recollection of the person should recall the name.[8] But when Addie thinks of the person Anse, she

---

[7] "Words are not terms [*Die worte sind keine Wörter*], and thus are not like buckets and kegs [*Eimer und Fässer*] from which we scoop a content [*Inhalt*] that is there," writes Heidegger; words are wellsprings (*Brunnen*), *What is Called Thinking* 130. Addie's jars look suspiciously like Heidegger's "terms." Yet their jarlike (juglike, thinglike) capability of "taking [*nehmend*]" and "keeping [*behaltend*]" "what is poured in [*Einguß*]" ("The Thing" 171) deadends into their unjarlike self-dissolution, their setting-free of what they have received in an entirely unthinglike way (compare Heidegger's description of the thingness of a jug, 166ff.). The effect is comparable (but not equal) to Heidegger's words "as the gathering which first brings what presences to its presence [*die Versammlung, die Anwesendes erst in sein Anwesen bringt*]," "Words" 155.

[8] As for memory, Heidegger connects it radically with knowing, as having-seen. Recalling is more than recollection; it is the "thoughtful maintenance of Being's preserve [*das denkende Gewahren der Wahrnis des Seins*]" ("The Anaximander Fragment" 36) and it is "devotion: a constant concentrated abiding with something [*An-dacht: das unablässige, gesammelte Bleiben bei*]—not just with something that has passed, but in the same way with what is present and with what may come. What is past, present, and to come appears in the oneness of its own *present* being [*Das Vergangene, das Gegenwärtige, das Kommende erscheinen in der Einheit eines je eigenen An-wesens*]," *What Is Called Thinking?* 140.

recalls a blank. The experiment seems to corroborate her theory that names function to signify doings ("Anse" recalls Anse to presence), while doings function quite healthily without reference to names (Anse does not recall "Anse" to mind). Another implication concerns the character of Anse. When Addie thinks of the word "Anse" (and of Anse's word "love"), the form (filled jar) is like an empty doorframe. An empty doorframe is a base for a door, the preparation for a door, and it implies the intention of a door; but ultimately it functions to signify the absence of a door. Like words in themselves, outside their function, like a mere doorframe, Anse is "a significant shape profoundly without life."[9]

Now when Addie forgets Anse's name and tries to recall it by thinking of him, she thinks of sexual intercourse, according to her violation-of-aloneness principle (doing). But in spite of the fact that he has fathered her two children ("I was three now"), in spite of the profound significance that these two "violations" have had for her, still Anse himself has never touched her according to her violation-of-aloneness principle; thus he has no meaning. The name "Anse" is a sign signifying nothing: a shape signifying a lack.

It is different with "Cash" and "Darl," although the function of names remains the same. When Addie thinks of "Cash" and "Darl," the names "die and solidify into a shape and then fade away," as "Anse" did. But "it doesn't matter what they call them." She learned when she was pregnant with Cash "that words are no good; that words dont ever fit even what they are trying to say at" (163). The names "Cash" and "Darl" are shapes which function to signify (recall, bring), but the shapes in themselves are not significant; in Addie's view names in themselves are arbitrary and unnecessary. "When [Cash] was born I knew that motherhood was invented by someone who had to have a word for it because the one that had the children didn't care whether there was a word for it or not. I knew that fear was

---

[9]Compare Sutpen's empty doorframe in *Absalom, Absalom!* where the ironies of intention misdirected, misapprehended, thwarted, and shattered are multiplied *ad infinitum* (New York: Random House, 1936).

invented by someone that had never had the fear; pride, who never had the pride" (163-64). The significance in "Cash" and "Darl" is the reality of "having" these two children. Cash and Darl, with or without names, are genuine *doings*, according to her violation-of-aloneness principle.[10]

There is one more active understanding of life and of words that Addie achieves before she must clean her house. This time the doing is passion and the word is "sin." Motherhood has provided the key to ("terrible") living, Anse has "died," and now she interprets her duty in life as duty *to* life, to "the alive." (Cora will castigate her for neglecting her Christian duty, but Cora's "duty" is another high, dead sound in the air.) "I believed that I had found it. I believed that the reason was the duty to the alive, to the terrible blood, the red bitter flood boiling through the land" (166).

"Sin" is the word people who haven't sinned use to cover up what-sin-is. "Sin" is for people who have to have a word for something they never had. It is a shape to fill a lack. But for Addie, the sinner, "sin" is a "gallant garment already blowing aside with the speed of his secret coming," a garment her lover and she lay aside in order "to shape and coerce the terrible blood to the forlorn echo of the dead word high in the air." The deed that "sin" displaces is a living, life-forcing doing.[11]

---

[10] Addie's "words" seem to function as Heidegger's "signs [*Zeichen*]" *Being and Time*, Section 17—to indicate, refer—and not as his "words." The priority Addie gives to what-is over what she calls "words" compares with the priority of "what calls for thinking [*Was heißt uns denken?*]" in *What Is Called Thinking?* (113ff., e.g.).

[11] Heidegger's discussion of resoluteness in *Schelling's Treatise* offers an interesting gloss: "But in the Moment of the decisive fundamental experience of human being [*Im Augenblick der maßgebenden Grunderfahrung des Menschenwesens*] we are, as in no other experience of self, protected from the vanity of self-overestimation and the self-righteousness of self-depreciation. For in the decidedness of our own being, we experience the fact that no one attains the height of what is his best as little as he attains the abyss of what is his evil, but that he is placed in this Between [*Zwischen*] in order to wrest his truth from it [*seine Wahrheit abzuringen*] which is in itself necessary, but, precisely for this reason, historical [*die in sich notwendig, aber gerade deshalb geschichtlich ist*]. It stands beyond the distinction of a truth for everyone and a truth for 'special individuals.' Only a wrested truth is truth. For it wrestles

The meaning of words is for Addie only the doing of human living. Words like "sin" and "love" and "fear," which have lost their connection with doing, which have flown off from doing (which is clinging to the earth) into the wild, dark air, have become falsifiers and expropriators of life and language. Thus Addie's injunction against substituting words for doings and her warning that people will never experience doings until they forget words.

But does the principle enjoin silence? Does it address literally all words? As we have already noted, Addie's principles of life and language are themselves "terms." Having examined these directly, we peruse her chapter again for further implications about the function of words.

There are the words of Addie's father, his dictum: "the reason for living was to get ready to stay dead a long time." Addie contemplates this sentiment at the beginning, in the middle, and at the end of her narration. What her father says in this dictum is at the beginning an ironic witticism to which her experience gives a bitter, humorless interpretation. If *this* (teaching school, hating and whipping the children, unmitigated aloneness) is the only way to get ready to stay dead, she wishes her father had not "planted" her. In the middle of the chapter the words occur again. After the "trick"—Anse's, "love"'s, life's—of a second pregnancy, this violation violating the consummation of the first, and after Darl's birth, Addie extracts Anse's promise that when she dies he will take her back to Jefferson where her people, presumably her father as well, are buried, "because I knew that father had been right, even when he couldn't have known he was right anymore than I could have known I was wrong." Now she knows the doing to which the dictum refers, knows that violation-of-aloneness is not "the answer" to living after all. At three moments of bitter revelation Addie interprets her father's dictum as each wave of violation overwhelms the last. Perhaps with the second she begins to know the

beings out into the open [*sie ringt das Seiende heraus in das Offene*], and orders that open so that the bond of beings may come into play [*damit die Bindung des Seienden ins Spiel komme*]" (155).

inherent self-contradiction life is, the violation that it commits against itself—continuous moving precluding the possibility of arrival, continuous getting precluding the possibility of attainment, continuous process precluding the possibility of product, until afterward.

At the end of her narration, after the secret "sin," when she discovers the new pregnancy, Jewel, and its price, cleaning up the house afterward, Addie "knew at last what [her father] meant and that he could not have known what he meant himself, because a man cannot know anything about cleaning up the house afterward." Her father's dictum signifies a doing which he could not have "known." She has speculated at three different points as to the meaning this saying had for him, who, as far as we know, authored the words. At each point the saying has come to mean something different for *her*. The saying is always comprised of the same words, words of her father who is dead; but their meaning is not fixed, has not solidified, died. If Addie's experience with her father's words is an indication of the legitimate function of living words, then the difference in old words that are dead and old words that are living is not in their age nor in their sound or sense, but in their relationship with living doing.[12]

Addie has illustrated the difference between dead and living words. In both cases the name (word) is a given shape that has an arbitrary relationship to what it names. But dead words are only given shapes; and what-they-name, what Addie's "jar" holds, is inert or

---

[12]Compare Heidegger's "manifold validity [*die Vielgültigkeit*]" in *Nietzsche*, Vol. I, 147-48: "supposing that the essence of truth did change [*das Wesen der Wahrheit wandelt sich*], that which changes could always still be a 'one' which holds for 'many' [*dann kann das Gewandelte ... das Eine werden, was für vieles gilt*], the transformation not disturbing that relationship. But what is preserved in the metamorphosis is what is unchangeable in the essence [*das Unwandelbare des Wesens*], which essentially unfolds in its very transformation. The essentiality of essence [*die Wesentlichkeit des Wesens*], its inexhaustibility [*Unerschöpflichkeit*], is thereby affirmed, and also its genuine selfhood and selfsameness [*Selbstheit und Selbigkeit*]. The latter stands in sharp contrast to the vapid selfsameness of the monotonous [*der leeren Selbigkeit des Einerlei*], which is the only way the unity of essence can be thought when it is taken merely as the universal [*das Allgemeine*].

nonexistent. Living words are dead names/shapes too (names/shapes *in themselves* are dead),[13] arbitrary too, and forgettable, but what-they-mean is living, real. Name them or not, name them something particular or something else, in any case what-they-mean "is," is memorable. And what the words mean is memorable *by way of language*, as Addie's experience with her father's words has shown.[14]

In fact, there seems to be an ambiguity principle operating in living words—not that the meanings of words are not determinable or clear, but that they are not fixed, not static, not complete, finished, totaled.[15] We have seen it in Addie's father's words living out of the past. We find it again, for example, in Addie's conversation with Cora on the subject of her refusal to confess, even under the ardent admonitions of the sanctified Brother Whitfield (158-60). Addie's words (e.g., "I know my own sin. I know that I deserve my punishment. I do not begrudge it") are extremely provocative to poor, spiteful Cora, whose nose for iniquity is quite reliable, but who is helpless to get a hold here without a "word" from Addie. And though Addie is confessing in words, words that have the meaning that both she and Cora understand, she nevertheless withholds the word outright (the confession, naming the party) that would satisfy Cora's malicious

---

[13]"The word—no thing, nothing that is, no being [*kein Ding, nichts Seiendes*]; but we have an understanding of things when the word for them is available" [*zur Verfügung steht*], "The Nature of Language" 87.

[14]For Heidegger the word not only "makes a thing appear as the thing it is, and thus lets it be present [*ein Ding als das Ding. das es ist, erscheinen und also anwesen läßt*]," but also "holds and sustains a thing in its being [*ein Ding in dessen Sein hält und erhält*]," "The Nature of Language" 65-6.

[15]"[M]ultiplicity of meanings [*Die Mehrdeutigkeit*] is the element in which all thought must move in order to be strict thought [*ein strenges*]. To use an image: to a fish, the depths and expanses of its waters, the currents and quiet pools, warm and cold layers are the element of its multiple mobility [*vielfältigen Beweglichkeit*]. If the fish is deprived of the fullness of its element, if it is dragged on the dry sand, then it can only wriggle, twitch, and die. Therefore, we always must seek out thinking, and its burden of thought [*das Denken und sein Gedachtes jeweils*], in the element of its multiple meanings [*Mehrdeutigkeit*], else everything will remain closed to us," *What Is Called Thinking?* 71.

curiosity (and perhaps atone for the fact that Addie has sons and can cook).

Ostensibly Addie is returning to Cora language of her own kind. Cora uses words no one can refute, religious phrases straight from the mouths of the likes of Brother Whitfield, hardened empty "jars" the church has handed around to everyone and stands every day to authorize.[16] And her use of these empty truisms is fairly transparent; a bully, she uses them like clubs. But the tantalizing, maddening thing about Addie's use of such words is that they are not empty forms when she says them; they are living, and for Cora they are brimming with a salacious mystery. Addie's words accommodate, house, what she means: a doing. Cora's words deny, belie, her doing-meaning.[17]

The ambiguity principle that allows dead language to serve the living, to live again, operates in reverse as well, allows living language to serve the dead, to die. Anse is fond of characterizing Addie in such

---

[16]Heidegger's description of "Idle Talk," *Das Gerade*, the everyday discourse of Dasein, in *Being and Time*, Section 35 (H. 167-71), assists my satiric remarks here; for example, relative to my Bro. Whitfield shaft a fortuitous remark: "The Being-said [*Gesagtsein*], the *dictum*, the pronouncement [*Ausspruch*]—all these now stand surety for the genuineness [*Echtheit*] of the discourse [*Rede*] and of the understanding which belongs to it [*ihres Verständnisses*], and for its appropriateness [*Sachgemäßheit*] to the facts. And because this discoursing has lost its primary relationship-of-Being towards the entity talked about [*den primären Seinsbezug zum beredeten Seienden*], or else has never achieved such a relationship, it does not communicate in such a way as to let this entity be appropriated in a primordial manner [*ursprünglichen Zueignung*], but communicates rather by following the route of *gossiping* [*des Weiter-*] and *passing the word along* [*und Nachredens*]. What is said-in-the-talk as such [*Das Geredete als solches*], spreads in wider circles and takes on an authoritative character.... Idle talk is constituted by just such gossiping and passing the word along" (212).

[17]Compare the distinction Heidegger makes between speaking and saying, "The Way to Language" 122: "To say and to speak are not identical [*Sagen und Sprechen sind nicht das gleiche*]. A man may speak, speak endlessly, and all the time say nothing. Another man may remain silent, not speak at all and yet, without speaking, say a great deal [*kann im Nichtsprechen viel sagen*].... 'Say' means to show, to let appear, to let be seen and heard [*'Sagen' heißt: zeigen, erscheinen-, sehen- und hören-lassen*]."

phrases as "She was ever a private woman"; "She was ever one to clean up after herself" (18-19). In such remarks Anse states words whose meaning is true, i.e., going-on, doing. Addie *has been and is doing* what these words indicate. Nevertheless, the words in Anse's mouth are the solidified forms that Addie despises. The words are dead, for Anse is dead. He says the words, as Cora says her platitudes; but he means nothing by them. That is, the words mean what *he* means, which is nothing. They serve at best as an excuse for not-being, a substitute for being. At their most positive, Anse's words are a complaint. Anse's arduous trek to Jefferson to bury Addie is his ultimate (most-doing) word (deed) of this kind; he seems glad that the task is impossible, absurd, indecent. The degradation is his manifest abdication of responsibility for his own doing (he disapproves of doing, we know): this obscene advertisement of ignorance and stupidity is *her* idea, *her* wish, *her* command ("It's a trial.... But I dont begrudge her it," 156).[18]

Where is the living in living words? Are the words doing the living? Anse says words that are "true," that say doing, and yet his words are empty. When we, readers, read his words, we understand that they are living by Addie's standards even though Anse does not know it. The answer seems to be that words belong to speakers and hearers. For Anse the words are dead; for us they are living, just as Addie thinks the words of her father were dead to him though they are living to her. *Living* does not belong to any abstract or objective "reality" and not to words in themselves, but to whoever is living, doing.[19] And living words are unfinished, are ambiguous; they allow

---

[18] We see the principle in small when in the passages I have cited both Anse and Addie use the word "begrudge," with different motivation and to different effect. Anse's word conceals his meaninglessness (not-doing), at least from himself; Addie's word indicates her meaning (doing), at least for herself, for us. We note that Addie's word does not reveal her meaning to Cora, for whom living language can indicate only mystery—and menace.

[19] Although Addie is an essentialist, Faulkner is something more. In this novel the uprootedness of language from traditional time and space and from "meaning"

doing to happen in them. Like the words of Addie's father, they accommodate changing, living doing.

The legitimate use of words, to hold a place for meaning to go on, has been shown above. But is the use of words, even the legitimate use, necessary? What is the effect of words? The novel shows in many cases the point of origin of words. That is, characters approach a word and break off—refuse to say it. Why?

> "It's laying there, watching Cash whittle on that damn …" Jewel says. He says it harshly, savagely, but he does not say the word. Like a little boy in the dark to flail his courage and suddenly aghast into silence by his own noise. (Darl 18)

> When they get it finished they are going to put her in it and then for a long time I couldn't say it. I saw the dark stand up and go whirling away and I said…. (Vardaman 62)

Before the word, at the point of origin, there is an approaching. Jewel approaches *coffin*; he stops short. We recall that earlier he could not stand the sound of Cash's hammer. "One lick less. One lick less. One lick less until everybody that passes in the road will have to stop and see it and say what a fine carpenter he is" (15). Jewel is right; for Cash the coffin does amount to a good job to do well. But for Jewel, who cannot bear to finish his sentence, the completion of the job would mean: coffin. The sound of the hammer, the deed (doing) of the making of the coffin, is a sound he hates, for he hates the sequel—denies, refuses the spoken or carpentered reality. He suppresses the word—denies, opposes the deed—as he will suppress, deny, oppose the truth (doing) of his own identity that Darl knows; as he will suppress, deny, oppose Darl who could say the word.

---

as well as its dependence on and relatedness to living people has fundamental Heideggerian resonances.

Before the word, we have said, at the point of origin, there is an approaching. Vardaman approaches *nail-her-up*. He says it: "Are you going to nail her up in it, Cash? Cash? Cash?" A breathless space and he says it again, this time discovering where the emphasis is: "I got shut up in the crib the new door it was too heavy for me it went shut I couldn't breathe because the rat was breathing up all the air. I said 'Are you going to nail it shut, Cash? Nail it? *Nail* it?'" (62).

What is the principle here? It is expressed by Darl, telling Dewey Dell (in their unspoken language), "'You want her to die so you can get to town: is that it?' She wouldn't say what we both knew. 'The reason you will not say it is, when you say it, even to yourself, you will know it is true: is that it? But you know it is true now'" (38-39). This story is full of secret knowledge, private and shared knowledge, subconscious motivation and determination of what characters say and do, knowledge that could perhaps subvert dead forms that their lives are trapped by, made impotent and crippled by. Saying it would drag it into the light, bring it into view, expose it. Saying it would mean seeing it. Saying false words fixes falseness, nothing; fixes a blight, death. Saying doing words means seeing doing, establishing it in view so that one, and others, can continue to see it. We find ourselves at something of an origin here: to say words is to create reality.[20]

An ontology of language has been traced in this novel to the problem of a beginning. In such a novel, which treats such a subject, we should at least glance briefly at the question of art. If language

---

[20]Besides the references above to the *word* as *es gibt*, see an interesting Heideggerian interpretation of Nietzschean maxims, in which "believing" is taken as "thinking" and "thinking" as "fixation [*Festmachen*]" of "a projection of Being [*Entwurf des Seins*]"—"the securing of permanence [*Bestandsicherung*]." Here it is not a thing that is "fixed," but a *possibility* (*Möglichkeit*); "to hold firm in this thought [of a possibility] is essentially to co-constitute its being true [*das Sichhalten in diesem Gedanken für sein Wahrsein selbst mit wesentlich ist*]," *Nietzsche*, Vol. II 128-29. We do not forget that in Heidegger the permanent is the transitory, "Holderlin and the Essence of Poetry" 280-81.

functions to create reality, then the makers of language are gods. How does this novel characterize the artist?

The artist is Darl—the rejected seer, oracle, prophet; separated from the others, apparently uncaring and uninvolved, alienated, and finally excommunicated. Jewel and Dewey Dell, the others abetting, get him, fix him. Like the abortion Dewey Dell wants desperately to get to town for, this "fixing" will eliminate the tell-tale indicator of the truths about themselves. The truth could set them free? Crucify him! Darl's last word is mad, ironic laughter.

Vardaman's experience of making language to articulate Darl's disappearance is suggestive. His words break off again and again when they approach what-has-happened-to-Darl. The blank/stop seems to run into a genuinely empty space—not horror or fear, but incomprehension, enigma. He says "crazy" without difficulty, but that does not finish the matter, the thought, the syntax. There is more *doing*, not brought into words yet. Darl my brother went crazy and was sent to Jackson *but that is not all.*

And there is another ambiguity. I have suggested that the Bundrens are suppressing and denying self-knowledge. They might drag themselves out of the mud primeval by making words, creating life, I have implied. Perhaps they could. They are profoundly guilty for their own condition and for the loss of the artist and for his immolation. But their fear of the truth is not simple perversity. Something fearful does lie beneath the language of the novel.[21] Darl's vision from time to time takes on Faulknerian tones, pessimistic: "How do our lives ravel out into the no-wind, no-sound, the weary gestures wearily recapitulant: echoes of old compulsions with no-hand on no-strings: in sunset we fall into furious attitudes, dead gestures of dolls" (196-97); or "Life was created in the valleys. It blew up onto the hills on the old terrors, the old lusts, the old despairs. That's why you must walk up the hills so you can ride down" (217). We pause before

---

[21] Compare groundlessness, untruth, death, nothing—all prior to world, truth, and being in Heidegger.

the artist Faulkner to consider the novel for a moment in terms of its own treatment of language. What kind of language does it use—dead or living?

Innumerable conventional "words" are employed in the construction of the novel: conventions of epic, of tragedy, of comedy, of romance, of allegory; motifs of the journey, descent into the underworld, hell, Christ, the scapegoat. There are techniques borrowed from the art of painting—impressionism, cubism, pointillism: comparisons to paintings (Darl often sees life *like a painting*, life imitating art), literal descriptions that exclude perspective, stream of consciousness, lack of narrator, collage of many narrations, many voices, points of view. Language theory, Freudian thought. No doubt the list could go on till the last echo from the past has been transcribed. The crucial question: Are these forms solidified fossils, deadweight, or are they living? Do the words define a space where "doing" is happening still?

The difference between the old meanings of the words and the new ones is part of what the new ones mean. The new living (doing) words stand here in a dialogic relationship with the past. We can make a few generalizations at once. There is a falling off. Whereas epics deal with heroes and warriors, and tragedy with men of elevated rank and superior character, the Bundrens represent the very lowest elements of human society. They are shabby and ignorant and grossly insensitive as they bear the stinking corpse across the country, the buzzards unnecessarily advertising what every bystander's olfactory apparatus has already told him. The motives of the family are shabby too. Tull says during the crossing of the river episode, "Just going to town. Bent on it. They would risk the fire and the earth and the water and all just to eat a sack of bananas" (133). Bent on going to town—Anse for teeth, Cash for a talking machine, Dewey Dell for an abortion. Their episodic odyssey is a spectacle of stupid heroics, "putting out" neighbors along the way and offending every sentient being. The elements of this story would be appropriate for comedy, but they are treated here with seriousness and often, as in Darl's chapters and Vardaman's, informed with a grotesque or naked beauty. The effect is a painful comedic irony.

Tragic heroes fall and in the falling grasp at last a bitter self-knowledge. If Jewel—who is Addie's savior from the flood and the fire—is taken for the hero, we must note that he extinguishes the oracle—"fixes" Darl who is the sign of his true identity. Oedipus, awakened, blinds himself. Jewel blinds himself to prevent awaking.

How does the novel reflect upon itself? We may set the first scene into contra-diction with the last. In the beginning Darl is dogging Jewel. Addie—the one signifier of truth for Anse, the central focus of meaning for Jewel and Darl—is dying, and a storm is coming. Surely crisis is at hand. At the end of the story the family is standing on a street corner eating bananas. There are two obvious changes. First, there is a new Mrs. Bundren, a substitution for Addie (a shape to fill a lack). Second, Darl is gone. The artist-character, always suspect, alien, has been declared crazy and *he will be crazy*. If Addie functions in the story as something of a center (her chapter occurs at about the center of the book; her meaning in the lives of the others is the meaning of the story; her death is the event of the story) and as fundament (her voice is given the first and last word as it gives the title, precedes and outlasts the story), then "I" as center, as self-consciousness, is what does die in this story, since the only seers, Addie and Darl, are put away in Jefferson (though seeing endures as potentiality in Vardaman).

The substitution for the traditional prophet-priest is Cash—Cash, whose first principle is precision and whose fine art is perfect, me-thodical carpentry. The last words of the story are his. His simple meagre soul is pleased with the new Mrs. Bundren's graphophone (signifier of a new kind of word, technological), only one brotherly ripple of a doubt disturbing the bucolic peace.

Appendix B: Heideggerian Insights

Everything spoken stems in a variety of ways from the
unspoken [*Das Gesprochene entstammt auf mannigfache
Art dem Ungesprochenen*], whether this be something
not yet spoken, or whether it be what must remain
unspoken in the sense that it is beyond the reach of
speaking [*was dem Sprechen vorenthalten ist*]. Thus,
that which is spoken in various ways [*das auf vielfache
Weise Gesprochene*] begins to appear as if it were cut off
from speaking and the speakers [*vom Sprechen und den
Sprechenden abgetrennt*], and did not belong to them,
while in fact it alone offers [*entgegenhält*] to speaking
and to the speakers whatever it is they attend to [*wozu sie
sich verhalten*], no matter in what way they stay within
what is spoken of the unspoken [*sie auch im Gesprochenen des Ungesprochenen sich aufhalten*]. (Martin Heidegger, "The Way To Language" 120)

Addie would have little patience, I think, with Heidegger's notion
that the word gives Being, less patience or none with the suggestion
that untruth is prior to truth, the undisclosed to the disclosed, and
in general she would dismiss without a hearing his "way" of *thinking*
about language. She has her own way; she *experiences* the lie that
"love" is, the empty shapes of "mother" and "fear" and "sin," for she
experiences the "words that are the deeds," i.e., the "doing" that words
miss. And from her point of view, just where she finds herself, and
in her own way, knowing little or nothing about such things, she
theorizes and ontologizes with the audacity—and power—of a poet.

In whose "way"? Experience is a dimension that Heidegger too
insists on in his metaphilosophy, although the concept changes character. He uses the word discussing Kant's emphasis on the encounter

or the "experience" with the "thing" in his analysis of the conditions of the possibility of the thing. When Heidegger reads Kant's formulation, we hear Heidegger's own formulation of the problem since *Being and Time*: "Experience is in itself a circular happening through which what lies within the circle becomes exposed (*eröffnet*). This open (*Offene*), however, is nothing other than the between (*Zwischen*)—between us and the thing" ("What Is a Thing?" 242). In Heidegger's early works Dasein itself provides the "there" of the open (language) which is the world. In later works language will more explicitly outreach and surpass Dasein (it never "outstrips" or abandons it, although that possibility is pending). But from the beginning it is not Dasein that "gives" Being; and language, which does, does not belong to Dasein; it is a "dimension ... which lies between the thing and man, which reaches out beyond things and back behind man [*die über die Dinge hinaus und hinter den Menschen zurückreicht*]" (244). Heidegger would contribute this "between," the "open" (language), as the condition of Addie's "experience" of "doing."

Heidegger shares with the unlikely schoolteacher not only the ground of her rebellion, but also some important points of contention. Addie's renunciation of words, which are "no good," in favor of the "dark voicelessness" of the "dark land talking," a language in which the words are deeds, is a demand that language answer "life." But "life" is no simple question, and what an "answer" might be cannot be decided until it already has been—the circle again. Nevertheless, Heidegger has addressed Addie's demand. First, his works trace and retrace the history of the ontology of language in the West from Plato (language as mimetic or representational, taken to agree with or correspond with [the truth of] its objects—"life") to Nietzsche (among the first to claim that "words dont ever fit even what they are trying to say at"). Then Heidegger questions the nature of language anew. His descriptions of the working of language evoke an experience of the uncanny—the poetic experience and, in his works, the thinking experience as the same (not the identical). I have sketched some of his notions about language in Chapter 1. Compare Addie's insomniac ruminations on the function of words in this chapter. Addie's assertions stand in opposition to Heidegger's. Words don't work; the relation between words and things is arbitrary; words are not necessary to things. But when Addie's uses of words are examined alongside her opinions about them, their broader field of operation suggests that her criticism applies to the language she finds in the world about her, language purporting to represent the truth, and that her uses and phenomenological descriptions of language stir up Heideggerian possibilities that lead thinking about language into a region previously un-thought.

One of the most intriguing networks of notions in Heidegger involves the word as it-gives, presencing, and spatiality. Addie's thoughts about words invite some comparisons. I have discussed the nature of the word as no-thing and its work of "giving" thingness/being. I have noted some of the implications for time. But in the matters that Addie invites us to consider, it becomes especially interesting to notice what is happening to spatiality. Addie lies in bed beside Anse thinking about words, "Anse." The word, as she claims, receives Anse and releases him into presence. Heidegger claims this much and more:

> To name something—that is to call it by name [*beim Namen rufen*].... What is called appears as what is present, and in its presence it is brought into the keeping, it is commanded, called into the calling word [*in das rufende Wort geborgen, befohlen, geheißen ist*]. So called by name, called into a presence, it in turn calls [*Das so Geheißene, in ein Anwesen Gerufene, heißt dann selber*]. It is named, has the name. By naming, we call on what is present to arrive [*Im Nennen heißen wir das Anwesende ankommen*]. Arrive where? That remains to be thought about. (*What Is Called Thinking?* 120).

For Heidegger the place where the being will arrive will not be
"in the mind" or "in consciousness," as this passage about thinking,
written at about the same time, indicates:

> We do not represent distant things merely in our mind
> [*bloß ... innerlich*]—as the textbooks have it—so that
> only mental representations [*nur Vorstellungen*] of dis-
> tant things run through our minds and heads as substi-
> tutes [*als Ersatz für die fernen Dinge in unserem Innern
> und im Kopf*] for the things. If all of us now think from
> where we are right here, of the old bridge in Heidel-
> berg, this thinking toward that location is not a mere
> experience inside the persons present here [*ist das Hin-
> denken zu jenem Ort kein bloßes Erlebnis in den hier
> anwesenden Personen*]; rather, it belongs to the essence
> of our thinking *of* that bridge [*gehört es zum Wesen
> unseres Denkens an die genannte Brücke*] that in *itself*
> thinking gets through, persists through [*durchsteht**],
> the distance to that location. From this spot right here,
> we are there at the bridge—we are by no means at some
> representational content in our consciousness [*Wir sind
> von hier aus bei der Brücke dort und nicht etwa bei einem
> Vorstellungsinhalt in unserem Bewußtsein*]. From right
> here we may even be much nearer [*weit näher*] to that
> bridge and to what it makes room for [*was sie einraümt*]
> than someone who uses it daily as an indifferent river
> crossing. ("Building Dwelling Thinking" 334-35)

Heidegger goes on to disclose with new force the "there" (*Da*)
where things appear in their being. The where of the "there" is not a
space, is not "here," but is a "way": dwelling (*Wohnen*).[22] We can say

---

[22] See Gerald L. Bruns' discussion of spatiality in Heidegger, e.g.: "Space becomes
an event, temporalized as a worlding and a thinging; literally it is a taking place
(*Ereignis*)," *Heidegger's Estrangements: Language, Truth, and Poetry in the Later
Writings* (New Haven: Yale UP, 1989) 93. See also *Being and Time* H. 55.

that "there" names where things arrive into relatedness: "When we say something about something [*etwas von etwas sagen*], we make it lie there before us, which means at the same time we make it appear [*lassen wir es als das und das vorliegen und d.h. zugleich erscheinen*].... The essential nature of language is illumined by the relatedness of what lies there before us to this letting-lie-before-us [*Das Wesen der Sprache lichtet sich aus dem Bezug des Vorliegenden zum Vorliegenlassen*]" (*What is Called Thinking?* 202).

Addie's first contention, that language has gone wrong when it fails to effect communication, community, accords also with this wider view of Heidegger's that essential language is "the relation of all relations [*das Verhältnis aller Verhältnisse*]" ("The Nature of Language" 107), the "house of Being [*Haus des Seins*]" ("Letter" 193, "The Way" 135), which brings together and holds: Dasein and (-in) the world, Dasein with other Daseins, Dasein and thing; eventually language holds in mutual relatedness the fourfold—earth and sky and gods and mortals ("The Thing"). (Language is not a glue, and entities held there cannot be considered simple, unified, or whole beings; language as relation is the relating of these entities; "being," not as the truth of presence, but as the event of presenc*ing*. Relating as presencing opens up any moment, any thinking, not merely to being/beings, but also to Being in general, to not-being, Nothing. The violence of the absoluteness of this actual, active opposing forbids any sense of closure to the world, the fourfold, and to belonging, i.e., relatedness.

And we find that the Faulkner story is "placed," essentially as uneasily, in or over some dark, all-but-silent, unfathomable dreadfulness, which moves the story as from behind, giving the characters and the story the character of Heidegger's anxious Being-toward-death. Though it is Addie who dies in the story, it is her life, placed at the center of the story, which offers thematically some show of force, vitality, and her vision and decision without faith could be measured against Heidegger's *Being and Time* resoluteness.

My Heideggerian reading of Addie's "language theory" begins with her practical deconstruction of representational language, peruses her essentialist correction (with Plato: the speaker gives meaning to language and the hearer), and moves on to discover a Heideggerian kind of priority that the novel gives to language itself, functioning to "accommodate living doing," to "create reality," and to implicate something other than itself, unthinkable.

James: Another Sense of an Ending

The following essay is a Heideggerian reading of Henry James's *The Turn of the Screw*. In Appendix C, I point out explicitly some of Heidegger's insights that I am finding among James's insights here.

Critics have characterized language in *The Turn of the Screw*[1] as "ambiguous" since Edmund Wilson provided the epithet and the "diagnosis,"[2] as Shoshana Felman put it (105), of the governess's—or James's—case. The term has come to mean "undecidability." The story ends where the moderns always lead us and leave us—in "ambiguity." The word betrays a trace of irritation, a sense of giving-it-up, that seems to suggest that one *should* be able to decide, and beyond that, that the issue *should* be decidable. Both the reading and the story seem to be somehow at fault—weaker than they should be in general muscle, strength to do the job, or know-how, skill, or character, will. There is a sense that the issue *is decidable*—it is only language that cannot decide; or that if it is not decidable, then effort is lost, wasted, in trying to understand. Ambiguity that implies loss of an

---

[1] Henry James, *The Turn of the Screw and Other Short Novels* (New York: Signet, 1962), Sixth Printing, 291-403.

[2] "Turning the Screw of Interpretation," *Yale French Studies* 55/56 (1978): 105. Edmund Wilson, "The Ambiguity of Henry James," *The Triple Thinkers*, rev. and enl. ed. (New York: Oxford UP, 1948) 88-132.

object and failure of an action is haunted by ghosts of the notions of being as presence, of teleology, form, meaning, the rational—the Western metaphysical paradigm before Nietzsche. As John Carlos Rowe observes, undecidability itself has become a critical concept, inadvertently defining a new center, reasserting the logocentrism it thinks it deconstructs.[3]

Felman takes the issue to its rational conclusion in her reading of the James story: she concludes not that language in this story is ambiguous, but that in this story James figures and enacts the dilemma of literary language *per se*:

> [Literary] mystification is a game, a joke; to play is to be played; to comprehend mystification is to be comprehended *in* it; entering into the game, we ourselves become fair game for the very "joke" of *meaning*. The joke is that, by meaning, everyone is fooled. If the "joke" is nonetheless also a "worry," if ... mystification is also "tragic," it is because the "error" (the madness of the interpreter) is the error of life itself. "Life is the condition of knowledge," writes Nietzsche; "Error is the condition of life—I mean, ineradicable and fundamental error. The knowledge that one errs does not eliminate the error." (202-03)

Felman's conclusion (Nietzsche's) does not resolve the issue: it dissolves it, the question along with the answer; only the questioner remains, inaccessible, silenced. For, as she lucidly but helplessly points out, her own discourse, the discourse of linguistics or psychoanalysis, answers to the same description and diagnosis. The whole linguistic project falls apart in this reading, and if there is anything left in its place it must be anguish.

---

[3] *The Theoretical Dimensions of Henry James* (Madison: U of Wisconsin, 1984), chap. 1.

It is this impasse of Felman's (not the irresolution but the stoppage) that my reading of the story questions. I shall agree that when language is taken to be representational—words corresponding in some wise with the thing (Aristotle) or words agreeing in some wise with the concept, which is intrinsically different from the thing and therefore lying, like the words that signify them, outside the possibility of essential correspondence with things themselves (Kant, Saussure)—then the "joke" of "*meaning*" is unavoidable. But when that notion is abandoned, as Felman's work brilliantly argues that it shall be, it becomes possible to take language to be Heidegger's non-representational worlding, decision-making (playful but not capricious), Being-granting "it gives." Or, to describe my method here more accurately (and more soberly), it becomes possible to suspend judgment about the nature of language and, according to Heidegger's "letting-be" approach, allow James's "literality" to speak for itself.

> That we cannot know the nature of language—know it according to the traditional concept of knowledge defined in terms of cognition as representation [*nach dem überlieferten, aus dem Erkennen als Vorstellen bestimmten Begriff des Wissens*]—is not a defect, ... but rather an advantage by which we are favored with a special realm [*wir in einen ausgezeichneten Bereich vorgezogen sind*], that realm where we, who are needed and used to speak language [*die zum Sprechen der Sprache Gebrauchten*], dwell as *mortals*. (Martin Heidegger, "The Way to Language" 134)

Now language can hope to move beyond Felman's point of impasse.[4]

---

[4]My objective here, to move beyond Felman's conclusion, has been attempted with some success already by Ned Lukacher in a Freudo-Heideggerian reading which in a fashion something like the Jamesian use of forms I describe above uses the

That point of impasse is the point of subject-object confrontation. "Seeing"/Knowing (meaning) belongs to the subject-object relationship; we understand or "grasp" something when we stand outside it, get it in its totality in view and in hand, command it.[5] Stories, like all entities, have depended on the ending (totality) for definition since the Greeks proposed the identity principle. The notion of ending as definition (totality) has prevailed until this century, when thinking may be represented by Roquentin in Sartre's *Nausea*, who reconceptualizes "story" as the error at the origin of the modern dilemma. "Life," "existence," is not a story, contains no stories. Stories are human representations employed to veil the void, diversions from the knowledge of meaninglessness. The "end" as definition slips away from the thing, object, and becomes "end" as human purpose. The principle extends from story to concept to form (though Roquentin salvages something, a scrap of melody, an antinovel). If there is no source from which to draw the ending, if no connections intervene, if the "ending" occurs with no valid relation to anything preceding, then the story, the concept, the form, is indeed from "beginning" to "end" a gruesome Christmas Eve "joke" to conciliate or titillate the ladies.

But even in a multiverse that tends to chaos, the mind insists on "seeing"; though we relinquish "truth," we cling to focus. Endings

---

thought of Freud, Derrida, Heidegger, Felman, and others, to go on to a position of his own, *Primal Scenes: Literature, Philosophy, Psychoanalysis* (Ithaca: Cornell UP, 1986).

[5] Heidegger explores and rejects this concept throughout his works (as the present-at-hand in *Being and Time*, e.g.) and re-envisions the site of this human-other confrontation in several ways: as existential horizon; as Kant's ob-jectivity revised; as a human letting-be of beings or bringing beings to stand-before; as the appearing (*eidos*), arising (*phusis*), or presencing of beings, e.g. At perhaps its most violent the relation is given in *An Introduction* as "wresting" being from nonbeing: "being-human is *logos*, the gathering and apprehending of the being of the essent: it is the happening of that strangest essent of all [*das Geschehnis jenes Unheimlichsten*], in whom through violence, through acts of power [*Gewalt-tätigkeit*], the overpowering [*Überwältigende*] is made manifest and made to stand" (171).

(definition, form) are useful as a knife-edge test technique, if not to identify entities then to approach them, to get them in view.

Sense of an Ending: Genre

The customary sense of an ending (as definition) in regard to literature is the literary form, genre. We set the story against generic form to get its measure. There are thousands of clues. There is the gothic set, the biblical, the psychological, or the romantic. The romantic set has not been exploited as thoroughly as the others, but its significance is primary in my view. In brief, the governess—ignorant, young, and sentimental—reads life like the novels she finds in the library at Bly; but just as among the romances she chances upon Fielding's *Amelia*, so she falls into something at Bly more real than romantic. The disaster in the ending is, in this reading, the shattering of the attempt to bring "evil" to account in romantic terms. Though I shall not offer a systematic explication of such a reading, I shall imply and embellish one when I turn the screw one more round to interpret the governess as romantic artist, below. Our problem here, however, is to determine the significance or function of generic structures. The genre summoned above cannot give us a sense of ending, definition, of ground or grounding—for they have been uprooted themselves in this century. These historic, religious, literary, and social paradigms are no longer taken to convey an original archepattern (theologic, mechanic, organic), signature of the universal. In this case, what is their source or ground and what does it signify for us?

For modern thinkers, as I suggest above, cultural paradigms serve subjectivity; form inscribes point of view.

Sense of an Ending: Subjectivity

If we consider *The Turn of the Screw* as a representation of subjective point of view, we seem to have found the key to its structure. The story presents—and undermines—the governess's personal narrative imbedded in a social, cultural, historical perspective.[6] The Eden myth, for example, belongs to the governess's tradition and personal history (and James's, ours), though it is revised, deviated from, or reversed in the story. The romantic motif mimics and satirizes the literary tradition (and especially the state of the novel as sentimental Victorian claptrap). The psychoanalytic pattern is James's modernist turn of the screw; he plays with this latest "lie" and subverts it, dumps it into the same subjective wash with the rest. He has concocted a modern polyglossia that performs before our very eyes a polished little all self-conscious suicide.

But we cannot settle on the usual death sans resurrection theme in this case, for we find that subjectivity cannot satisfactorily account for the matter here.

First a Heideggerian account of the subject-object concept[7] and a review of the modern situation. Descartes grounded the objectivity of objects in the subjectivity of the thinking "I," giving ontological priority to the subject (and to its mathematical mode of knowing, pure reason), but at the same time separating it ontologically from the objects of its knowledge. Now the subject stands opposite objects and sees them in their entirety. But Kant "saw" that subjects had genuine—objective—access only to objective phenomena. The mind cannot bring itself into agreement with things in themselves but can see them only as they stand in agreement with itself. The subject's access to objects is limited, thus deficient. Hegel united subject and object in a dialectical convergence tending inevitably, historically, to transcendence; and the collective romantic imagination, political and social as well as literary, exploded into Renaissance. But revolutions

---

[6] Compare Heidegger's they-self (*Man-selbst*) in *Being and Time* H. 129, for example.

[7] Heidegger discusses this concept in work after work, beginning with *Being and Time*. It is treated in detail in *What Is a Thing?* trans. W. B. Barton, Jr., and Vera Deutsch (South Bend, Indiana: Regnery-Gateway, 1967). Kant is interpreted directly in *Kant and the Problem of Metaphysics*, trans. James S. Churchill (Bloomington: Indiana UP, 1962), and Hegel in *Hegel's Concept of Experience*, trans. Kenley Royce Dove (San Francisco: Harper and Row, 1970).

and world wars would ravage the possibility of certainty and of hope, and in the West all the patterns that had comprised a universe would seem to disintegrate, and with them the feasibility of pattern itself. Modernists in art and literature have been interpreted as presenting fragments of perspectives on a world that fell apart.

What philosophy has called subjectivity modern psychoanalysis defines in terms of the unconscious. The "I" in subjectivity is here the projection of a self-image that occurs as one of several stages of displacement, all of which represent a vain attempt to return to or to replace an original totality of unity with the mother in the womb. Whose projecting, attempting, returning? Psychoanalysis goes behind the subject to a pre-conscious (pre-language) entity or energy. In Julia Kristeva's use of Lacan's neo-Freudian analysis, the "subject" is continuously reposited, reconstructed, by the generating activity of physical drives, is never present or permanent but is always "in process/on trial."[8] This always-being-posited subject is the precondition for the development and function of language, and language is necessary to receive and guide the force of the drives (failing means revolution or destruction of language, of subjectivity—means madness, death). This conception of subjectivity is compatible in part with the view that the James story evokes, except that it stops (with Felman's) at the threshold of the story, of the matter, with a distrust for the use of language to differentiate beyond that point. In my reading of *The Turn of the Screw* psychoanalytical notions assert themselves again and again, partly no doubt because James is making deliberate use of such notions and partly because they are often compatible with his insights into human phenomena. But my attempt is to follow James as he makes a way past theory, I claim, and by means of language.

---

[8] *Revolution in Poetic Language*, trans. Margaret Waller (New York: Columbia UP, 1984). Kristeva's analytic attempts to salvage subjectivity for science by including it in objectivity. The effect is that language-making is recognized, but what language says is discounted. As Felman points out (199), this assumption negates itself since psychoanalysis, like science, objectivity, exists in or via language.

The site and indeed the element of the story is the governess's subjectivity. At the beginning the governess characterizes her position along with the others': "... I had the fancy of our being almost as lost as a handful of passengers in a great drifting ship. Well, I was, strangely, at the helm!" (302). Indeed her progress through the story suggests the movement of the prow of a ship projecting itself ahead of itself:[9] an anticipation moving now hopefully, now fearfully—"a succession of flights and drops," as she calls it, "a little seesaw of the right throbs and the wrong" (298)—an expecting that gets surprised, stopped, diverted, aided, and obstructed by other things. We may take these interruptions as the suggestion of the *fact* of objectivity; yet it is impossible to disentangle objects from her subjectivity.

> ... The terrace and the whole place, the lawn and the garden beyond it, all I could see of the park, were empty with a great emptiness. There were shrubberies and big trees, but I remember the clear assurance I felt that none of them concealed him. He was there or was not there: not there if I didn't see him. I got hold of this; then, instinctively, instead of returning as I had come, went to the window. It was confusedly present to me that I ought to place myself where he had stood.... (316-7)

This is indeed the element we wish to examine—the shifting, ephemeral human site, and dilemma. Things which according to our paradigm exist in themselves occur here inside and inter-related with her consciousness. We know that we are restricted to the governess's *story* (convenient lie), the embodiment of subjectivity, cut off and entrapped in its delusion. We suspect also that the governess represents the fallen romantic, half-fabricating what she half-perceives.

---

[9]Compare "projection" in *Being and Time* H. 145 as an existentiale of Dasein, wherein "it *is* its possibilities as possibilities [*es seine Möglichkeiten als Möglichkeiten ist*]" not in understanding or planning ahead thematically, but in Being-toward its own Being, significance, and world. This structure does not belong to "subjectivity."

We find the central clues to the meaning James gives to subjectivity in the governess's relationship with the ghosts, for in Freudian terms they represent projections of the governess's actual and unrecognized nature, the unconscious, and James is making use of such concepts. The figure on the tower makes its advent as a literal displacement of the master in the governess's fantasy (her imagination turns real, she says). He appears to be a total stranger, an Other who, however, stares into her own gaze in a profoundly disturbing, knowing exchange. The relationship established in this encounter deepens in the second meeting when he appears at the dining room window, more familiar and at closer range. Then at the third confrontation, at the "heart" of the "darkness" on the stairway to the bedrooms just before dawn, she meets him and knows and denies him measure for measure. She is drawn to, into, his seeing-knowing (his seeing-knowing *her*) as fully as she is coming to, into, seeing-knowing his nature as "evil." Her gathering decision to oppose the evil, to offer her self to shield the children, is at the same time—and not in a separate conflicting tendency—a drawing into, absorption of and by, the evil. Thereafter a kind of relish for its appalling depths infects even her solicitude for the children.

> How can I retrace today the strange steps of my obsession? There were times of our being together when I would have been ready to swear that, literally, in my presence, but with my direct sense of it closed, they had visitors who were known and were welcome. Then it was that, had I not been deterred by the very chance that such an injury might prove greater than the injury to be averted, my exultation would have broken out. "They're here, they're here, you little wretches," I would have cried, "and you can't deny it now!" The little wretches denied it with all the added volume of their sociability and their tenderness, in just the crystal depths of which—like the flash of a fish in a stream—the mockery of their advantage peeped up.... (356-7)

The event: obsession, possession. Her resistance to the evil is not a Hawthorne making-do with making-way among complexities and contradiction or a Conrad-Marlow restraint, but a total opposition, as she believes: a rigor of denial, suppression, which is at the same time a total drawing toward/into the evil, identification (342).[10] She absorbs the evil—into the timeless silence that is the force of her own rigid will. The governess possesses Quint, or the evil possesses her. In the end she is the violator if she is not the savior, and this uncertainty is the horror of the story. The possibility of innocence is by this time as dreadful as the presence of evil.

The second ghost, Miss Jessel, appears to the governess after she has with Mrs. Grose's assistance interpreted the first one; this time the governess identifies the ghost for herself, *as* herself: as beautiful young woman, as governess implicated in a relationship with Quint, as guilty, mad creature, doomed. But the governess resists the fatalism in this ghost in a different and more effectual opposition: outbreak, outcry, which clears the air so that she recovers her self (365-6). The self-image that Miss Jessel re-presents to her seems insubstantial, unelemental, can disperse and disappear. Subjectivity as self-image is a secondary, refutable adversary, whereas the attraction-repulsion of a libidinal Other is altogether essential and formidable. Both appear to be purely subjective, offer no clues or connections to objectivity except as they are effectual.

The governess's relations with the ghosts intervene in her relations with everyone and everything. Her duty is to shield the children from them. Her relationship with Mrs. Grose becomes a collaboration for the purpose of bringing the ghosts to terms (literally). Her relations with the children are bi-level; beneath a surface of order and conventionality and congeniality runs an undercurrent of difficult and troubled and contradictory intercourse. The consequence of these duplicitous intercommunications is an inner excitement and a rich resurgence of intelligence and creativity. And the movement of the

---

[10]Compare Felman's Freud-Lacan concept of sexuality as "division and divisiveness," 112.

story occurs among and takes its direction from these "subjective" interrelationships.

But if we have only the governess's story from which to ascertain events, happenings, can we ascertain them at all? The governess is on her own testimony easily "carried away," "led on." With a proclivity for gothic or sentimental novels she "reads into" things meanings that they then, obediently perhaps, enact. She "sees" with absolute clarity at dusk or in the middle of the night and by the light of the moon, candles, matches. What she actually sees "in clear noonday light" is Miss Jessel, that specter, who can be made to disappear at a "wild protest," above (365-6). We watch while innocuous, perhaps random, suggestion turns into "monstrous" event. We see that everyone and everything is a mirror to everyone and everything else, reflects *itself* back from what it takes to be *Other*. The story seems to be a set of random reflections set in motion and crazily perpetuating and perplexing a single ungraspable tautology. Subjectivity, the element of the story and the setting, is also the ground and the motivation for and even the "reality" of fact and event.

When we take subjectivity to mean interpretation, the content of consciousness, and when "truth" is attributed to objectivity, then subjectivity means "lie," since it fails to correspond with truth. But subjectivity in James's work encompasses human event or the happening of human reality, and it enters the realm of objectivity on something of an equal footing, not that the two become identical but that they co-operate or inter-operate in the making of "reality." The story is loosening its grasp on the Cartesian-Kantian paradigm.

The governess is a *naif* —a truthsayer; she asserts with absolute self-certainty the truth of her observations. (Indeed her observations are often so sensitive or incisive that we can not dismiss her as a fool or a madwoman.) But her "truth," her account—her justification—is somehow inadequate to the events it sets forth, for the doubt and all the complexities to puzzle or contradict her claims lie open in her narrative among the things she thinks she presents. It is in her connections and self-justifications and exclamations of certainty that we find the possibilities of breaks, gaps, lapses, coverups.

> Miss Jessel stood before us on the opposite bank exactly as she had stood the other time, and I remember, strangely, as the first feeling now produced in me, my thrill of joy at having brought on a proof. She was there, and I was justified; she was there, and I was neither cruel nor mad....

> ... The revelation then of the manner in which Flora was affected startled me, ... To see her, without a convulsion of her small pink face, not even feign to glance in the direction of the prodigy I announced, but only, instead of that, turn at *me* an expression of hard, still gravity, an expression absolutely new and unprecedented and that appeared to read and accuse and judge me—this was a stroke that somehow converted the little girl into the very presence that could make me quail. I quailed even though my certitude that she thoroughly saw was never greater than at that instant, ... (380-81)

Perhaps her story is a sheer gauze over the happenings she actually relates, a respectable facade under cover of which she can present the horrors that are the burden of her communication. The governess can not hope to, though she may intend to, convince anyone of her story, but by means of its machinery (machination) she can "confess"; the real stuff can "come out." "Story" seems to be a shield through which the governess dares to look at things, like the paper masks we cut to watch an eclipse of the sun. Function is the objectivity in the story. The lies and evasions and excuses are part of the same objectivity as the "truth." Reality in the story is not a world of objective facts which collide with the objective fact of the governess (whose nature is subjective), so that an objective (pure) view could discover, distinguish, dissociate them. For "objective" event occurs in the "subjective" human encounter, enters into existence in reference to it and in relationship and interrelationship with it. The human "subjectivity" is as effective, as real, as much agency and consequence as un-human "objectivity." Our knife-edge technique, setting the subject-object paradigm against the story, has brought a Jamesian difference to view. The Cartesian-Kantian paradigm seems to pertain in that subjectivity is prior and "truth" is out of the question. But James takes the "subjective" to the limit where it is no longer a notion and where both subjectivity and objectivity are transformed. When the identification of subjectivity with consciousness is abandoned, then subjectivity becomes a kind of activity, co-instigator of the event called "reality."[11]

Stories mean form—no one more exacting than James on this point. I am approaching this story using the question of form—generic, conceptual. Genre has given way to subjectivity, and subjectivity has passed outside the limits of formality. What, then, is the nature of form, of ending, definition? Let us examine James's conception and appropriation of literal forms in the story and attempt to derive the principles of form that operate in the story. We do not abandon the site-element-function of "subjectivity"; we approach it more closely.

---

[11] See Heidegger's comparison of realism and idealism in *Being and Time* H. 202-208, for example, or his account of the encounter of objects in the context of Being-in-the-world, H. 366. See H. 318-323 for a summary of Kant's subjectivity and Heidegger's revision of the concept.

Sense of an Ending: Forms

Mirrors[12]

One literal form, already mentioned, is the mirror, the "glasses" at Bly in which for the first time in her life the governess can see herself "from head to foot" (299). Freudian theory identifies the mirror-stage as a crucial step in the development of self-consciousness. This is the principle that brings us round by the end to the beginning of this story, for the story is the governess's self-portrait, her attempt to make out definition and value, i.e., proofs and justification. But self-portraiture is an ironic figure, for seeing herself is what the governess does not do.

We trace the pattern. The story delineates a developing self-consciousness. In the interview between the governess and the master, as Douglas relates it in the prologue, a new sense of self is awakened in the governess, reflected to her from the master's charming manner, the pressure of his hand, his appeal for the assistance of someone capable of independence and judgment. A surprising, flattering self-image, one which somewhat allays her apprehensions, is suggested to her by the manner in which Mrs. Grose and Flora receive her at Bly "as if I had been the mistress or a distinguished visitor" (299).

---

[12]For a Heidegger-Schelling account of a kind of mirror-stage in God's emerging as self, bringing Him*self* before Himself in His own image, see *Schelling's Treatise on the Essence of Human Freedom*, trans. Joan Stambaugh (Athens: Ohio UP, 1985) 125-26. There are no reflections, displacements, in this mirroring, but active self-seeing/achieving instead. Heidegger describes mirroring of the fourfold in "The Thing" (179-80), but again the effect is not illusion or refraction. Each participant mirrors the presencing of the others and in doing so is also presencing. All are involved in "mutual appropriation [*Vereignung*]" within which each is "expropriated [*enteignet*] ... into its own being [*zu einem Eigenen*]" in its freedom while it is bound to the others in essential mutual belonging. This "mirror-play [*Spiegel-Spiel*]" Heidegger calls "world" [*die Welt*].

And the sense of "greatness" that marks her first impressions reflects to her the vision of a fulfilling duty ahead, "To watch, teach, 'form' little Flora" (300). In further iterations of these preliminary self-appraisals, her duty to the children and her motivation of earning the master's approval deepen and widen to sinister proportions. She sees herself reflected in the ghosts—in Quint's progressively more challenging, more dangerous exchanges; in the mournful figure of Miss Jessel. She comes to see her cruelty reflected in Flora's distress, her ugliness in Miles' beauty. But all the mirrors in the world set up about her on all sides (and the phrase seems to describe her situation) can not show her her own monstrous metamorphosis and effect, though they reflect them to her.

The governess's incapacity and imprecision can be explained, however, if not "justified," by the complicacy of her situation. That is, the awakening and intensification of the governess's self-seeing is one thread in a veritable web of reflections and cross-reflections, in which all the characters and situations and events catch each other in perpetual, essential, and actual inter-view, inter-course. The web is discernible, for example, in a kind of remark that punctuates the story. "I saw him [Quint] as I see you," the governess says to Mrs. Grose (319), and again later, "Oh, for the effect and the feeling, she [Miss Jessel] might have been as close as you!" (329). Such remarks set up a series of equations, identifications, which serve to illuminate or obfuscate the nature of the ghosts and/or the nature of the governess's "seeing." The two examples above associate Mrs. Grose and the apparitions, especially in the governess's apperception. And indeed the source and the meaning of the ghosts is inextricably bound up with the memories and fears and dreads of Mrs. Grose. Further passages of the same kind associate Mrs. Grose with whoever is present and with the reader, who by a similar cross-reference has been identified in the prologue with the evil in the story, "general uncanny ugliness and horror and pain" (292). In the web of counter-reflections, it is equally possible to "see" that Mrs. Grose and the children are reflecting the evil from the deluded governess, and that the simple governess is reflecting the evil that preceded her at Bly, from Mrs. Grose, the children, or perhaps from the reader of the story.

Other cross-indexes associate situations, actions, events. Here the perspicacity of the governess is brought into doubt: "I saw him [Quint] as I see the letters I form on this page," she writes (312). One implication is that when she thinks that she is "seeing" (reading), she is projecting (writing). What the governess offers as proof of authenticity doubles back to cast doubt on her grasp of reality (both romance theme and subject-object paradigm subverted).

Now mirrors give inaccurate reflections. And mirrors mirroring mirrors, multiple mirrors, multiply the errors and overwhelm the understanding. The reflections and counterreflections that complicate and variegate the surface of this story can not verify or clarify objective "reality"; instead they create a delightful or distressing confusion where our instinct struggles for focus. Nor can objectivity be located in an original figure, fact, or source. It is possible to turn the story about the figure of the governess or Mrs. Grose or Quint, or even Miles, so that the reflections seem to emit from that center; but each temptation is a trap. (The trap is a motif that surfaces into literal language as the governess and Miles engage each other in a chesslike complex of moves and checks, challenges and captures.) There is no point of origin that can accurately or adequately account for the rest. But the issue goes beyond a subversive subjectivity or an undecidable ambiguity. Despite the irreality of appearances, the lack of verifiable connections—cause, cohesion, linearity of sequence—a "reality" seems to be originating or moving, changing, all the time. Certainly event, disaster, makes its discernible approach and shatters illusion, the ideal of literal coherence, in the end, enacting the rational tautology that this work is setting forth—and setting off against a vision of form as function.

The complex of mirrors is a trap to catch and to entangle not only the governess and the seeming constituents of her situation and story, but also the reader and life outside the story. The most immediate "proof" besides this sentence I have begun is the similarity in all my sentences and in those that other critics have written about the story.[13] Our interpretations are all "seeing" and "proofs," justification and self-justification. As deluded and destructive as the governess appears to be, her motives, her seeing and saying, even her actions, seem to reflect something essential in the human condition:

> The great thing is indeed that the muddled state too is one of the very sharpest of the realities, that it also has colour and form and character, has often in fact a broad and rich comicality, many of the signs and values of the appreciable. (1934 "Preface to 'What Maisie Knew' " in *The Art of the Novel*, Northeastern UP ed., 1984, p. 149)

The most significant aspect of this essential reality for my study is its comprehensiveness. That is, pure objectivity has no more separate integrity in James's world than psychological subjectivity, fact no more than fiction; they are caught together in the same network, comprise an interacting, inter-changing "reality."

Frames

Another literal form in the story is the frame, which figures form itself and demonstrates the function of form not only to contain and close but to disclose, to open.[14] To the governess the figure

---

[13] Felman elaborates this point (98-102). The mirror image of the reader has become a received component of the story.

[14] See "The Origin of the Work of Art," *Poetry, Language, Thought* (64f.) for Heidegger's account of figure (*Gestalt*) in the context of placing (*Stellen*) and framing (*Ge-stell*). Framing or Enframing as the technological in "The Way to Language" (131f.) and in "The Question Concerning Technology" (*Basic Writings* 283-317) is a particular use of the term, not comparable here except in its contradictory nature. Enframement has the effects of concealing, blocking, and threatening being and truth, and yet it belongs to the grant of destining, to unconcealment, and thus to the human again as guardian of being.

on the tower appears "as definite as a picture in a frame" (311). I began to discuss definition in terms of endings, as limitation, identity. Now when the governess is concerned with the problem of identity outright—the identity of the apparition—she avers her clarity, lucidity, and certainty by an appeal not to factual objectivity but to a picture in a frame. Of course, the governess is a romantic; what she takes for "real" is a "picture" (a mimetic representation is suggested, a concept not consonant with James's notion of art) separated from life by that frame. The frame marks the difference between the real "real" and the governess's concept of it. Her remark serves to satirize sentimental "art" and its debilitating effects on weak, young things. Art is fallen in the story too.

Frames mark boundaries, differentiate. Quint appears twice in frames that admit him to view only from the waist up; we have noted that he displaces the master in the governess's imagination. He appears at first on the tower high up and far away (ideal, remote) framed by the turret wall and the tower. His next appearance, at the window, brings him nearer—right up to the glass (again like a painting, the glass another frame—and mirror, medium of and barrier to access) and broadens his significance when the governess senses that he is looking for someone else, Miles. The governess rushes outside and, missing the intruder, stands in his place outside the window frame looking in—looking in, it occurs to her, as he did earlier—just as Mrs. Grose comes into the room. Now the governess is framed in the window behind the glass. The glass works both ways: Mrs. Grose's stricken face mirrors to the governess what her own face must have shown to Quint ("I had the full image of a repetition of what had already occurred"); and now the governess is the apparition behind the window framing and mirroring for Mrs. Grose something dreadful of hers ("I wondered why *she* should be scared" 317).[15] From this

---

[15] For Bruce Robbins ("Shooting Off James's Blanks: Theory, Politics, and *The Turn of the Screw*," *The Henry James Review* 5.3 [Spring 1984]: 192-99) the conflation of identities among ghosts and servants discloses a latent utopian thematic, the desire for a classless, otherless, society. In Tobin Siebers' reading ("Hesitation, History,

time the governess is intermediary between Mrs. Grose and Quint, frames and mirrors him to her (as the story mediates between the reader and something of his/hers). Now Mrs. Grose hurries out, joins the governess on the outside of the window, and applies her face to the glass. The glass as frame intermediates—delays while it facilitates confrontation; separates while it communicates. The glass as frame brings something to view, gives it definition, while it inhibits unity, the merge (loss) of identity. Note what happens in the story when the frame is missing at Quint's third appearance.

The governess meets Quint the third time on the stairway just before dawn. There is no frame—no barrier, no distinction. Each time they have met they have exchanged a mutual challenging stare; this time she meets him totally and denies him—subdues and absorbs him. He disappears into the silence which is the "element" (342) of her strength. Formerly frames (tower, window) worked to separate, to distance, rendering Quint's appearance partial, selective. Absence of the frame means the loss of differentiation, of mediation, means merge of identity. The form—apparition—of Quint becomes an empty form, an "it" that now belongs to her (see the final chapters where Quint is often "it," "the thing," and something that *she* no longer "[has]" outside the window, 401-03). And merge of identity means loss of distancing, of point of view, of seeing, loss of "I," subjectivity. The governess thinks that she triumphs—but *she* is possessed now.

As the governess noted, a frame makes definite-ness appear ("as definite as …"). Without a frame a painting, say, is not prohibited from integrating into the rest, into what is not-painting. A frame functions to set off a work of art from the "real world." It makes a distinction, a difference, a boundary; and it makes a beginning, an

---

and Reading: Henry James's *The Turn of the Screw*," *Texas Studies in Literature and Language* 25.4 [Winter 1983]: 558-73) the ordinary displaces the uncanny when Mrs. Grose becomes identified with the ghosts and the governess, not to dissipate evil but to reveal it, both thematically in the story and functionally by the story, as the "moment of hesitation" in which the reader may discern the threat of violence that inhabits and haunts history and literature.

introduction, a point of encounter. Art has been taken to represent life, to reproduce it, to interpret it, to transcend it, to attempt and fail to meet it, to miss it; but it is always conceptualized in reference to it. When art is not set off by a literal frame, as in music where time inheres but space more problematically, or as in the novel, as Bakhtin, Lukacs, Ortega y Gasset, and others define it as a form that opens onto life, then the difference dims and the antagonism or community of life and art is harder to discern.

We can put the question to test immediately. The story in our hands is a prodigious little work of art, and it is set into a frame by the prologue.

In *The Turn of the Screw* "story" gets separated from "life" not by the governess, not by her sentimentality or ignorance or naiveté, nor by her error or delusion, but first and essentially by death, by time, by historicity, memory or forgetting, by the story's passing from hand to hand, from generation to generation. In a Jamesian analogy ("Preface to 'The American'" 33-4), when the rope connecting the earth with the balloon of experience (to which we are connected in the car of the imagination) lengthens or disappears, then "experience" becomes "romance." In the prologue we watch the process occurring as the story passes from experience to record, from record to story, from story to ghost story. It drifts farther from its origin or source and from personal memory or association; the story moves on and leaves the governess's life behind.[16] Each re-telling accumulates story, acquires

---

[16]Lukacher has made the point: "By presenting his text as a veritable palimpsest of a multiple scene of writing, each layer of which distances us from the voice of the governess, James at once discloses and conceals the question of the origin" (128). This problem of the lost origin is Lukacher's subject, which he addresses using Freud's psychoanalytical strategy, i.e., by constructing (not re-constructing) the primal scene to serve in its place. The analysis is subtle, but constructing a primal scene in *The Turn of the Screw* means supplying the fact of what really happened, who is really responsible, brushes dangerously near dreaded presence.

In any case the unknowability and irretrievability of the original event ("the real") do not in themselves efface or change its ontological status as "truth"; it is that status that delivers the alienation in its "unknowability," its "irretrievability," and requires

and accretes new voice, motivation, setting, each rendering bearing less of whatever fidelity the governess's little narrative ever bore to an original experience. This story is "romance" by its distance from "life," and the more romance as it drifts farther away. The prologue and the series of prologues demarcate as frames do a kind of distinction, separation, between the story and life, a separation associated with death, forgetting, the passage of time; or perhaps more essentially with suppression, repression, locking up (precipitating ghosts, breaking out, the return of the dead).

On the other hand, each prologue by which the story is passed along offers itself as a new presentation of actual life outside the story. As the story loses touch with experience, the prologue seems to continue to renew its hold, and to provide a new measure of the widening gap between the two. As each prologue moves farther from the story, adding a new threshold, a new audience, for a new perspective onto the story, the increasing difference should continually "correct" the romance, error, of the tale. But instead each prologue presents another reflection or, indeed, reduplication, reiteration, of the original story. In each segment of the chain of re-presentations, all the themes and motifs of the governess's tale are repeated, or introduced. The problems of seeing and the nature of seeing, inter-view, interchange of view; problems of interpreting, of writing and reading; the problems of ghosts, the return of the dead (already the governess and Douglas have joined the ranks of ghost), of good influence and "evil," the latter identified in mirror-exchanges between the respective narrator and his/her audience, eventually with *us* as the last audience in the chain, as "uncanny ugliness and horror and pain..." (292). These problems suggest in turn the problems of memory and forgetting, suggesting also the question of the influence of art, that repository of the dead, of the forgotten or suppressed, the unconscious. Above all, the prologue enacts the theme of story as form (and art) and form (art) as containment (the Grecian urn enigma so compelling

---

a substitution, the fictitious primal scene that will allow the thinker to go on as he would have done with ontological certainty. Here his security is removed, but his metaphysics is not.

to moderns)—containment in and by and against which the matter contained breaks out. Each prologue enacts such an outbreaking.

The prologue to *The Turn of the Screw* is a frame which appears to distance the story from life; but language which tries to present the difference between fiction and life can only reflect or repeat not life but its own attempt; form forms. However, though art is separate from life and different in its character as form, it is at the same time form that works to disclose the difference, life. Life is not captured, circumscribed, not reflected or repeated; but it is connected or engaged via this tenuous, confrontational negotiation.

Frames are a principle of seeing as interpreting—differentiating something from other things, and connecting and relating it to them. We noted above the frame of expectation. Bly exceeds the governess's expectations, and we have described her progress through the story as an ongoing projection of expectations. But though what appears upon the horizon of expectation may appear by dint of its difference, its appearance does not dissolve the expectation; instead, what appears maintains its appearance in relationship to that projection. Expecting (desiring) the master's face the governess sees the apparition on the tower; but though she quickly adjusts her impression, the displacement underlies and colors her subsequent reflections and reactions. Expecting Miss Jessel out the window she sees Miles, but, as we note below, her dread is not eased but redirected. Expecting Flora at the lake she finds her, a rare, treasured "proof" of her own prescience. Her expectations, we may conjecture, stem from her limited previous experience, her youth, her sentimental proclivities, private fancies, and later from her need for justification. The most inclusive frame for her seeing/interpretation is the commission that the master gave her and her hope of fulfilling it, winning thereby his "grateful" approbation (295).

Windows

Another frame, as we have mentioned, is the window. We have considered the window as glass, as mirror, but it figures more essentially as aperture, opening, and as limiting structure, point of view (frame). We take for example the scene cited above (345f.): the governess awakens; Flora has blown out the candle, arranged her bedclothes artificially, and is partially hidden behind the curtains at the window peering out at someone—the governess "knows" whom, Miss Jessel—on the lawn below. The governess steals out of the bedroom, hovers for a moment at Miles' door, and spurred by one of those fearful glimpses at the possibility of his innocence, passes on to dispose herself at a window that will give her another view of the lawn. To her utter dismay, the figure she sees below is little Miles, whose gaze is fixed on something above her window, on someone, she suddenly "knows," standing on the tower where she last saw Quint. Though she sees this "lovely upward look" (357) as a proof of Miles' ongoing guilty relationship with Quint (we note that he turns the same sweet gaze up into *her* face shortly afterward back in his room), she finds later that it is merely a part of the "trap" which the children have set for her, a little dramatic invention—to catch a king, perhaps. (There are many Hamlet echoes in the story, and in this one the governess all but betrays herself—as does Miles, 349-51).

A window is an aperture; one looks *out* a window onto "the real world." But not all of the real world. A window is already situated to "take in" a certain limited vista. It is situated in a place, from which it opens out and into which it brings the things it opens to view. The governess chooses a particular window for the purpose of taking in a certain view in a certain way; i.e., she chooses a window in the bedroom of the old tower, chill and musty with disuse (but kept in perfect order by Mrs. Grose), and she approaches the window with a particular, fearful expectation—that she will see Miss Jessel below, that "horror." From this perspective, the past steeped in tradition, and anticipating evil, she looks out below. As we have noted, with the discovery of Miles her horror is not simply vanquished or corrected but is transferred. What she sees is "aided" further by the restrictions of her window. She sees Miles' gaze directed past herself to a point above, to, as she is immediately and horribly certain, Quint on the tower. But she cannot look directly at the tower; what she brought to the window, associations of memories and fears and desires, for example, informs her vision. The knowledge and capacity (which windows figure) which are the only means and guides to identifying and interpreting appearances work here to rush upon and overwhelm the small figure. The place where her perspective is situated does not disappear and become inoperant when the governess looks out from it; the meanings, associations, that inhabit the place are the functional and limiting means and manner of taking in the view of what is outside. Window is a way of approaching and also of appropriating. It brings the place and its furniture with it and by means of these it meets and engages, articulates and appropriates, what it opens to view.[17] James expresses similar notions in the New York edition of "Preface to 'The Portrait of a Lady' " when he compares "a number of possible windows" in the "house of fiction" to as many novels, and at each window the particular consciousness of an artist, restricted and enabled by the particularities of his window to see what he sees (45-6). What psychology calls "projection" is indeed "pro-ject," throwing out before, but here it is not essentially or merely flawed subjectivity; it is essential mode of access.[18]

---

[17]Tony Tanner offers this etymology: " 'Speculation' was a key word for James and it is perhaps fitting that the etymology of the word gives us *specula*—a watch tower, and *speculari*—to watch. More than that, of course, the word means to reflect, conjecture, theorize: it also means, to borrow the OED phrasing,"to undertake a business enterprise or transaction of a risky nature in the expectation of considerable gain." And a speculum is "a reflector for seeing inside people, a surgical aid" (*Reign of Wonder: Naivety and Reality in American Literature* (Cambridge: Cambridge UP, 1965) 310.

[18]See Heidegger's "projection [*Entwurf*]]" as a structure of the understanding in *Being and Time* H. 145 and esp. H. 151 in terms of "framework [*Gerüst*]"; see also "The Essence of the Mathematical Project (*Entwurf*)" in *What Is a Thing?* (88-95)

Screens, Bars, Fences

Windows are a principle of seeing, of reciprocity, engagement. Though windows may be used as mirrors, in which case they reflect a self image, when they are used as windows proper they open the view onto an outside, though limited and easily turned to the service of preconception or prejudice. A counter-device to windows is the screen. The governess undertakes to screen the children from the vision of evil; she herself will be the screen, shielding them by intercepting the view. After her third encounter with Quint, however, she feels barred, herself, from the evil with which she "sees" the children freely communicating. Bars and fences are more counter-devices to windows. The governess fences the children about more tightly than ever; she hardly sleeps, never lets them out of her sight. Fences enclose them now, and yet the governess feels that it is *she* who is "barred": from the vision of evil.

Of course she is contained, fenced about, too; the children are "in possession" of her now (355). She and they are bound together—on the wrong side of the fences, bars. They are closed in—with evil. The governess cannot *see* evil because it is within her now. The children are in presence of evil for she (and not only she) brings it with her. The surprising consequences, noted above, are that the children are more radiant than ever, outdo themselves—and her—in creative invention and in feats of intelligence and learning. But the governess continues to tighten the vise of her obsessive possessiveness, and something must out.

Screens and bars are doubtlessly effective, but not to contain evil. They are part of some essential tendency to hide, lock up, close off, and they function not so much to contain or prohibit things as to construct and proclaim a limit; and eventually in each case they precipitate a reaction.

---

and a footnote by the translators regarding Heidegger's use of the word "project" in terms of "frame" (88-89).

Perhaps Miles' is the primary case. After Miles has betrayed signs of impending rebellion, the governess sets him free—relatively. He is freed from their regimen and from a kind of delay or suspension of normal expectations. For a couple of days he ranges over Bly. Though he has told the governess that he wants her to "let [him] alone," that he wants to go away to be with people of his "own kind," he seems to equivocate now, comes back to be near her, needing, she feels, to break their silence. He proposes that they stay on together (395). In the final scene in the dining room before the windows through which the evil broached (via the governess) the children and Bly, the governess senses that Miles feels *barred* by the windows and screens (figures of her means of receiving and containing the evil) from something he needs to see. The media that mediate seeing are forms (frames) of the governess's kind, belong to a limiting, defining capacity, not to the freedom that Miles knows to distinguish his kind. Miles manifests something like human potentiality, whose essence is freedom but whose realization requires seeing as well, whose seeing requires forms.

Form as ending, as definition or as enclosure, works in the story as frame (frames per se, windows, screens, fences, bars), and frame works not merely to mark a place, but to work an intermediation and to produce an action, reaction.[19] This story eludes or escapes the very forms it *uses*. It uses forms to get past them. But my description so far falls short of a certain violence which forms mark and precipitate in the story.

---

[19]Siebers suggests that the story restores the historical sense of hesitation between the rational and the supernatural and contends that a relationship between the supernatural and violence is the fact against which the rational and the fantastic are opposed and are structured. His notion of the "radical discontinuity" of "founding oppositions," which inhabits or haunts social and literary structures, and his characterization of literature as "[teaching] ... what literature is" (571-72), i.e., a response to and an incorporation of the violence of superstition, accord at least in large with my reading here.

Propriety

Propriety is a form at whose borders lie the gross, the queer, monstrous. Quint, for example, is no gentleman, wears no hat, is "too free ... with everyone." Near the end of the story when forms are rupturing all round, the governess and Mrs. Grose dash after Flora—all without hats; even the appearance of decorum is abandoned. But impropriety is not all of a kind in the story. The women exhibit one kind. In the scene at the lake all of them—the governess, Miss Jessel, Mrs. Grose, and even Flora as she makes her choice—share in their separate and several senses a "gross" character, i.e., a tendency toward the vulgar, the ordinary, the literal.

Mrs. Grose represents an essential aspect of it. "Grose" suggests "gross," and descriptions of the housekeeper link her unmistakably with ordinary common sense. Unable to read or write,[20] she depends upon the spoken word for knowledge (303-04, 329). As for understanding, seeing into things, she takes (or the governess takes her to take) the spoken word of the governess.

> I had made her a receptacle of lurid things, but there was an odd recognition of my superiority—my accomplishments and my function—in her patience under my pain. She offered her mind to my disclosures as, had I wished to mix a witch's broth and proposed it with assurance, she would have held out a large clean saucepan. (348)

Mrs. Grose is intent on holding truth at the level of appearances ("See him, miss, first. *Then* believe it!" ... "You might as well believe it of the little lady. Bless her," she added the next moment, "*look* at her!" —But Mrs. Grose is dissembling.) Thus she is content with the

---

[20] The word "illiterate" could be applied to this character, whom I take to figure the literal. But the "literal" and "literal-minded" often imply an *overly*-literal grasp of things, an understanding not up to symbolism or abstraction.

appearance of well-being, with orderliness, propriety. She is presented in capsule in this passage:

> I found her sitting in pained placidity before the fire. So
> I see her still, so I see her best: facing the flame from her
> straight chair in the dusky, shining room, a large clean
> image of the "put away"—of drawers closed and locked
> and rest without a remedy. (366)

Mrs. Grose's lack of refinement of sensibility, her proclivity for suppressing or ignoring the troublesome, suggest that "grossness" tends toward the undifferentiated, toward stasis, inertia. This "grossness" is mitigated, however, or modified by another aspect of her character, also suggested in her name and in the portrait above. "Grose" given a "rose" pronunciation says "grows." She is the mother-protector of children and the home. There is something fundamental in Mrs. Grose's unexamined impulses toward propriety (propriety as what is proper to something in its nature, ownness). Indeed the governess depends upon the "justification" of Mrs. Grose's commonsense experience.

> There could have been no such justification for me as
> the plain assent of her experience to whatever depth of
> depravity I found credible in our brace of scoundrels.
> (352)

"Grose" as "grows" puns "rose." The word "rose" and rosiness appear in the story in connection with appearance, *mere* appearance (e.g., 302, 314, 360). Appearance is the measure Mrs. Grose takes of things and the object of her concern. "Grows" also brings Flora into association with Mrs. Grose as it links both of them to nature, the natural. In the scene at the lake Flora identifies herself and is identified by the language of the narrative with Mrs. Grose and the "gross." Flora "falls," losing her radiance, her beauty, her youth—"with a strange, quick primness of propriety" "united" with Mrs. Grose "in pained opposition" to the governess: "I don't know what you mean. I see nobody. I see nothing. I never *have*..." (382). I interpret Mrs. Grose's commonsense grossness and Flora's nature principle as different kinds of fundamental resistance to "seeing" or to the radical change that vision might precipitate. In the scene here the governess, hopelessly entangled in "seeing," responds bitterly to the opposition of these two: "I've been living with the miserable truth, and ... you've seen ... the easy and perfect way to meet it."

Thus "grossness" in the story is an unseeing, unreflecting, unassailable predilection for mere appearance; propriety in a fundamental sense fallen to ordinariness. Now when the borders defined and maintained by "gross" propriety are violated, another kind of "grossness" appears. The governess and Miles follow Quint past these borders and wander into the "unnatural," the ugly and the manacing, the "hideous obscure." The governess, the commissioned guardian and perpetuator of propriety, oversteps, violates, its borders in its service. Against the reality and force of evil she sets her rigid will, but though she is violated and becomes violator, she never relinquishes her original motivation: the hope of justification—in her view the fitting of her "truth" inside the borders of propriety, respectability. Alongside or underneath this motivation is, of course, the desire for the master's approval, which carries the governess past the border once again to the fundamental potentiality principle that she finds so compelling in Quint and in Miles.

Miles' character presents the clearest definition of both propriety and grossness. Throughout the story he manifests propriety in its most refined possibility: even after he announces his intent to rebel, the narrative notes that his table manners are impeccable (393). But in the last violent scene he mirrors the "coward horror" of the Quint apparition: his "white rage" reflects Quint's "white face of damnation"; the movement of his head as "of a baffled dog's on a scent" echoes Quint's "prowl of a baffled beast" (398-403). Perhaps the soberest question the story raises is whether the artist *should* open the eyes of "the children" to evil, whether it were not best to suffer its ill effects along with its fertilization, and to do so in the dark.

Propriety, I am claiming, is one of the forms used in this work to declare and use borders, not for ending but for crossing. Propriety per se is not a form with essential qualities, but a way of forming a border for living, for "reality"—a way of justifying ways of moving or not moving about. Mrs. Grose uses it to define a limitation of "reality," a point of far-enough, the governess to move into the strangest of fabulous worlds. Propriety works like a border for Mrs. Grose and defines safety; but for the governess—easily carried away, fanciful—it is more; it stands as both an ideal form and as an unexamined appeal to the master. Propriety, mere appearance, is what the governess most adores. But her own initiation into the vision of evil, a seeing past mere appearance, carries her to the border between form and disaster which is the site of the story.

Propriety belongs with the many dissimulations, pretenses, and the governess's rigorous imposition of her "rigid will," all attempts to control or order or end (define) things as they are—i.e., without order, end (definition)—and to control by means of form, appearance. It is the notion of propriety that defines the violation in Quint's impersonation of the master, his hinted relationship with Miss Jessel and/or with Miles, or in the governess's subliminal attraction to the master, to Quint, and to Miles, or in her relationship with Mrs. Grose.

The principle in propriety is *literality*, which is characterized in the prologue: "The story *won't* tell," said Douglas; "not in any literal, vulgar way" (294). Felman has worked out this definition of the literal as the limited consciousness, language. But the story reveals another aspect of literality as well. I shall examine literality, grossness, first for something essential in it. Literality is crude as Mrs. Grose and the governess evince it, yet in itself is not necessarily or merely so. Mrs. Grose, seeing only the "literal," represents a mundane, coarse sensibility; yet, as I have suggested, she represents at the same time an organic and a vital mothering principle. The governess, "seeing" with visionary conviction what she needs to see, represents literality as deficiency; yet in crossing the borders of the "natural" into a grossness that is ugly and monstrous discovers for our sensibilities something fundamental: the border and what borders.

Literality

There is a literality in the story which can be examined like frames and mirrors—the fact of letters. In the beginning there is the letter from the master, which contains another letter from the headmaster at Miles' school. Later the children write letters, never posted, to the master. Finally there is the governess's letter to the master, destroyed. And there is talk about letters: first Mrs. Grose and later Miles threatens to write to the master.

After the initiatory communication *from* the master, all the letters imply impulses (blocked) to get in touch *with* the master, impulses to reach outside Bly or the story to a responsible authority or power. The problem of the absent master invites analysis from several perspectives (see especially Felman 144ff. and Rowe 125ff.).[21] The phrase "presence of absence" has been overworked, but it was fresher when

---

[21] Psychoanalysis proposes that the symbolizing faculty, thus language, is made possible and necessary by the loss, absence, of an original totality, unity with the mother. This loss and absence secretly motivate, control, and limit (define) the nature, and in particular the linguistic aspects, of human being. Idealism is transferred to a new physical, quasi-scientific ground. In the James story the absent master may be seen as surrogate father, as the natural and legal fact of an historical link to the existence of authority that at one time inhered naturally and politically in the father. However, John Carlos Rowe's Derridean analysis raises problems of legitimacy, of illegitimacy, indeed finally of "the essential ambiguity of illegitimacy" (135) in the story, that break up or preclude the possibility of predicating reliable lines of relationship here. After Lacan's problematization and fertilization of Freudian thought, Felman interprets the master in this story as fundamental indeterminacy governing, i.e., disrupting governance, in all the master metaphors/displacements in the story.

Todorov traced the figure in this story,[22] and it predicted a predominant theoretic preoccupation that followed a few decades later. It names the uncanny, the demonstrable existence in some wise of what we "know" cannot "exist."

In James's story, letters are addressed to the absent master, but, except perhaps in Mrs. Grose's view, it is not his absence itself that motivates the acts of writing; it is the particular deteriorating state of affairs which occurs in his absence. The master to whom Mrs. Grose would appeal is the figure of propriety institutionalized: he is the embodiment of the principle of legitimacy. The master to whom Miles would appeal or the master that the governess is enjoined against addressing represents what remains of mastery (the original master is dead) as underlying source, as origin, and as enduring potentiality (not-language, below). The master seems to represent a point where the literal as we have discussed it occupies the same space as lawless potentiality. The master—such as he is: absent surrogate of dead father—embodies in one uncertain point of unstable equilibrium two adversarial human features: (1) the propensity for institution, legitimation; language, law, the literality-compulsion in my discussion; and (2) an underlying state, which seems to suffer no deterioration at all: pure potentiality (freedom). However, the attempts to solicit the intervention of the master are little more than hapless gestures after a receding past. It is altogether unlikely that they can effect a return to or a restoration of the legitimacy or integrity of an original mastery. The appeals to the master signify a desperate tactical resolve in the face of catastrophe, a last ditch effort to avert ("skirt") disaster.

One characteristic common to all the letters, even the first packet that reaches its destination, is that they are not so much communications in themselves, as indications of communications withheld. The master's note accompanying the letter from Miles' school, the packet

---

[22]Tzvetan Todorov, *The Poetics of Prose*, trans. Richard Howard (Ithaca: Cornell UP, 1977) 143-178.

sealed with such a heavy seal that the governess must spend some time and effort to get to it, reads:

> 'This, I recognize, is from the headmaster, and the head-master's an awful bore. Read him, please; deal with him; but mind you don't report. Not a word. I'm off!' (303)

This note introduces the enclosed letter. But it also refers to and reaffirms the terms of employment established in an earlier interview between the governess and the master in London, of which we know from Douglas's introduction. The master's letter does not communicate, but rather *indicates*, the complete withdrawal of the master from whatever shall happen at Bly (from the story), giving the governess total authority and responsibility for it, and giving her, perhaps inadvertently, her primary motivation as well: the underlying guiding principle of all her courage and decision as well as her temerity and indecision. It is (as she interprets it) the hope of winning the master's grateful appreciation or (as we, more likely, do) a libidinal compulsion we labor these days to analyze.

The conditions at work in the story, that found and guide and limit it, proceed from an original interview, to which the literal terms of this letter point in confirmation. At the same time this note introduces the headmaster's letter which introduces the problem which it will be the governess's duty to resolve. The master's letter is functioning as a frame, to enclose and to set off, to connect and to separate, to relate and to distinguish, to begin by ending and to end by beginning. And we can see in this framing the violence that frames do: in literally setting off the story from its origins, Bly from the master, the frame founds a new order: the governess as (unlikely) governor.

The letter from Miles' school, the governess says, states that Miles is dismissed and absolutely may not return after the holidays. This is a statement of literal terms which in their literality attempt to contain or limit the matter to which they pertain. But the major impact of the letter is its indication of what is unstated, the matter that remains contained, locked up: i.e., the reason for the dismissal, the nature of Miles' misdemeanor—the mystery which will be the focus of all the governess's occupation and preoccupation in the story. The letter in its effort to contain provokes the first eruption into view of the matter it would conceal or restrain. Letters, not simply or directly but inadvertently, as it were, not "literally" but functionally, indicate.

The governess's letter to the master signifies to Mrs. Grose and to Miles the direct action that they both have urged her to take, which they both have threatened to take themselves. Things, the ending, having gone out of her control, only outside intervention can prevent the catastrophe. But the letter is construed by each to signify a different action. For Mrs. Grose literal letters are a secondary reality, measures of emergency; the governess's letter is the means of invoking the contravention of the master; that is, the power of "respectable" order, appearance, to dominate or destroy the "monstrous," the "horrible," i.e., mystery, ambiguity, uncertainty. For Miles, however, the letter to the master means the possibility to escape the literality-compulsion of the governess, which "unnaturally" (339-40, 359-63) encroaches more and more upon his freedom, blocking his access to an appropriate education for an appropriate future among others of his "own sort," i.e., male, powerful, free. And yet a contradictory impulse draws Miles *to* the governess's literality: "love," he calls it (362), perhaps his own need to see. When he steals and reads her letter, what he wants is "to see what you said about me." (Later Mrs. Grose will identify Miles' original misdemeanor at school: "He stole *letters!*" 389-90.) Here it is himself he wishes to see and hopes to see by means of her letter. But the letter does not say something about him; it merely indicates that there is something to be said. Later, as we have noted, he feels the need for the governess's assistance again in order to see something outside and Other; but in both cases the governess's literality itself bars him from seeing what he wants to see.

Mrs. Grose desires the reign of literality and Miles desires freedom from literality. To both, the master represents correction of reality—to Mrs. Grose institutionalized respectability (order) as representation of reality, a principle of "gross" literality; to Miles power, freedom, a potentiality principle. Both desire rescue, deliverance, from the state of affairs at Bly and take the governess's letter to be the means of access to that end. But both desire from the letter more than it provides. Measured against their expectations her letter indicates a mere intention to act, a substitute for action, at most future, delayed action. But for the governess the measure of their disappointment is the measure of her success, for the ultimate literal achievement for the governess would be *not-writing* the letter, indicating positively her faith to her charge and implying successful governorship. The governess's procrastination in composing and posting the letter succeeds at least to delay defeat; for the "action" which the others desire would mean self-extinction for her (see tomb images, 363f.), whose literal function (as governor) is, according to her sense of the office, to manage, control, contain what-is and what-happens at Bly. The letter to the master which states "nothing" would, if it were posted, *indicate* the governess's failure and impending disaster. It would *act* to sound the alarm, to announce, as the headmaster's letter did, the existence or the advent of something. It would *act* to violate the conditions of the governess's employment, to break her commitment to the master. Here the literal functions not only to indicate and to evoke, but also to maintain or violate the contract which is the basis for the order of things at Bly.[23]

But there are the letters to the master which are written by the children and valued and preserved by the governess as "but charming

---

[23] The literal is operating as a frame about the human condition founding its difference from and its interrelating intercourse with "life." In Heidegger's works language is given as the open, the clearing, world, which is always actively contested by self-refusing, self-containing, "irreducible spontaneity [*Zunichtsgedrängtsein*]" (earth). "The Origin of the Work of Art," *Basic Writings*, trans. Albert Hofstadter, ed. David Farrell Krell (New York: Harper and Row, 1977) 143-87. References to "The Origin" hereafter, as heretofore, cite the essay in *Poetry, Language, Thought* unless otherwise indicated.

literary exercises ... too beautiful to be posted." In view of the master's injunction against direct petition, these letters are purposeless
"exhibitions" of meaningless potentiality inspired by false hope. The
letters are merely beautiful and thus irrelevant to what really happens. They belong to the story's satiric treatment of the romantic
governess, of the romantic. Art, represented in these letters, has the
venerable esthetic character of existing for its own sake, but in the
governess's hands art is nonfunctional or dysfunctional. In a time
of need, when these letters might work (work literally, according to
our definition) to make connections and change the course of the
story, they are suppressed by the governess in her own interest, to
indicate positively by their absence her commitment to the master's
charge. The essential difference between these letters and the others
is their (Kantian) purposelessness ("I let my charges understand that
their own letters were but charming literary exercises," 358) and their
beauty ("too beautiful to be posted"). The governess "preserves" these
letters (locks them up), she claims; but it is herself she is attempting
to preserve. These beautiful letters are capable of the literal function
of indicating, announcing, and precipitating event.

Beauty is mere appearance, a delusion, trap, in the governess's
view; the beauty of the children themselves is deceptive, for she asso-
ciates it with divinity and purity, according to her frame of reference,
and when she perceives that the children are not the paragons they
appear to be, she becomes "disillusioned." Even so, she sometimes
flees into the beauty of their presence for sheer refuge against the
doubts and dreads that beset her (314-15).

But the story offers other clues to the character of beauty.[24] When
Flora opts for mere appearance, the everyday, her beauty falls away.
When Miles looks directly on "evil" in the last scene, he mirrors the
mad, bestial "thing" at the window. As the beautiful young governess
slips deeper into her obsession, she sees a progress of ugliness mir-
rored back to her. Beauty occurs in the story most radiantly along

---

[24]Compare beauty in Heidegger's "The Origin" 56, 81; *An Introduction* 131-32.

with the creativity, intelligence, and vitality that mark the community the governess and the children sometimes share, all the more richly as that intercourse, defined by expressions of geniality and care, is fertilized by the influence of the ghosts. Either order or chaos, language or not-language, the governess's option or Miles'—either alternative alone is inimical to beauty, which seems to belong to the potentiality in things that inheres in a commingling of both.[25]

Douglas has said, "The story *won't* tell, not in any literal, vulgar way." Telling in a literal, vulgar way would be the bailiff's way. When Mrs. Grose threatens to write to the master (Mrs. Grose cannot write), the governess asks her how she communicates. " 'I tell the bailiff. *He* writes.' " The governess returns sarcastically, " 'And should you like him to write our story?' " At this, Mrs. Grose "[breaks] down": " 'Ah, miss, *you* write!' " An express distinction is made between writing in a literal way and writing a story.[26] If the bailiff writes to the master, his letter will certainly sound the alarm, announce and precipitate the defeat of the governess, after which the master must intervene at Bly, take matters, the ending, into his own hands. The problem, which the women see at once, is that such a letter cannot "write [their] story." The literal will not do justice, the ladies sense, to what is happening. Is the literal merely inadequate, or is it antagonistic, to the ladies' needs? We must of course inquire into the ladies' needs.

We know that the governess needs justification. She "sees" what no one else verifies. Her justification for her role in the unraveling of "health" and "security" at Bly is the "horrible proofs," foremost of which is Mrs. Grose's identifying the governess's apparition as Quint. Inasmuch and insofar as Mrs. Grose identifies, or identifies with,

---

[25] Compare Heidegger's account of "creation [*Schöpfung*]" when "the ground [as longing] ... comes to word," *Schelling's Treatise* 129, and the enriching effect of the tension in the unity.

[26] Compare the preference that early James critics expressed for "story" (a reliable idealism) over "analysis" (a threatening realism to be resisted), in Tony Tanner, *Henry James I: 1843-1881* (Burnt Mill, England: Longman Group Ltd., 1979) 5-8. It is this popular preference that the governess figures.

the ghosts, she too is responsible for what happens (368). Justification would mean that the ladies' behavior would prove manifestly appropriate to, commensurate with, the facts of the matter. Now the bailiff's letter would bring the situation at Bly to light, precipitate change, but it would not supply the master with the proper, i.e., justifying, point of view, interpretation. (Of course, we could show that the bailiff's communication too will be an interpretation, as are all of the "literal" letters above, as all assertions and implied assertions are. But the bailiff's effort will be clearly minimal, and serves us like the others to reduce and expose the literal about as far as possible.) The literal as we have defined it is not in itself hostile to point of view, but is simply inadequate, in its essential function, to produce it. For that, as the ladies agreed, one needs a story. Stories, the ladies imply, may represent the "truth"—an appropriate interpretation of life providing the appropriate focus, coherence. *Vulgar* literality is the covering-over (locking up) of life by language that substitutes itself instead—language as representation (romance).[27]

There are other instances in the story where the essential function of the literal to evoke event is suppressed for the sake of coherence, order, ease. The governess locks away in her room the "horrible letter" from Miles' school; its "grotesque" suggestion of a "bad name" is "swept away by [Miles'] presence" (307). The governess chooses to deal with this matter in Mrs. Grose's characteristic manner, i.e., to settle for appearances. ("It doesn't live an instant. My dear woman, *look* at him!" 307) But the charge discharged in the letter is not rendered nonexistent by the governess's suppression; it lives in and moves the story more vigorously, and more insidiously.

---

[27] One aspect of falling [*Verfallen*] (an existentiale of Dasein) is "idle talk [*Gerede*]," *Being and Time* H. 167-70, which "serves ... to close [Being-in-the-world] off [*verschließen*], and cover up [*verdecken*] the entities within-the-world" (213). In H. 214-26 Heidegger distinguishes truth as Being-uncovering [*Entdeckend-sein*] from truth as agreement between "an ideal content of judgment [*idealem Urteilsgehalt*] and the Real Thing [*realen Ding*] as that which is judged *about*" (259).

The "vulgar way" of literality is the way of the plans, framed proposals, and theories (schema, the literal, which may function essentially or secondarily) set out at the beginning of the summer in regard to studies and lessons for Miles, all thwarted by what just happens when the governess assumes authority for the first time (308). Again, the governess's "literal" self-indulgent self-analysis ("my discretion, my quiet good sense and general high propriety," 309) is already at odds with the impulsive, egoistic tendencies which are moving her toward the obsessed, aggressive possessor/savior she will become. Her scheme to screen the children by intercepting the evil hovering about them is mocked soon enough by her own hovering evil. Her romantic impressionism is yet another example of the same phenomenon; things appear to her first invariably in a cloud of fiction, then more problematically, and finally more cruelly as they near.

These instances and others signify in a motif of oppositions between languag-ing which draws toward form (in the romantic governess the tendency toward mere appearance, re-presentation as coherence, story as en-closure) and life (not-language, chaos, abyss): oppositions which occur at and by means of a border.

Sense of an Ending: Border

… there were times when it might have struck us that almost every branch of study or subject of conversation skirted forbidden ground. Forbidden ground was the question of the return of the dead in general and of whatever, in special, might survive, in memory, of the friends little children had lost. (355)

I shall call this point where language, formal or informal, skirts forbidden ground a "border." This border defines a difference between language, form-tending, and something forbidden to language that resists it.[28] At this border lies (1) "the question of" the return of the dead, the general question, and (2) the particular question of the possibility of the survival in memory of the friends of children, e.g., Quint, Miss Jessel, eventually the governess (355). "[The] return of the dead" as a general question encompasses the question of survival of the dead in memory. Both returning and surviving defy death, surmount or reverse or conquer it. Thus they transform it, since death that one can pass through and out from again is not death. Now the question that lies at the edge of language seems to be the question of the relationship between the present and the past—the present governess and the former governors, for example—and the effects this conjunction has upon "little children." No language can represent the relationship, for language stops at the question, "skirts" it. Language avoids not-language, and not-language is forbidden or forbidding to it—a double injunction, from inside and out. The border between language and not-language does not limit, define, separate, end: the border is where language stops before a questioning, an opening—which is the chief preoccupation of the governess and the story and our interpretation: the question of occurrence and recurrence. We cannot "say" whether Quint is a projection of the governess's or she is an instrument of his, though we can say that his evil recurs in her as Miss Jessel's "poisonous" presence does.

An interesting problem is the entanglement of past and present time in this vision of border as question. The question as to whether the present projects the past or vice versa, and the evidence justifying both ways, unsettles our usual concept of time as a sequence of now's and replaces it with a vision of time as involvement of past and present and future in each other, inter-counter-involving—the past appearing in a futural perspective (desire) or the present occurring as the past's

---

[28] Heidegger's vision of the hostilities at the border between language and not-language is affirmative; in the violence of this confrontation lies the possibility of the emerging of essents. The governess's (inauthentic) form-imposing tendency is fundamental in the achieving and establishing of world (*An Introduction* 161ff.). See also "The Origin" 54f. For language as abyss see "Language," *Poetry, Language, Thought* 191f.

(the ghosts') making its (their) way via the governess into the future. Time is not the issue; yet time is unseated and revitalized in this question of the border.[29]

The question as quest, as dreadful searching farther into not-language (the venture of consciousness, call it, or subjectivity, into not-language) is the adventure of the governess in this story. As her "seeing" moves reciprocally against and into not-language, relationships among things conceptual and factical change, break up, reform to re-break-up: reality happens. Once again the concept of subjectivity loses its integrity. The interdependence that mirrors mirror in this work is the figure of the happening of reality (here and in the Jamesian element generally). There is never a direct seeing or a pure knowing or an independent action or event. Subjectivity reaches into extrasubjectivity, involves and changes objectivity. All is entanglement, interdependence (note the motif of aid, assistance, to seeing and interpreting). Nothing *is*. All *is happening*.

The problem of not-language and its repositories—the past, memory, history, art—and the function of the border are all implicated in the governess's first encounter with the first ghost. When the governess "sees" this apparition, she sees the uninterpreted "evil" more immediately than it will ever appear again. The stranger displaces the master in her imagination, noted above, interrupting her general consciousness with a sense of immediate presence. He appears in the place of her futural expectations (desire), but in many ways his appearance in the context of the tower and the evening brings with it the past—a history of incongruous ancient-to-new structures, "battlements," which "[loom] through the dusk" unified with her in one moment. There are evidences, as we have noted, that the apparition is a projection of her own fancy. The governess's first impression is that her "imagination had, in a flash, turned real" (310). "I saw him as I see the letters I form on this page," she writes. The passage details a dawning of subjectivity, "I"-ness: a total solitude, the projection

---

[29]Compare Heidegger's " '*ekstases*' of temporality" in *Being and Time* H. 329-331; see *On Time and Being* (New York: Harper & Row, 1972) 10f.

of an object of desire, a point of view (he appears, as we noted, "as definite as a picture in a frame"). What the subject "sees" is, however, not her self as self (Miss Jessel will provide that view) but her self, or someone else, as Other. There are evidences that the stranger is not or not merely an extension of her own nature. Her second impression which she senses as a correction to the first is that he is *not* what she at first took him for, the master, but is a total stranger, at least to her knowledge. He looks back at her with an intensity like her own; their inter-penetrating gaze is a mutual challenge. When he finally turns away he "still markedly fixed me. He turned away; that was all I knew" (312). This language evokes another ghost on battlements calling from beyond the grave, "Mark me"—calling young Hamlet to another quest beyond the same borders. The point is that this encounter does not resolve into pure subjectivity; the question of the nature of the ghost is the question of the border between language and not-language, e.g., between present and past.

What the first meeting between the governess and the apparition figures in small, the story—as the governess's self-portrait, self-consciousness—treats from start to finish. The comprehensiveness of the story's elaboration of this network of inter-reflecting and interacting returns us again to the problem of form. The complexity of design in this work achieves the esthetic effect of poetry or of tapestry, embroidery, painting, to use the work's own similes—the effect of perfected form. Not only does the work present itself as the governess's story, perhaps a projection of her unconscious, but it brings along with it a series of similar pretensions or projections—Douglas's, our narrator's, James's. This widening image brings us to the most fundamental form available to our examination, the figure of story as work of art and the governess as author.

Sense of an Ending: Work of Art

The governess is an author literally in that she is writing her story. Within the story she is author figure as she assumes responsibility for

Bly and author-ity over what happens there. She represents the author, perhaps primarily, in her "dreadful liability to impressions" (321), in her extraordinary capability of seeing as well as saying (introducing into reality) what others cannot see, i.e., the actual presence and influence of the dead.

The governess as author takes on the task "authorized" by the master (we have mentioned the master's remote, reluctant relation to original authority above). The substance of the task is to govern ("form," as she terms it) the children at Bly—with the assistance of Mrs. Grose, the housekeeper, whom I take to represent the reader, an unlikely interpretation since Mrs. Grose cannot read (303-04). But though Mrs. Grose cannot *see* beyond mere appearances as the governess can—an active, participating reading that is half writing—she does seem to the governess to receive what the governess "writes" with perfect passivity (noted above), and her collaboration seems essential to the governess's own reading/writing, seeing/saying. Of course, Mrs. Grose is not as purely passive or receptive as the governess imagines. Though the governess-author "sees" best and interprets most confidently and cordially with the "assistance" of Mrs. Grose, i.e., with her reactions and remarks and silences, we see that the governess often misses or ignores or revises these to her own purposes. We may say that Mrs. Grose represents the reader in the working imagination of the author.

I take Bly, Be-lie, to be the place of fiction. Much is made of the "place"; it is in itself a large part of the problem in the story: "healthy and secure," says the master (296), but infected and endangered by the return of the dead, by guilt, desire. Whether the governess as author (Mrs. Grose as reader, aiding) is diagnostician or carrier of the infection or both is uncertain, but we can say that the story brings the question to a fine focus. Mrs. Grose, the matriarch of commonsense, removes the absolutely irreconcilable Flora (blind nature principle) from the story to the safety of the world from which Bly is cut off (of course, it is never verified that such a world is still attainable or secure); and the elemental contenders, form and freedom—the governess and Miles—carry their differences to the limit: and do so within the confines of Bly, i.e., the place and condition and function of fiction.

The governess purports to retrace her conscious experience as governor at Bly (the author gives an account of her work as author—according to our figure a double exposure of the image). Along with a certain uncertainty that attended the venture from the outset, a doubt so persistent that it assumes in retrospect the aspect of foreboding, the governess remembers the appeal that the task held for her: the dignity of such an enterprise ("the making of a happy and useful life"); the richness, the elaborateness, of the possibilities in the adventure ("the scene had a greatness that made it a different affair from my own scant home"). Add an intoxicating sense of freedom, and sweet remuneration (308), and these heady possibilities effect a profound temptation:

> ... a trap—not designed, but deep—to my imagination, to my delicacy, perhaps to my vanity; to whatever, in me, was most excitable. The best way to picture it all is to say that I was off my guard.... (308-09)

She speculates about the "situation" she has accepted and the course of events that can be expected to follow, anticipating with satisfaction her own power to compel them: "I was under a charm, apparently, that could smooth away the extent and the far and difficult connections of such an effort." She senses the ending toward which events must tend ("how the rough future [for all futures are rough!] would handle them and might bruise them"), and recognizes the proper genre for the project, romance (309). But the simplicity of this design is disrupted by the sudden intrusion of something "Other," some potentiality beyond her authority:

> It may be, of course, above all, that what suddenly broke into this gives the previous time a charm of stillness—

that hush in which something gathers or crouches. The change was actually like the spring of a beast. (309).[30]

Her attempt to exclude this element from the garden (her fiction, in our analogy) is the problem of the story, whether "story" is taken as her experience as governor (author) or as her written memoir. "Evil," shall we call it, appears first as perhaps an hallucination (Quint on the tower), which she must handle personally without relation to the story. But when it reappears at the window, looking past her for, she "knows," the children, she confides in Mrs. Grose, who identifies the apparition as Peter Quint. Quint belongs to the (hi)story of Bly, to *Mrs. Grose's* memory of that hi/story, to *Mrs. Grose's* hi/story, at any rate (for Mrs. Grose is haunted too). Bly has a memory, a past, a guilty past, and the governess is relieved to think that the evil is not an aberration of her own but an aberration of Bly's, a threat to the children, giving new purpose to her commission to govern them. Dealing successfully with the evil will solve the problem of Bly (the story), achieving at the same time the grateful appreciation of the master. The two projects (fiction and "life") elide into one.

---

[30]The "spring of the beast" will reappear in "The Beast in the Jungle" (*The Turn of the Screw and Other Short Novels* [New York: New American-Signet, 1962] 404-51) where again "beast" represents some richness and strangeness in "life." John Marcher postpones life for the sake of a "sense" he has "of being kept for something rare and strange," etc., something he is "to meet, to face, to see suddenly break out," changing, perhaps destroying, everything. At the end of the story he "sees" himself and his life as void. This "hallucination" gathers as the long-awaited beast to spring. In his (characteristic) attempt to evade event, Marcher hurls himself face down upon the tomb of his (missed) beloved. Choosing not to "face" what he "sees," he fulfills his fate: to be "the man of his time, *the* man, to whom nothing on earth was to have happened."

In our story the all-"seeing," all-will-ing governess defies, contests, denies (absorbs), the beast, and by way of her "gross" application of the literality principle diverts its force, surviving the ordeal, for good or ill, to govern another little girl with another brother. Miles, however, facing all, seeing all, loses all; coerced by the governess to yield all his "potentiality" to her "seeing," his total self-confrontation means total annihilation.

At first she is psychologically detached from her charges (characters, story). The children invent their own stories, using her as an occasion or a prop; her character and her history seem irrelevant. Gradually, however, she becomes personally involved and enthralled. Miles is the very epitome of the force in the master and in the Quint apparition that compels her. We recognize in Miles the traditional male principle (*mīles, militis,* Cain)—freedom and privilege, power, shadowed or colored by the potentiality for evil. Like Miles, Flora represents an elemental force that compels while it baffles the governess's artistic intention. Flora (flower), like nature, exhibits an inscrutable and unbroachable beauty. It is she who introduces the governess to Bly, "[telling] me so many more things than she asked" [302]. Of the Quint episode that shadows Miles' and Mrs. Grose's consciousness Flora "never heard or knew" [323], and in her final scene she persists—stubbornly, in the governess's view—in seeing nothing. But something in the nature of the male—irresponsibility, perhaps, or freedom, potentiality—engages the governess more profoundly. The combat between Miles and the governess will figure the combat between the author's authority and the subject's freedom in the making of a work of art.[31]

But the configuration is not static. The governess does not represent form or form-tending as a distinct and separate entity or tendency, nor Miles freedom as a pure or fixed state or function. The governess exercises freedom in a fundamental way in her function as author, and the "evil" that haunts her is the very potentiality that Miles reflects to her; in counterpoint Miles manifests decorum in a primary way, noted above, as the master represents respectability at its height. Still, in the design of the novel the dominant tendencies in the character and behavior of the governess and Miles figure the respective forces of form-making and freedom-seeking.

---

[31] Compare James's notion of the work of the artist with Heidegger's, e.g., in "The Origin" 62f., where the work is a "figure [*Gestalt*]" wherein is established the conflict between world and earth.

The governess's narrative is the story of the author entering into her characters. We may call this invasion an unconscious one, or an invasion of her unconscious (her unrecognized potentiality, freedom, her "evil"). Ostensibly her story is about her attempt to separate her characters from *their* guilt, memories, past. But progressively she herself enters into the story, becoming obsessed with it, possessed by it (342). The author psychologically violates, and is violated by, the characters; she submerges in the story. Meanwhile she and they contest control of the event.

Miles, the most compelling character, is stronger, more intelligent and more creative than the governess-author herself. She cannot master him and she cannot follow him in his freedom. In the maneuvers and counter-maneuvers of these two contenders in the last chapters, their fundamental conflict is worked out in the open. The "eternal governess" (360, form-maker, author as master-principle fallen to romantic authoress as female principle, gross literality) engages in mortal combat with the potentiality principle—power, freedom. In the governess's compulsion to force Miles' confession, *to her*, she attempts to en-close him; in each case he manages to elude her. The movement of each against the other precipitates eruption, explosion. (We note that the smothering syndrome, locking-up, is the very tradition from which the governess escaped into the story in the first place, suggesting fiction as repetition, mirror, or recurrence, or story as frame, above.)

The governess's effective maneuvers are verbal, Miles' nonverbal. When her insistent inquisition brings him to the brink of confession, he shrieks and blows out the candle, plunging them into darkness. He wins (373). Or he wins time for Flora to slip away to the lake when he lulls or lures the governess into forgetfulness with his music (373).

The governess-author attempts by means of form to master the unruly element in her story. She succeeds. Winning Miles' confession, forcing the evil into the open, the governess dispels the beastly apparition at the window. The governess's narrative figures the event of stories: the need and the attempt to govern, to formalize a potentiality that exists outside language ("evil," "love"), the effect of which is to necessitate and to provoke the escape, outburst, of the matter under compression. Though the story is a constraining, a forming, what it constrains—not-form, freedom (evil, love)—is at work inside it. The story (work of art) sets forth the struggle of these antagonists. But to what end?

At the end of the story (confession) lies the abyss.

> With the stroke of the loss I was so proud of he uttered the cry of a creature hurled over an abyss, and the grasp with which I recovered him might have been that of catching him in his fall. (403)

This ending, which depicts recovery and possession, does not define, limit, totalize the story; the success of the governess's literality does not spell the triumph of story. The triumph of story is not victory or transcendence but the "exhibition" (as the governess is fond of calling the children's inventive facades) of its own defeat.

> ... at the end of a minute I began to feel what it truly was that I held. We were alone with the quiet day, and his little heart, dispossessed, had stopped. (403)

Containment succeeds to contain only with the absolute surrender of what it contains, and at that point it contains nothing—the final vignette of the story. Absolute containment is *not* containment. Story cannot exist purely, alone, cannot "triumph." Story as containment, possession, stops where non-story, disaster, abyss, death, begins. At the end (everywhere story is, it is ending), where the battle wages, where story moves against life, there the nature of both story and life is declared; there "reality" works its meaning (i.e., happening). But though their nature is exhibited in the confrontation, their separation is prohibited. Non-story—the stuff, call it "life": all that containment wants to contain—demands story in a strange way. Both the master's original appeal to the governess and Quint's unnatural visitation have shown that the males in the story have found it convenient or desirable to appropriate the offices of the governess. We have noted Miles' case; when the governess grants him freedom he returns to her, feeling *barred* from what he wants *to see* (394-95). For its own differentiation, its escape from chaos, freedom, which cannot see, requires "seeing."[32]

Sense of an Ending: Outbreak

Perhaps the fundamental principle of "story" and of the work of art is the principle that we have found at the end of every path of exploration: "outbreak," as the prologue terms it, "coming out" (294, 297), "saying." The prologue presented the governess's story as a manuscript that had been locked away for years; Douglas's reading and his prologue were characterized by the listeners as an "outbreak after all these years ..." not only of the governess's love story but of *his*. In general *The Turn of the Screw* is a story about love locked up breaking out. Miles' secret guilt is the primary case, his secret "capacity" locked up and gathering against the governess's "rigid will"— to catastrophe. The ghosts as they appear to the governess in silence are already an outbreaking, but the governess's anxious or mad attempt to contain them is the problem of her story.

Saying as outbreak is a complex phenomenon. As speaking, saying belongs to the literality principle in this work and has the effect

---

[32] Compare Heidegger's description of the relation between longing (a " 'nameless' " "striving" [*Streben*] without understanding which is "lacking the *possibility of words* [*ihr fehlt die Möglichkeit des Wortes*]") and the word ("Longing is the nameless, but this always seeks precisely the word"), a relation and a unity denominated "Spirit" here, "the unity of the ground in God and his existence [*diese Einheit des Grundes in Gott und seiner Existenz*]" in Schelling's terms (*Schelling's Treatise* 124-29).

of ending indeterminacy. Compare an essential encounter between the governess and the two ghosts. In her third meeting with Quint the governess does not speak and Quint does not, and their silence is the element of their interview, the element into which he disappears, becomes locked up, hidden: absorbed. Her "self" is no longer her own. On the other hand, when the governess has decided to flee from Bly (as Miss Jessel did) and upon entering her room finds Miss Jessel at her desk, the very image of herself, she "[recovers] [her]self and [clears] the air" by "actually addressing her" in a "wild protest" (365). Thereupon she discovers, moreover, that she has decided not to run away. Both these apparitions bring something dreadful of hers to appearance along with something compelling of an Other. In the first case she seeks merge/emergence, in the other insists upon difference. The contest between language and not-language wages not at the border between human subjectivity and not-human objectivity, but seems to occur everywhere "reality" is occurring, in intra-human, as well as inter-, perhaps extra-, human experience.

Another effect of saying is that it brings along more saying and more seeing. When the governess "tells" things to Mrs. Grose, brings them into the open, and again later as she writes her story (projects it into the letters before her on the page), she "sees" things she missed at the time the thing happened, and with the (qualified, above) "aid" of Mrs. Grose's responses, spoken and intimated, sees more; the saying-projecting enables and engenders more seeing, for good or ill.

The ultimate effect of "literal" saying is to bring the ghosts into the open among people. After the governess tells Mrs. Grose about the apparition, they two are "in presence of what we had now to live with as we could." In the churchyard Miles alludes to the forbidden topic of school; speaking outright is not his forte, as we have noted, and his seemingly "harmless" speech is remarkable here for "something in" its "intonations" rather than its articulation as speech, yet this "saying" evokes "something new, on the spot, between us.... The whole thing was virtually out between us" (360). Having followed Flora to the lake the governess "[brings out]" the dreaded name of Miss Jessel and "the whole thing was upon us . .." (380). Saying projects, as writing does, the appearance of something. In the last chapter of the novel the principle is carried to the limit when Miles' guilt is forced into the open, word by word, down to the dreaded names themselves.

Miles was expelled from school for "saying things… to a few … whom he liked… ;" things "too bad … to write home." Flora is taken out of the story, away from Bly and the governess, after a night of feverish raving ("I've *heard*…. From that child horrors! … On my honor, miss, she says things—!" 388). The governess too is saying things, things "beyond everything. … For general uncanny ugliness and horror and pain" (292), as Douglas put it in the prologue. Douglas, now deceased—a "ghost" then—is himself a primary character in the ghost stories drawing an audience before the fire in the prologue, a character whose own love story is "coming out" ("outbreak" 293-94) as he introduces and reads the governess's story to our narrator and a select few ["select" since the silly ladies have left]. Eventually it is James who is "improvising" this little "excursion into chaos" for "those not easily caught …, the jaded, the disillusioned, the fastidious" ("Preface to 'The Aspern Papers' " 172).

There are two principles at work in each of these renderings. The "gross" literality principle (language as representation) which the governess forces upon Miles is the principle that James's author-ing of Douglas's reading and our narrator's "exact transcript" of the governess's beautifully handwritten account all engage in order to fabricate and maintain the story. But against this principle of form another literality principle is at work: saying happens. From "for-bidden ground," the "element of the unnamed and the untouched" (354-55), the dead return, eruptive, destructive. Gross literality is containing; saying as projecting is doing more.[33] Gross literality is the movement of form over against life to find it, force it; saying

---

[33] James's "saying" "recalls the worlding world contending against the sheltering earth in the work of art in Heidegger's 'The Origin of the Work of Art' or the violent 'wresting' of being from nothingness in *An Introduction to Metaphysics*." (From Appendix C).

bursts through form. Form precipitates appearance as it pushes life to its own limits. But what appears is not form; instead, against form not-form appears. The frame of language makes possible and actual the saying of not-language.

This effect of "saying," the effect of this story, is a release of things locked up—for the governess exorcism, and since the governess stands in the place of the master and eventually of James as author, for them exorcism too: discharge of, call it, guilt. What this story releases into appearing (the question that opens onto not-language at the end of the story) is the disastrous effect of "saying" upon "the children." (The culpability of the artist is a familiar Jamesian theme.)

> ... to "put" things is very exactly and responsibly and interminably to do them. Our expression of them, and the terms on which we understand that, belong as nearly to our conduct and our life as every other feature of our freedom; these things yield in fact some of its most exquisite material to the religion of doing.
> ... the whole conduct of life consists of things done, which do other things in their turn, ... (*Preface to* "The Golden Bowl" 347)

The "literal" function of language in the "The Turn of the Screw" is to bring living mysteries out into the open. Not that it resolves the mysteries, as though mystery were a cloud that could be dispelled so that something could stand clear; language reveals mystery in its mystery, and admits it here "in the midst" of us (perhaps a biblical allusion to the upper room where the dead Christ appeared to his disciples, 329). This novel's language, its own form-tending literality, declares a new sense of an ending—ending as ambiguity, as prow, as frame, as border, as outburst: ending as a kind of leverage that language (counter-) exerts against not-language, i.e., the past, the dead, the unsaid, to force its appearance, its re-appearance—a sense of ending as the perpetual turning of a screw.

Appendix C: Heideggerian Insights

Longing is the nameless, but this always seeks precisely the word [*Die Sehnsucht ist das Namenlose, aber so gerade das Wort immer Suchende*]. The word is the elevation into what is illuminated, but thus related precisely to the darkness of longing [*das Wort ist die Erhebung ins Gelichtete, aber so gerade auf das Dunkel der Sehnsucht bezogen*]. (Martin Heidegger, *Schelling's Treatise on the Essence of Human Freedom*,Trans. Joan Stambaugh, Ohio UP, 1985, 127)

In his criticism as well as his fiction James articulated his artistic vision with such fineness of detail, richness of nuance, that a phenomenological exploration of his work can never exhaust its paths and mazes. (A rational analysis could make shorter work of the project, for it would reduce or discount a great deal of the matter.) Against critics who have faulted him for excess verbiage I maintain that there is scarcely a word to spare. The scope and complexity of his rendering of things could support a Heideggerian comparison of equal scope and complexity, but comparison is not my purpose here. I can, however, point to some Heideggerian issues and characteristics which I encounter when I read *The Turn of the Screw*[34] as one is forced to read Heidegger—suspending habits of thinking and following as closely as possible: the language.

We usually agree that subjectivity is the realm that James inhabited and explored. Heidegger, as we know, eschews the concept. One of the major events in *Being and Time* is the *destruktion* of the Cartesian-Kantian subject-object paradigm. Yet the operation of subjectivity in *The Turn of the Screw* is resonant if not consonant with Heidegger's extrasubjectivity, particularly in his early works where

---

[34]Henry James, *The Turn of the Screw and Other Short Novels* (New York: Signet, 1962), Sixth Printing, 291-403.

we find, e.g., the structures of Being-in-the-world, Being-with, Being-toward, Being-there, and the "there" as language, as the "open" of Being and history. The terms *subjectivity* and *objectivity* have no referent in Heidegger; I can find no referent for them in *The Turn of the Screw*, where relations among characters (including the dead, the ghosts) involve such mutual reflecting-projecting interrelating that a definition of "reality" has to settle on such movement and change as these structures will allow—and produce.

In a similar re-vision of the rational tradition, Heidegger unties time from the clock and sets the past and future *in motion* (and that means: *into the present*); historical time becomes a futural having-been. In James's story the active presence of the ghosts, their intervention into present affairs from fore and aft, and their intercourse with the living, work to invite a similar reconsideration of the question of time.

What I explore in James primarily is the nature of language. I take language not only as writing or as speech, but as a principle of literality that the novel employs in an elaborate complex or array. James's uses of formal structures in the story—from literal forms to figurative ones and on to the governess's motivating principle—invite several comparisons. For example, an implicit analogy is drawn between James's uses of literal forms in the story (taken figuratively) and certain structures that Heidegger defines in Dasein's approach to the interpretation of entities and the world (fore-having, fore-sight, and fore-conception),[35] presuppositions and preconceptions that anticipate and guide the understanding.

Formality per se belongs to the metaphysics Heidegger seeks to overcome; in his work forms become beings and work primarily instead of secondarily.[36] His ontology of the work of art and some of the notorious stylistics of his literary hermeneutics declare the

---

[35] *Being and Time* Sect. 32, e.g.

[36] From *An Introduction to Metaphysics*: "Form as the Greeks understood it derives its essence from an emerging placing-itself-in-the-limit [*dem aufgehenden Sich-in-die-Grenze-her-stellen*]." My redefinition of "ending" in this chapter is akin to

difference (metaphors are not read figuratively, e.g.; such things as colors, marks of punctuation, or placement of structures are read not according to literary convention but as they lead and are led by the reader's listening questioning). In my reading of the James novel the ultimate disclosure is a similar overturning of linguistic *representation* and literary expectations in favor of a "literal" *function*: to bring to appearance, to do.

The nature of the governess herself figures the issue, her anxious determination to contain or deny what draws and eludes her ("love," "evil"). Hers is a form-tending nature that works in opposition to a fertile, formidable formlessness. It is James's familiar principle of art—the artist insisting, the stuff resisting: the contest between the two appearing to be the very ground and the nature of the work of art; and it recalls the worlding world contending against the sheltering earth in the work of art in Heidegger's "The Origin of the Work of Art" or the violent "wresting [*entreißen*]" of being from nothingness in *An Introduction to Metaphysics* (110, 161f.), where the same practical as well as philosophical consequences are at stake. Heidegger's radical *destruktion* of totality, unity, closure, is dramatized in the climactic collapse of these notions in the last lines of the story, while the event of the story enacts a Heideggerlike function of language to give, to do.

I explore literality as a motif, a figure, and an idea, and interpret many aspects of it articulated in the story as well as the principle (or the event) of its operation. In many respects Heidegger's explications of language, of the word as "it gives," and of the work of art are comparable. This chapter attempts a kind of *Being and Time* introduction to the other readings in this book, exhaustive (exhausting as well,

---

Heidegger's definition of this limit or "end." "Here 'end' is not meant in a negative sense, as though there were something about it that did not continue, that failed or ceased [*etwas nicht mehr weiter gehe, versage und aufhöre*]. End is ending in the sense of fulfillment (*Vollendung*). Limit and end are that wherewith the essent begins to *be* [*Grenze und Ende sind jenes, womit das Seiende zu sein beginnt*]" (60).

alas), elementary, and essential in its reconsideration of language and "reality."

> The ambiguity of this poetic saying is not lax imprecision [*das Ungenaue des Lässigen*], but rather the rigor of him who leaves what is as it is [*die Strenge des Lassenden,* who has entered into the "righteous vision [*gerechten Anschauens*]" and now submits to it. (Martin Heidegger, "Language in the Poem" 192)

Death in the Afternoon:
The Ontological Difference

The following essay is a Heideggerian reading of Ernest Hemingway's *Death in the Afternoon*. In Appendix D, I point out explicitly
some of Heidegger's insights that I am finding among Hemingway's
insights here.

Hemingway's *Death in the Afternoon*[1] appears at first to be and
purports to be and has for the most part been taken to be a more
or less technical manual/handbook for the novice aficionado of the
bullfight. It has not often been treated as a serious work or as a
whole,[2] though biographers and Robert W. Lewis [3] have chronicled
Hemingway's careful crafting of the work over a period of seven years.
In particular, according to Lewis, the portions which have been taken
as literary "digressions" were added, revised, and polished, and it is
these passages which are often quoted, but as fortuitous interruptions
to the work's integrity. Nevertheless, in spite of the history of advice
to the contrary, I shall take the book seriously, in itself and as a

---

[1] New York: Charles Scribner's Sons, 1932.

[2] Allen Josephs' "*Death in the Afternoon*: A Reconsideration," *The Hemingway Review* 2.1 (Fall 1982): 2-16.

[3] "The Making of *Death in the Afternoon*," *Ernest Hemingway: The Writer in Context*, ed. James Nagel (Madison: U of Wisconsin, 1984): 31-52.

whole, claiming that its "tangential" passages are essential, that the "digressions" are the very signs that mark the way, the signals (winks, clues) that indicate the seven-eighths of the iceberg which is the substance and the support of the one-eighth that surfaces in the text.

I shall explore Hemingway's use of language in this work and the esthetics it expresses, as they indicate and articulate what John Hollander, after Wallace Stevens, calls a "poetics of extraordinary reality" (216), more interesting even than the interesting Aristotelian, possibly Kantian, and Eliotic reflections and corrections, or the vituperative broadsides addressed to fellow-literati. The poetic power that Hemingway's considerable art manifests here is not in any simple way to "put down what really happens," but to attempt to approach, to broach, the unspeakable as far as possible, to bring the finest edge on the encounter, to discover what can be achieved in the bravest attempt: to submit language as far, as close, as possible to oblivion.

For my money (values in this book are always partially market-dependent), the easiest way to submit language to oblivion would be to write a technical manual about the bullfight. *Death in the Afternoon* supplies all the information one could expect in such a handbook. Beginning with CHAPTER TWO (CHAPTER ONE is devoted to gentling the ladies and Anglo-Americans with reference to morality, esthetics, and, in general, feelings), the facts are enumerated: first the novillada, the non-professional bullfight in which technique, that knowledge which makes the event an artistic spectacle, is "most visible in its imperfection"; then a general outline of the procedure of the formal bullfight, leading to a tour of the country, Spain, the towns, the countryside, the girls, strawberries, wines, all of which converge at the bullfights in the afternoon; add facts about climate, the seasons, and several chapters about the history of the bullfight and modern decadence. Now the fight is briefly sketched in its three parts; on to the occupational diseases of the matador. Many chapters deal with the bull, the good bull, the bad bull, above all the brave bull ("the bravery of the bull is the primal root of the whole Spanish bullfight," 113), then with details and examples the breeding, feeding, pasturing, branding, and testing of the bull. Eventually there is the bullfight, the matador's work with the bull (art), his knowledge, technique, especially with the cape and the muleta, and cases upon cases for illustration and fine analysis. We go through the fight again, more slowly for detail: three acts, first the picadors; next the banderilleros and then the matador; and finally, in next to the last chapter, the killing of the bull—methods, rules, tricks. (The last chapter is a poetic, partially stream of consciousness rendering, with Joycean and Eliotic echoes, of the milieu of the author's experience in Spain following the bullfights.)

But in spite of the lists and paragraphs and pages of facts that appear to give a literal accounting of the innumerable particulars that comprise the complicacy of the bullring, in spite even of the eighty-one photographs that follow the text, the glossary of Spanish bullfighting terms, seven pages of brief accounts of fifteen individuals' first reactions to bullfighting, a critical evaluation of the American matador Sidney Franklin, and at last a calendar of bullfights regularly scheduled in Spain, France, Mexico, and Central and South America; in spite, I repeat, of this hoarding of fact and evidence, and in it and because of it, interrupting and surrounding it, a clear impression deepens that the literal fact of the bullfight is the merest, though eventually the purest, part to the work's whole. (Terms such as "pure" and "parts to wholes" are used after the author.)

In regard to the bullfight itself we find that a prodigious event has been attempted before us (readers) and in us: to carry us to and through the bullfight, not as simple or even innocent spectators but as participating aficionados; to traverse Spain, its regions, towns, dusty roads, high pastures and low; to gather it up in its noise and festival and rivalries in the barricaded streets and in the professional bullring where past and present personages—heroes, cowards, masters, toadies, and artists—in their cruelties, triumphs, graces, and corruptions mingle, coalesce, and disperse—nothing simple or pure except the fierce, often angry, and ultimately extravagant (and therefore magical or visionary) attempt to see. We are not thrust at once into the midst of a brutal exhibition, but are taught (in a literal and traditional, quasi-Aristotelian way at one level) to see ("This is not being written as an apology for bullfights, but to try to present the bullfight integrally" 7): first as from the gallery to see the whole, to understand the formalities, principles, purposes; moving closer to study the necessity and the value of technique and alternative techniques, and the difference and the loss in tricks; finally from the barrera behind the matador to learn to recognize danger and courage, and simulated danger, cowardice, to recognize and despise tricks; and to feel and to remember to express appreciation for art when it happens. But seeing, itself, is one subject under scrutiny—seeing as one way to scrutinize, to penetrate the inscrutable.

Death in the Afternoon evidently aspires to the condition of fact, accurate documentation on the order of history or social science. (We shall see how the author treats fact, on the one hand, and history, natural history, on the other.) Even the anecdotes, personal to the author or to the principals of the bullring, are supposedly "factual" or "true," are not at any rate fiction. Or, contrariwise, the work can be taken as an esthetics and a poetics, as I shall attempt to show, as it demonstrates or mimics, sometimes parodies and often contradicts the thematic it literally expresses. It confuses or conflates and at last renders essentially indistinguishable general "language" and art. It is fair then to take the work as a study on the nature of language in general as well as artistic language and as a practice, a demonstration of language and of art.

It is a commonplace that Hemingway's language is direct and concrete, that its simplicity or its "ruthless economy" (Weeks 1) is in some way responsible for its vigor, impact. In this work, which presents itself as the voice of an author talking directly to a reader, with no detour through fiction (art, artifice), an author simply telling the truth, the language seems relaxed, personal to Hemingway (we know his voice), digressing sometimes into personal anecdotes and

professional shoptalk, sometimes into amusing or not amusing parodies of stories, all settling into an informal but traceable continuity
(certain unsettling particulars of the subject matter aside—wounds,
deaths). In fact, the language seems most personal, most direct, sincere, most "altogether frank" (1) in the last chapter (I mean CHAPTER
TWENTY, discounting the last half of the book, the documentary evidence) where the author sounds like a character from a Hemingway
novel.

This suggestion draws everything at once into question.

> If I could have made this enough of a book it would have
> had everything in it. The Prado, looking like some big
> American college building, with sprinklers watering the
> grass early in the bright Madrid summer morning; the
> bare white mud hills looking across toward Carabanchel
> .... (270)

It seems that the narrator's voice, which simply assumed (put
on—like a mask; took for granted) our trust from the beginning,
mocks that trust in the end. Is this treatise on purity just one more
among the numerous tricks it has taught us to discover? Or is that
sound of unsoundness that we have sounded (and what does "sound"
mean?)[4] just one among the numerous alarms set in the text for the
discriminating reader?

At the beginning we too quickly presumed a simple literality.

> At the first bullfight I ever went to I expected to be horri-
> fied and perhaps sickened by what I had been told would
> happen to the horses. Everything I had read about the
> bull ring insisted on that point .... (1)

---

[4] For a Heideggerian discussion of the word see *What Is Called Thinking?*, New
York: Harper & Row, 1968, 128ff.

We understood of course that the narrator would debunk these notions. Now we see that we were warned in the first sentence not to trust what we were "told," what we "read," ergo what we were being told, what we were reading. The narrator offers the same lure from the beginning to both the simple reader and the wary.

But we were not gulled, or not long, not merely, by a naive sense of complicity with the author. We were guided by the text.[5]

> ... I was trying to write then and I found the greatest difficulty, aside from knowing truly what you really felt, rather than what you were supposed to feel, and had been taught to feel, was to *put down what really happened in action; what the actual things were* which produced the emotion that you experienced.... *the real thing, the sequence of motion and fact* which made the emotion and which would be as *valid* in a year or in ten years or, *with luck and if you stated it purely enough*, always, was beyond me and I was working very hard to try to get it. (2, italics mine)

This author persona has explained that he, a *real author*—not a character, not a persona—approached the bullfights *in fact*—in perhaps 1929, -30, -31, (eight trips from 1923-33, writes Meyers 117), in Spain—in order to "study" the ritual of the bullfight because it sets forth and formalizes "one of the simplest ... and the most fundamental ... [of] subjects that a man may write of," violent death. The object of the experiment was to see clearly, without shutting his eyes, what actually happened and what the actual things were which produced the emotion they produced; to see them in order to write about them.

---

[5] Gerry Brenner has explored the duplicitous or multifarious art of concealment in Hemingway's practice in *Concealments in Hemingway's Works* (Columbus: Ohio State UP, 1983). See a devastating example of this art pointed out in "The Snows of Kilimanjaro" by Earl Rovit and Gerry Brenner in *Ernest Hemingway*, rev. ed. (Boston: Twayne, 1986) 19-23.

Textual allusions invite a comparison; here is no Wordsworthian "contemplation" of emotions, their interrelations and proper association, conducing to "habits" of poetic sensibility ("Preface to *Lyrical Ballads*). This author's absorption and study and apprenticeship give priority to the *things* that *produce* the emotion. Wordsworth's concern to purify the instrument that receives a stimulus is replaced by Hemingway's emphasis on the actual occurrence of the stimulus. Wordsworth's poet works to represent passions, Hemingway's to reproduce them.

Two constituents of "the real thing," or not two since they include each other, both "actual" and in sequence: what-actually-happened and actual-things—only these and these purely were what the author wanted to write about (and at that time was unable to do so; this text is being written, he later tells us, five years or more after his stay in Spain [3-4]). No explicit philosophy, ontology, or semiology guides this thinking (though a literary tradition is developing or dissolving).[6] We could call the approach phenomenological except that the self-consciousness of the word would interrupt the particular "purity" in this author's intention to see.

Things happen. They happen as a sequence of motion and fact. The author in the barrera can see, if he has the courage to watch, what happens. He will be able to write it if he is an artist and writes purely enough. Terms such as *honest, true, sincere, honorable*, and, above all, *not-tricked*, are applied to the art of writing as to the art of bullfighting

---

[6]Much has been written about Hemingway's anti-intellectualism. Hemingway states in the Introduction to *Men at War* (1942):

Tolstoy ... could invent more with more insight and truth than anyone who ever lived. But his ponderous and Messianic thinking was no better than many another evangelical professor of history and I learned from him to distrust my own Thinking with a capital T and to try to write as truly, as straightly, as objectively and as humbly as possible (xvii-xviii, quoted in Jeffrey Meyers, *Hemingway: A Biography* [New York: Harper and Row, 1985] 134).

Other critiques: Lionel Trilling, "Hemingway and His Critics," *Partisan Review* 6 (Winter 1939): (56-7); and Steven K. Hoffman, "*Nada* and the Clean, Well-Lighted Place: The Unity of Hemingway's Short Fiction," *Essays in Literature 1*, 6 (Spring 1979): 91-110.

throughout the book; they do not signify moral principles, unless morality is defined the author's way, as "what you feel good after" (4), but they signify instead the rigor that guides the seeing and knowing of things that actually happen. These assumptions become more interesting and lose their simplicity when we too suspend prior definitions and theoretic assumptions and (after the author's method) watch what happens in this text.

What happened first was our too-credulous fall into the dream of simple language as transparent, univocal, then the awakening to duplicity. What happened next was a restoration of a kind of trust, modified and unsubstantiated, tentative and attentive.

Hemingway's critical readership have already made the analysis that Hemingway's language works on a minimalist principle. The criteria for purity include necessity and precision:

> No matter how good a phrase or a simile he [a writer] may have if he puts it in where it is not absolutely necessary and irreplaceable he is spoiling his work for egotism. Prose is architecture, not interior decoration, ... (191)

Two examples here elaborate the point: describing (and imitating) the arrogance and grace of the veronicas of the gypsy, Cagancho, the author apologizes for "the worst sort of flowery writing, but *it is necessary* to try to give the feeling, and to some one who has never seen it a simple statement ... does not convey the feeling" (14, emphasis mine). The kind of writing required to attempt the proper effect is "the worst sort of flowery writing," the phrase implying excess, superfluity. Therefore he writes that sort.

A second example:

> The third fighter was Miguel Casielles, a complete coward. But it is a dull and ugly story and the only thing to remember was the way [he] was killed and that was too

ugly, I see now, to justify writing about when *it is not necessary*. (227, emphasis mine)

But he writes about it at some length. He gives an anecdote about having unadvisedly told his young son about what happened at that fight, of his son's associating the matador's fate with his small size and the matador's size with his own, an analogy so disturbing that whenever he closed his eyes he would see what his father had described. The solution was for the family to substitute for "death" when the subject arose (they were reading a Dashiell Hammett novel together) a comic "umpty-ump," until the boy announced that he no longer thought about "the one who was umpty-umped because he was so small" (228). The author's introductory "statement" (the story is too ugly to write about when it is unnecessary to do so) diverts if it does not deceive, contradicts if it does not lie, and unsettles any ordinary notion of purity; for the personal anecdote that follows is an oblique "statement" that raises, even while it displaces or places at a remove, the "unnecessary" spectre of the matador's death. One implication is that "purity" in writing—writing only what is necessary and irreplaceable—demands fidelity to what-happens, not to an anterior principle. In this passage, by the shock of incongruity (an impurity, itself, by ordinary standards), an impurity in language—at worst euphemism, self-deception—is shown to be an essential language skill, a technique for handling danger. Comic or quotidian language may displace the thing that actually happens to effect a relief, postponement of the emotion that what-happened evokes. The substitution obstructs or turns away or filters the view of the real thing, holds it off in its danger without denying it altogether. Such language is a form of address, even of engagement or contention, which like the matador's cape or the muleta waves the danger by. (Compare the Natural History, below.)

Here is the often quoted statement of principle:

> If a writer of prose knows enough about what he is writ-
> ing about he may omit things that he knows and the
> reader, if the writer is writing truly enough, will have a
> feeling of those things as strongly as though the writer
> had stated them. The dignity of movement of an ice-
> berg is due to only one-eighth of it being above water.
> A writer who omits things because he does not know
> them only makes hollow places in his writing. (192)

If the author knows enough and writes truly enough, he may
deliberately omit seven-eighths of what he knows with no loss of
effect.[7] Unlikely advice in a work as generous with detail as this one
(until the last chapter indicates the volume of relevant detail omitted
and all detail becomes relevant). Upon this advice, that which is not
stated *is stated*, or is as effective *as though stated*. It is the bulk of the
substance of what is stated. It is its bulk that projects the one-eighth
that is stated.

That which is omitted because of ignorance is not stated either,
and this omission too enters the text: it marks it with a hollow place.
Both silence and ignorance indicate an absence, shadow of oblivion,
danger of death, but the absence marked by silence "states" the presence of what it withholds, while the absence marked by ignorance is
empty.

In the earlier quotation above (2) the function of writing is to
put down, to state; its perfection would be to state purely; in the

---

[7]Hemingway states the principle again and again. One working example is
quoted by Bernard Oldsey, "Hemingway's Beginnings and Endings," *Ernest Hemingway: The Papers of a Writer* (New York: Garland, 1981) 42, in which all mention
of war or of Indians is omitted from "Big Two-Hearted River" and the name of the
subject river is changed, without, the author claims, loss of the importance of these.
"The test of any story is how very good the stuff is that you, not your editors, omit."
Harry, in "The Snows of Kilimanjaro," waiting it out and unable to write, thinks:
"There wasn't time, of course, although it seemed as though it telescoped so that you
might put it all into one paragraph if you could get it right," *The Snows of Kilimanjaro
and Other Stories* (New York: Charles Scribner's Sons, 1962) 18.

passage here the dignity of stating is in not-stating, omitting or stating minimally. An example is the author's Hemingwayish "sketch" of a picador just returned from the sorting of the bulls, "a study in apprehension":

> If I could draw I would make a picture of a table at the cafe during a feria with the banderilleros sitting before lunch reading the papers, a boot-black at work, a waiter hurrying somewhere and two returning picadors, one a big brown-faced, dark-browed man usually very cheerful and a great joker, the other a gray-haired, neat, hawknosed, trim-waisted little man, both of them looking the absolute embodiment of gloom and depression.
> "Que tal?" asks one of the banderilleros.
> "Son grandes," says the picador.
> "Grandes?"
> "Muy grandes!"
> There is nothing more to be said. The banderilleros know everything that is in the picador's mind…. (56-7)

(What the author, the banderilleros, the picadors, and presumedly the reader know is that when a very large bull hits the picador's horse, the picador is certain to fall. What follows is "everything that is in the picador's mind.")

Here is a more typical example of the emotional effects that mark the entire work, moments of truth, deaths in the afternoon, which flash out at the turn of a phrase: "He was twenty years old when he was killed by a Veragua bull that lifted him once, then tossed him against the wood of the foot of the barrera and never left him until the horn had broken up the skull as you might break a flowerpot" (45).

To writing as stating, above, belongs purity; to writing as not-stating belongs dignity; and dignity, we learn at the outset, belongs to death, to tragedy.

> In *the tragedy of the bullfight* the horse is the comic char-
> acter. ... The comic that happens to these horses is not
> their death ...; *death is not comic, and gives a tempo-
> rary dignity* to the most comic characters, although this
> dignity passes once death has occurred; but the strange
> and burlesque visceral accidents which occur. ... if this
> animal instead of doing *something tragic, that is, digni-
> fied*, gallops in a stiff old-maidish fashion around a ring
> trailing the opposite of clouds of glory.... I have seen it,
> people running, horse emptying, one dignity after an-
> other being destroyed in the spattering and trailing of its
> innermost values, in a complete burlesque of tragedy.[8]
> (6-7, emphasis mine)

Now death or danger of death is one thing on icy city streets
where a shod horse must be rescued at great risk (4), or in the village
when a bull escapes from the herd and runs a cruel rampage (110-11);
it is life or history. But in the bullring death is ritual and tragedy.

The difference between death outside the ring and inside undergoes a revision in the narrative. In the first chapter the value *dignity*
is given to death outside the ring. Gertrude Stein shows the author
a photograph of the greatest bullfighter Joselito and his brother in
the bullring, and herself and Alice Toklas in the barreras above. The
author "had just come from the Near East, where the Greeks broke
the legs of their baggage and transport animals and drove and shoved
them off the quay ... ," and he tells her that he "did not like the bullfights because of the poor horses" (2). The bullfight is presented here
in a photograph; photographs in this work are a modern mechanical,
"flat"[9] representation which stops the movement of what it represents,

---

[8]The passage burlesques Wordsworth's Platonism as well, particularly "Ode:
Intimations of Immortality."

[9]George Plimpton interview, "Ernest Hemingway," *Writers at Work: The Paris
Review Interviews*, 2d Series, ed. George Plimpton (The Paris Review, Inc., 1963)
234.

i.e., what-happened. The photograph is presented by Gertrude Stein, the first of a series of homosexual subjects in the book who represent not something unnatural but something un*wholesome* in the lusty Old Lady's sense of the word or, according to the author's thematic, un*wholesome*, unwhole. The author anticipated the bullfight with the uninformed, untried, mistaken prejudice of most Anglo-Americans. Dignity was all on the side of real death, the ones he saw outside Smyrna, and the bullfight in Stein's photograph appeared artificial in comparison.

The revision occurs in his first actual encounter with the bullring, and the point is fundamental. One encounter suffices to bring into view the bullfight as the thing it is, as a whole—tragedy (some implications for essence are explored below).[10] The difference in death outside the ring and inside is not reversed; the opposition between them disappears. Death in the ring is the same as death outside, only the formalized ritual of the spectacle, tragedy, purifies and intensifies it, produces a clearer seeing. The tragedy of the bullfight brings death into a work of art. The association of the dignity that belongs to the movement of the mostly submerged iceberg, the figure for writing,

---

[10]There are numerous references throughout this work to the principle of the thing as a whole, of parts to wholes, and the prose section of the book ends with such a reference, which recalls the iceberg principle:

> Let those who want to save the world if you can get to see it clear and as a whole. Then any part you make will represent the whole if it's made truly.... (278)

Hemingway's notion of tragedy and wholeness enters into or draws into itself Aristotelian notions, but either they are brought in like ornaments or relics—and Hemingway eschews both—inessential, secretly contradicting or subverting Hemingway's thematic; or they are brought in like the Trojan horse, inhabited with alien meanings. Hemingway's tragedy differs as participation and confrontation differ from imitation, as an infinity of actual, changing, articulable, rankable "facts" differs from unity and totality, as living people differ from characters, as death differs from truth, as lucidity differs from catharsis. Comparing explicit themes in this work and in the *Poetics*—tragedy, mimesis, wholes, necessary and irreplaceable parts, plot as ordered sequence of incidents, spectacle, catharsis, rules—argues that Hemingway is answering Huxley's charge (190-2), and without becoming a popinjay.

above (art), and the dignity given from the beginning to "the tragedy of the bullfight" (death) is essential.[11]

The author first associated writing and death when he went to Spain to the bullfights in order to study the most fundamental of things that an author may write about, violent death, and in order to achieve in his writing "the feeling of life and death" (3). Later the performance of the matador in the slaying of the bull was presented in terms of art, as in many ways analogous to the art of writing, with art per se. Finally, treating the subject of the art of bullfighting serves as the occasion for an exhibition of the art of writing in precisely the terms set forth for the bullfight. That is, the work *Death in the Afternoon* imitates the bullfight. As we indicated above, the work gathers up the knowledge required to understand and teaches the reader to see, to know, to value, etc. Further, as some passages quoted here show, the language in the work often imitates the particular subject at hand.[12]

In general, this work treats its subject matter, the bullfight as art, as the principals in the bullfight treat the bull: as if the subject matter were the bull, it is admitted into the ring in the beginning, allowed to display its bravery and spirit in a more or less natural and uninhibited way; then when its tendency in one direction is detectable, it is opposed, corrected, by the insertion of disturbing barbs, i.e., the interruptions, interpolations, oppositions, enumerated above. In total and above all, the work is an orchestrated assault against the bull (against the subject of the work: violent death)—not for the purpose of assassinating (or overcoming) it, but to bring

---

[11] "The essential relation [*Wesensverhältnis*] between death and language flashes up before us, but remains still unthought [*ungedacht*]. It can, however, beckon us toward the way in which the nature of language draws us into its concern [*uns zu sich be-langt*] and so relates us to itself [*bei sich verhält*], in case death belongs together [*zusammengehört*] with what reaches out for us, touches us [*was uns be-langt*]" (Heidegger, "The Nature of Language-," *On the Way to Language*, New York: Harper & Row, 1971, 107-08).

[12] See for example the three conditions of the bull, levantado, parado, and aplomado, 145-7; quite techniques, 176-7; even killing, 244-5.

it to its finest concentration of power and bravery and hatred (its concentrated otherness); in order that it bring to the same fineness of concentration the bravery and skill and experience and knowledge and art and emotion of the matador, artist (98-99);[13] in order above all that the two of them, united by the sword (the power of art), shall force "the moment of truth" (68): the flash of emotion in which immortality and mortality are seen suspended in one figure. In this analogy the matador's sword passing through the bull and into death, the thrust which the eye of the spectator follows into the flash of emotion, is not an image but the actuality of violent death, ultimate opposition of man and bull, purified and intensified in the language or art of the ritual of the bullfight. The shock of the ultimate violence occurs at the point where seeing meets not-seeing. Against the absolute certainty of what absolutely does not "happen" and cannot be "seen" is projected the figure of man and bull, the appearing of what-happens.[14]

This is the point where Hemingway's "depiction" converges with Heidegger's point of ontic-ontological difference, the point where/ when beings appear (not in themselves but) *as beings*, or what-happens appears *in its happening*. It is not my purpose to thematize the comparison of the two so much as to evoke what the works of both authors evoke: the sense of the uncanniness of "seeing" "being," the happening of truth in language (art).

But we have claimed that this work does not purport to be art, but instead to present or to represent actual facts in the manner of description, explanation (see Bibliographical Note on the last page), i.e., non-fiction, non-art, just language doing what language does. As such a project the work not only states, in the sense of proposition,

---

[13]The old man and his fish reciprocate a similar violence and love in *The Old Man and the Sea* (New York: Charles Scribner's Sons, 1952).

[14]Compare Heidegger's discussion of the unity of *phusis* and *logos* and at the same time the separation and opposition between them (*Aus-einander-setzung*) in *An Introduction* 130ff. The "essential striving" between being and nonbeing (the "motion [*Bewegung*]" or "agitation [*Bewegtheit*]" or "happening [*Geschehen*]" 48ff.), which characterizes the work of art, is the subject of "The Origin." Compare Heidegger's "figure [*Gestalt*]" (64f.).

assertion, the difference between art and non-art; but it also at the same time demonstrates the difference, demonstrates non-art, language which does not set itself apart as a separate monument to itself as well as something else.

What language that is not art shows in this work, however, as we have seen, is its own duplicity, its incapacity to represent truly what happens. Non-art as non-artistic language turns false or turns up as false. For example, the author can "write like this" (135) for only so long, as though the perspective or the disposition "this" requires were artificial, uncomfortable, difficult to maintain. The phrase occurs in the opening section of "The Natural History of the Dead" where the same kind of language that renders the bullfight information is heightened or exaggerated to emphasize its impurity. This impurity, a not-true-ness, seen like the horses in reference to the whole work of which it is a part, renders non-art (natural history, humanist truisms, Whittier's poetry) in *Death in the Afternoon* as a comic burlesque of art. Both art and non-art deal with what happens and eventually with death, and the difference between them is a matter of purity, which is a matter of degree: "... the real thing ... would be as valid in a year or in ten years or, with luck and if you stated it purely enough, always ..." (2). The difference between non-art and art is (given luck) a measure of "enough."[15] Thus *Death in the Afternoon* surpasses the language of non-art which it exposes, and brings the problems of art, of non-art, of the bullfight as art, of life as art, into a work of art where they may (as problems) endure.

We have associated the work of the matador with the work of the author on the grounds of the dignity that belongs to the fundamental issue for both, death, and the purity of the work of both artists. The purity of the work depends on fidelity to the "rules" in each case.

---

[15] Michael S. Reynolds ("Unexplored Territory: The Next Ten Years of Hemingway Studies," Oldsey 11-23), comparing this work to *The Green Hills of Africa*, concludes similarly on the basis of the esthetics he finds there: "... although we call these books non-fiction, there is no non-fiction. All writing is fiction, in a sense" (17).

The following prescription for the matador's attention to "the rules" recalls the iceberg principle of the author.

Nota: Although the bull will certainly be killed, either in the ring or in the corrals after the bullfight, the odds are a hundred to one that the matador will not be killed unless he makes a mistake.

> … But the matador, if he knows his profession, can increase the amount of the danger of death that he runs exactly as much as he wishes. He should, however, increase this danger, *within the rules provided for his protection.* In other words it is to his credit if he does something that he knows how to do in a highly dangerous but still geometrically possible manner. It is to his discredit if he runs danger through ignorance, through disregard of the fundamental rules, through physical or mental slowness or through blind folly. (21)

The rules are "fundamental," not literal:

> Barrera's method of killing, while it keeps within the letter of the rules, is the negation of the whole spirit and tradition of the bullfight. (249)

We can compare the writer's "rules" (192-3), not arbitrary or inessential but necessary protection against the actual danger entailed in writing the true: write truly, purely, minimally, precisely and as necessary, withholding seven-eighths of what happened, consigning it to silence, not from ignorance but from knowing enough so that the proper one-eighth is strengthened and heightened to produce the true emotion. The rules describe an intention, an orientation, without prescribing technique or content. Both the matador and the author are addressing, handling, delaying, designing, creating a work of art in respect to: death. The ultimate achievement of both artists depends upon their personal integrity (no tricks), courage, skill, knowledge, experience, genius, artistry, as they bring death as close as possible, or bring their art as close as possible to death.

Originally, i.e., in the first anticipatory statement, above, what writing intends to state is "what really happened," the always-valid "real," which the author defines as a "sequence of motion and fact." He wants writing to state what happened, thereby to elicit the valid emotion. In the next passage writing tends less to statement or discovers an alternative technique, but its purpose remains to achieve the same effect ("as though the writer had stated"), i.e., to produce the emotions that things that happen actually do produce.

The act of writing begins and ends with an emotion, not an arbitrary one or a selected one but the real one, the true one.[16] This point is essential. Just as the ordinary sense of simplicity, of the literal, and of purity are being rewritten, so the sense of what-happens, of what *really* happens, and of what "really" means, is under revision. Here what-happens happens as it produces an emotion in the author who sees what-happens and might write it. All the pages of information about Spain and the breeding of bulls and the relative quality of wines inform, precisely, what actually happens in the emotional climax of the bullfight.[17]

---

[16]My reading is at odds with Nancy Comley's ("Hemingway: The Economics of Survival," *Novel* 12 [Spring 1979]: 244-53) in regard to emotion in Hemingway as well as to the economic principle.

[17]The sense of "really" here includes the "sense of place" which Carlos Baker describes: "Hemingway ... has trained himself rigorously to see and retain those aspects of a place that make it *that place*, even though, with an odd skill, he manages at the same time to render these aspects generically.... Hemingway likes the words *country* and *land*. It is astonishing how often they recur in his work without being obtrusive. He likes to move from place to place, and to be firmly grounded, for the time being, in whatever place he has chosen" (*Hemingway: The Writer as Artist* [Princeton: Princeton UP, 1972] 50, 148). This groundedness could be compared with Williams' emphasis on ground. Hemingway's evocation of place is more richly "actual" than Williams', but the sense of thisness and actuality takes precedence here over locality. Hemingway's notion is closer to Heidegger's "world" than to the "dwelling" with which we compared the local in Williams.

Ironically, the *author's* first experience of the emotion that the bullfight brings is the emotion of the *spectator or reader*. It is this response to this seeing that he wants to produce, to continue to produce: this emotion which is seeing—seeing which sees no object but sees instead the figure (appearing) of what-happens. This paradigm does not place the author as spectator or reader outside the spectacle; his involvement in it is the primary motivation for writing. In a passage quoted below (206-7) the matador "plays on" the spectator, and in other passages the spectator is united in one figure with the matador and the bull (213); in some sense (some sense of "actual") it is his death as well as theirs that is engaged by the sword. The importance or the culmination of the bullfight is not in the killing or the death of the bull in itself, not what-happens in itself, but the figure of what happens which appears and the emotion that ascertains and proves it (the point of ontological difference).

> ... the beauty of the moment of killing is that flash when man and bull form one figure as the sword goes all the way in, the man leaning after it, death uniting the two figures in the emotional, aesthetic and artistic climax of the fight. (247)

The emotion in the figure of the matador and the bull is not projected from the spectator but through him from not the artist but the work of art, the working of art (207, below), art catching up the artist and the spectator in the working of the project, the projecting of the figure which produces "the emotional and spiritual intensity and pure classic beauty" which leaves "you" empty and changed and sad. The most fundamental thing, violent death, is seen most clearly and purely in a work of art, defined by order and ritual, not as it has been already produced there, but as it is occurring there. Art preserves what-happens in its happening. And further, emotion as the ground of the work of art is the ground of the appearing of what-happens in true seeing.[18]

Thus emotion provides the means for judging and evaluating the true, the real. Traditional "truth" as correspondence or correctness deriving in ideality or in things themselves gives place to the "true" as real things really happening, announcing themselves and proving themselves on the ground of the emotion of a spectator. Compare the numerous counterpoint references to "accuracy" (e.g., 137, 189, 204), to histories and statistics (239-244).

But emotion per se is not pure and does not necessarily indicate the true. In an emotional critique of a book by the German art critic Julius Meier-Graefe written to compare paintings of Velasquez, El Greco, and Goya (written, the author says, "to have publishable ecstasies about them"; written, he says, to "exalt" the painting of Greco over both the others, 203), our author argues that an artist's power can be assessed only in works about subjects which he loves or hates or believes in strongly. He implies also both in remarks about the critic and about Greco that the loves, hates, and beliefs of the artist (or art critic) precede and inhabit the artist's-critic's works. The principle is being illustrated at the same time in the author's own contemptuous tone and at the end of the passage by his malicious epithets intended to deliver in one line a more telling judgment of a few artists than the "stupid" critic could produce in a book. Both the critic's and the author's judgment and writing are shaped, or distorted, by emotion that originates in prior opinion and predisposition, or perhaps we should find the critic's prejudice so but attribute the author's taste to a history of educating experience.

---

[18]The event of art as I am describing it here recalls Heidegger's description of the work(ing) of art in "The Origin," in that (1) art (a nonbeing grantor of being) is the origin of artists and works of art; (2) art is the mutual operation of createdness, creator, and preserver; (3) art is the site of the active appearing of the world-earth conflict (being versus not-being); and (4) art is a way in which "truth" as Being-uncovering happens.

Emotion does not originate in things and proceed from them to spectators (who write it), but is already in the spectator, is the stuff of seeing, as we have suggested, and the stuff of producing as well. The best matadors, for example, are emotional, work emotionally, produce emotion; the author's first objective is to learn to produce the emotion that actual things produce. This work itself is a drama of differing and conflicting tones, producing different emotional effects; compare the clean precision of certain pure, minimally sculptured "things that happen" (the clean, white bone, 20) with the increasingly emotional colloquial ejaculations ("This is Christ's truth," 242, "I swear," 243, "By Christ," 257). Emotion that inspires and informs the artist's work is not one undifferentiated force. To take an unequivocal example, the "nonsense" produced by certain mystic writers (53-4) is evidence of emotion producing writing instead of the other way around. This emotion, however, which blurs the writer's vision and distorts its objects, derives from an "unrelieved turgidness" which "a few good pieces" of a certain "sovereign specific" could easily clear away. "Erectile writing," the author calls it, characteristic of a certain American school of "mechanical experiment," now, happily, passing or past.

Further, though emotion is fundamental to seeing and knowing the true and to the appearing of what-happens, emotion alone cannot account for what-happens in the working of the work of art. What happens includes in addition to the emotion that is in the matador and in the spectator and in the working of art: the valor, art, understanding, and imagination of the matador, characteristics which "artistry and genius" add onto: the bravery, honor, knowledge, experience, and skill that even "day-laborers of bullfighting" must have to give a competent performance (207). Add the bravery and nobility of the bull, besides its health, condition, age, size, horns, and complete ignorance of the bullring. Add to these the innumerable particulars of Spain and its people and history, all that actually happens and has happened to provide the matador, the bull, the ritual—everything and, according to the last chapter, more, that appears in this book. Gather it all into the figure of the man and the bull seemingly suspended in time as it appears in the flash of emotion.

What appears is the figure of mortality-immortality.

> ... Now the essence of the greatest emotional appeal of bullfighting is the feeling of immortality that the bullfighter feels in the middle of a great faena and he gives to the spectators.... He gives the feeling of his immortality, and, as you watch it, it becomes yours. Then when it belongs to both of you, he proves it with the sword. (213)

He proves it. The eye follows the sword from the man into the bull and past toward that which does *not* "appear," does *not* "happen." What appears in the violence of that contradiction is im-mortality: man as not-death, not-nothing, man "taking to himself one of the Godlike attributes; that of giving [death]" (233), negating mortality.

In the spectacle of the bullfight the artist and the man, the two-in-one, meet the"wild animal" (21); the bull must be brave, simple, inexperienced (145), altogether alien to the instituted ritual of the bullfight. (Through breeding it has been possible to alter the bull's size, the length of its horns, even its spirit; the loss of the original large, brave, powerful animals is one aspect of modern decadence. In the art motif too, the domestication or hybridization of the wild means loss of an original subject, adversary.) The bullfight sets forth a fundamental, practical, actual thing: man and art contesting nature and death. In this contest man and art do not set themselves apart from and then against nature and death so as to dominate them, slay them, man and art the victors. For there is no sense of separating or objectifying, as there is no sense of stopping or of interrupting or changing what-happens or even of catching hold of it, holding it. Formalizing the death of the bull means purifying it of randomness, if possible of cowardice or ineptitude or of dissimulation; purifying the nature of the bull and the mastery of the man; purifying, then, the opposition between the two, intensifying the violence of what happens.[19] The power and intensity of the opposition renders clearer, purer, the appearing of the figure of what happens and more powerful and pure the seeing-responding emotion of the spectator. The heightened seeing makes possible the more powerful and purer "writing" that attempts to continue to produce it, to make it permanent, not as an object but as what-happens, for a long time or, with luck and if stated purely enough, always (2).

Lest restatement tend toward conceptualization, let us return to the violence itself. The complete performance:

> … the complete faena; the faena that takes a man out of himself and makes him feel immortal while it is proceeding, that gives him an ecstasy, that is, while momentary, as profound as any religious ecstasy; moving all the people in the ring together and increasing in emotional intensity as it proceeds, carrying the bullfighter with it, he playing on the crowd through the bull and being moved as it responds in a growing ecstasy of ordered, formal, passionate, increasing disregard for death that leaves you, when it is over, and the death administered to the animal that has made it possible, as empty, as changed and as sad as any major emotion will leave you. (206-7)

What happens in this performance, which the author often calls "ritual," happens in a bath of emotion, group or mob emotion, rising ecstatically toward death in the actual "performance" of actually killing an animal. Here held up in praise as pure art and as pure seeing and knowing of the most fundamental thing to "write"—i.e., to preserve in its happening—is the ghost of blood sacrifice rituals,

---

[19]Compare the world-earth contention in Heidegger's "The Origin" 42f., 55f.

perhaps the Christ mystery. And we "see" more clearly a problem
that has haunted this book beginning with the words of the title.

The subject of this work, the bullfight, climaxing in the killing
of the bull, has passed before us again and again, with less to more
particularity and clarity. Our emotion—a repugnance or fear—has responded to the disturbing imminence of the subject not only of death
itself but of "administering" death, of murder, the bloody violation of
life and history which civilized people manage as far as possible to
ignore, forget, to "umpty-ump," or to transform through religion.[20]
The measure of Hemingway's courage, his sincerity, honor, the purity
and trueness of his seeing and knowing and writing, the dignity of the
tragedy he presents perhaps an eighth of, is the measure—according
to his standard—of the true emotion his performance raises in us,
his spectators. We see the nature of the danger, of the death that
Hemingway is dealing with, working a work of art on—drawing us
into. Brenner calls Hemingway's intrepidity a "healthy" corrective for
especially American trepidation before the subject of death (70-74).
This is something like our author's suggestion (264-66), but in context the notion works not so much to settle as to quicken the reader's
response. Settling the unspeakable into terms of health or even into
current concepts of complexity or ambiguity diverts or diminishes
the force (the horns) of the phenomenon, eludes it again, eases the
emotion and turns away what might appear in it. The book intends,
I think, to bring the reader into an understanding appreciation of
the art of the bullfight and the subject of violent death and to engage
his/her emotion increasingly as the spectacle in this passage does.
As we noted above, the language becomes more emotional as the
book approaches the last (but one) chapter, about killing itself. But
the emotion is excitement, not ecstasy, inviting overreactions such as

---

[20] Joseph Waldmeir justly compares the bullfighter to the priest intermediating
the " 'feeling of life and death and mortality and immortality' " (166), but makes
no inference to the poet-priest intermediating what-happens, "*Confiteor Hominem*:
Ernest Hemingway's Religion of Man," PMASAL 42 (1956): 277-81, rpt. in *Hemingway: A Collection of Critical Essays*, ed. Robert P. Weeks (Englewood Cliffs, New
Jersey: Prentice-Hall, 1962) 161-68.

D'Agostino's (483-4) or Edmund Wilson's ("Hemingway" 223); given the weight of the habit of repugnance and fear against the untracked or the "true," in the author's sense, it will be some time before readers will go as far into the matter as the author may be going. I will set the issue aside as I go on, retaining the disturbance as the primary disclosure of this work.

We can say that emotion is in the artist and in the spectator and in the two and more at once when art is working, that what really happens produces this emotion, and that the emotion is or is the condition for and securing of a pure seeing. We can say that not all seeing is pure, not all writing (or bullfighting) is art, not all things really happen. Finally we can say that a pure seeing inspires and climaxes this book, the open gaze which follows the sword of the matador and receives the emotion; that the emotion proceeds in and from every part—matador, spectator, bull, spectacle—climaxing as they unite in the appearing of one figure and in opposition to death. In the working of art, life and death appear in their difference, at the point of difference, to produce the figure, the emotion, the seeing. Appearing and seeing unite where they collide against death.[21]

Now, in the style of the author, above, we rein the discussion in: "This seems to have gotten away from" the study of Hemingway's use of language. No, the object of writing is to produce the very emotion that what-happens produces. The author in this work has written about violent death, the most fundamental thing an author can write of, and to do so has written about it as it is set forth in the working of a work of art (the bullfight, this work). A double exposure accrues, explication and demonstration in the same.[22] According to the author's esthetic as I have read it, (1) we see the violent death

---

[21] Another implication for emotion in the passage quoted above: the power of the emotion aroused by the bullfight is not greater than or different from the power of "any major emotion." Emotions seem to be the stuff of seeing and knowing—not knowing about, but knowing in the sense of securing the seeing of, having.

[22] The effect is the same as in Heidegger's use of van Gogh's painting of peasant shoes in "The Origin." Inquiring into the nature of equipment (his primary inquiry addresses the work-being of the work of art) Heidegger takes the painting as a

most purely and may study it as it is set forth in an impermanent work of art (the bullfight), which purifies the view and intensifies the effect; (2) we see the bullfight (a working of art) most purely as it is set forth in a permanent work of art, *Death in the Afternoon.* There are two implications for language or art. Language or art is the institutionalizing, formalizing that (1) allows the encounter with violent death, a facing if not a seeing, without annihilation, and (2) allows the appearing of *things* as opposed to *nothing* (death). We see that one sees what-happens most clearly and purely when one sees it in a working of art, impermanent art working in life first, and then again and again in a permanent work of art, the subject of our own study.

Writing preserves what-happens in its happening. It does not represent, after Aristotle's formulation of mimesis (*Poetics*), and the emotion that Aristotle reserved for the spectator is the element in which Hemingway's writing begins, goes on, and ends. It is not emotion purified through contemplation and a habit of refined emotional associations, which then "gives importance to the action and situation," as Wordsworth argued ("Preface" 281-82). The importance is in the actual appearing of what-happens; emotion is the site and the means of the appearing. Writing does not fall upon "a set of objects, a situation, a chain of events" to evoke the proper emotion Eliot's way ("Tradition and the Individual Talent"), for the emotion that Hemingway's writing elicits is the very emotion that what-happens elicits, and no formula could construe the actual things that actually produce it (as Baker observes, *The Writer as Artist* 56-7). Language or art is not a faithful mirror or a realist denotation. It is closer to Heidegger's charged language-dependent "presencing," which occurs and is preserved via the work of art. It is "statement" which preserves

---

convenient representation of such an entity. The nature of equipment is indeed discovered, but this discovery is embedded in another one: it was the painting (as art work-ing) that disclosed the being of the shoes. Thus the thinking finds that it has "unwittingly" already learned that disclosure is the work-being of the work of art.

somehow an actual "fact" as it "happens."[23] Obviously this book is full of "motion" and "fact" in the literal sense, but beyond that is Hemingway's modified sense of the literal which we are trying to understand.

Facts, the "actual things" that produce the emotion, have not so much an austerity or rigor of identity as a purity, essence. The fact which this author writes about is violent death. What actually happens to produce the emotion when at the climax of the bullfight the matador thrusts the sword is the fact which these pages of detail and history and fable and speculation make up. Writing will preserve ("[make] permanent," 3) the fact that happens, will produce the *same* emotion. Now "flowery writing" produces emotion—for novices. For example, after a figurative and technically showy (as to rhythm, pacing, euphony, mime) description of a veronica (14), we read, "Any one who has seen bullfights can skip such flowerishness and read the *facts which are much more difficult to isolate and state*" (emphasis mine). The narrator classifies flowery writing with the "picturesque," useful only for growing out of, into experience and knowledge of the better "true," the truer ungarnished "fact." "Erectile writing"

---

[23] Hemingway's insistence on the actual is modified in the case of character, as we note. Baker traces the author's apprenticeship in writing the truth; first a strict "observation of action, set forth in unadorned prose" (*The Writer as Artist* 60): "You see I'm trying in all my stories to get the feeling of the actual life across—not to just depict life—or criticize it—but to actually make it alive. So that when you have read something by me you actually experience the thing." (1925, Carlos Baker, ed., *Ernest Hemingway: Selected Letters 1917-1961* [New York: Charles Scribner's Sons, 1981] 153)

Eventually, however, with accumulated knowledge and experience he allows "guesses, fiction, motivations, imaginations" to inform his "inventions," though the purpose remains the same, to seize and project for the reader what he often called "the way it was," to, Baker quotes Hemingway, "produce a truer account than anything factual can be" (*The Writer as Artist* 64). In the Plimpton interview in 1963 Hemingway states similarly: "From things that have happened and from things as they exist and from all things that you know and all those you cannot know, you make something through your invention that is not a representation but a whole new thing truer than anything true and alive, and you make it alive, and if you make it well enough, you give it immortality..." (239).

too, above, is emotional, but it does not produce the emotion that actual things produce; on the contrary, emotion produces the writing, emotion originating not in the fact but in the writer.

The purity of facts is their actuality. As things that happen, facts always occur individually and experientially, and yet seen truly a fact appears repeatedly essentially the same. Thus the author can claim that the reason why "the bullfight has never been explained" is that people have not "admitted" such unconventional things as the comic effect of the disembowelled "old-maidish" horses (7); the implication is that the horses' part in the tragedy is truly incongruous, that forthright accounts would agree. But though facts reappear essentially the same, different spectators will have different reactions to them. The *fact* about personal reaction is that it is immediate and unpredictable. The author gives his own experience as evidence (and appends to the text a catalog of testimonials), not "because of a desire ... to write about himself and his own reactions, considering them as important and taking delight in them because they are his, but rather *to establish the fact* ... that the reactions were instant and unexpected" (8, emphasis mine). The most essential point is that facts occur in experience, not idiosyncratic but "true" experience, and cannot be conveyed in language until they have been "seen," responded to. "... you will know when you first try it whether you like it as a thing or not from the effect it will have on you" (12). And, "It is of no use [unnecessary] to describe the state of ... , nor speak of the aspects of this ... because every one has some contact with them sooner or later ..." (85).[24] The primary application:

---

[24]Bloom calls Hemingway one of the "late and dark ... negative theologians" of "the Emersonian religion of self-reliance" (*Modern Critical Views* 2-3), but in my view what Bloom calls Hemingway's "Real Absence" indicates not a negative meaning (this is his difference from Melville) but a context of unconceptualized, nonconceptual, factical relationships working in what happens. His Real Absence marks the point of ontological difference all right, but an ontology does not follow; refusal to fill in the blanks renders his "void" anomalous if not absurd in the tradition. (It is something like Nietzsche's or the young Heidegger's radical revision.)

At this point *it is necessary that you see a bullfight.* If I were to describe one it would not be the one that you would see, since the bullfighters and the bulls are all different, and if I were to explain the possible variations as I went along the chapter would be interminable. There are two sorts of guide books; those that are read before and those that are to be read after and the ones that are to be read after the fact are bound to be incomprehensible to a certain extent before; *if the fact is of enough importance in itself.* So with any book on mountain skiing, sexual intercourse, wing shooting, or any other thing which it is impossible to make come true on paper, or at least impossible to attempt to make more than one version of at a time on paper, *it being always an individual experience,* there comes a place in the guide book where you must say do not come back until you have skied, had sexual intercourse, shot quail or grouse, or been to the bullfight *so that you will know what we are talking about.* So from now on it is inferred that you have been to the bullfight. (63, emphasis mine)

Seeing fact truly is already a kind of *knowing*, after and only after which "it is of [any] use" for an author to "describe" it. Seeing-knowing experientially means seeing-knowing essentially[25] so that

---

[25] Heidegger uses words associated with seeing and with light to denote the character of Dasein as clearing ("*Aletheia-Offenheit-Lichtung, Licht, Leuchten,*" *Being and Time,* footnote H. 133); existential understanding takes the place that intuition or "pure beholding" held in metaphysics from Parmenides to Hegel as the ground of "seeing." (See "Moira.") Seeing and essential "knowing" are explicitly conjoined in *techne*: "To know [*Wissen*] means to have seen [*gesehen haben*], in the widest sense of seeing [*weiten Sinne von sehen*], which means to apprehend what is present, as such [*vernehmen des Anwesenden als eines solchen*]" ("The Origin" 59; see also "The Anaximander Fragment," *Early Greek Thinking,* Harper & Row, 1984, 36).

As for experience, Heidegger gives priority to being-there (*Dasein*). For example, in order to understand (evil) one must have a "preconcept [*Vorbegriff*] of it," which "can take hold [*zugreifen*] only when what is to be conceived has already been

once one sees-knows, "[one] will know what we are talking about"
however it may afterwards appear in whatever variation of experience possible; and every experience is different. This is the principle
that explains why "people will know the first time they go [to the
bullfights], if they go open-mindedly and only feel those things they
actually feel and not the things they think they should feel, whether
they will care for the bullfights or not" (10).[26] The restrictions about
feelings are essential to the definition of fact, the essence of fact, as
we have seen.[27] But the seeing-knowing essentially, which may occur
at the first encounter with the fact, is not the seeing-knowing which
does not just "occur," but develops with time and careful apprenticeship, learning. The author's first seeing-knowing experience with the
bullfight:

> I remembered, at the first bullfight I ever saw, before I
> could see it clearly, before I could even see what hap-
> pened, ... in the midst of this confused excitement hav-
> ing a great moment of emotion when the man went in

experienced [*das Zubegreifende zuvor erfahren ist*]" (*Schelling's Treatise* 106). See
especially *What Is A Thing?*, in which Kant is interpreted as bringing "experience"
into rational metaphysics (summary 238ff.). "In short, being is no longer determined
out of mere thought [*bloßen Denken*]" (240), but involves also "the letting-stand-
against (*Gegenstehenlassen*) of experience [*des Erfahrens*], and, therefore, of the
actions of the subject [*Handlungen des Subjekts*]" (241).

[26] It is also the principle that offers a non-psychological basis for Tom Stoppard's
observation that Hemingway's prose "[makes] the reader do the work," proving for
us that "prose in itself does not describe at all.... In fact, it is the associative power
of words rather than their 'meaning' that makes prose work on its ultimate level,"
"Reflections on Ernest Hemingway," *Ernest Hemingway: The Writer in Context*, ed.
James Nagel (Madison: U of Wisconsin, 1984) 22.

[27] Compare Heidegger's "mood" in the "there" in *Being and Time*. From "The
Origin" (*Poetry, Language, Thought*, Harper & Row, First Harper Colophon ed., 1975,
25): "Perhaps ... what we call feeling or mood [*Gefühl oder Stimmung*], here and
in similar instances, is more reasonable [*vernünftiger*]—that is, more intelligently
perceptive [*vernehmender*]—because more open [*offener*] to Being than all that
reason which, having meanwhile become *ratio*, was misinterpreted as being rational
[*mißdeutet wurde*]."

with the sword. But I could not see in my mind exactly
what happened and when, on the next bull, I watched
closely the emotion was gone and I saw it was a trick. I
saw fifty bulls killed after that before I had the emotion
again. But by then I could see how it was done and I
knew I had seen it done properly that first time. (234-5)

In the first experience the novice spectator could not see clearly
owing to obstructions and confusion; yet the "moment of emotion"
occurred because the killing was "done properly."

It is impossible to believe the emotional and spiritual
intensity and pure, classic beauty that can be produced
by a man, an animal and a piece of scarlet serge draped
over a stick.... But if you should ever see the real thing
you would know it. (207)

The real thing evokes an essential seeing, even if unclear and partial. At the next bullfight, watching closely, the author "sees" (without
emotion; the emotion does not come) that the killing is a trick. He
sees accurately. The killing *is* a trick. He watches fifty bulls more,
until he can "see in [his] mind exactly what happened," and then with
the next bull he experiences the emotion again; now he knows that
the very first killing had not been tricked. There is a seeing without
and a seeing with emotion. The "real thing" produces the latter. The
flash of emotion, which is not perception and not cognition, enables
and validates true "seeing." The essence in this essential seeing is the
essence of the thing, the "fact." It is not a platonic Real. This essence is
"actual," is what occurs in what-happens. It is not a God-guaranteed
essence; indeed, the author distances himself from the Christians at
the beginning and maintains a steady, often acerbic opposition thereafter. It is explicitly set against a romantic or an egotistic individual
identity (against Huxley, 190-92), though things are always individual and unique (against Eliot, 99-100). This seeing as the ground of

experience is not Kant's transcendental apperception, for its law of ordering, which means purifying and intensifying encounter, the rule that orders parts to wholes, names essence which is without content, and wholeness which is without definition, and produces neither perceptual representation nor conceptual knowledge. It is not Derrida's trace, for though meaningless it is not objectless; without content it is nevertheless not empty. It is more nearly the pre-Socratic *eidos* (Heidegger's interpretation, e.g., *Being and Time* 61) or the moment of the Heideggerian ontological difference, not only as the occulted non-origin but also as the groundless ground of beings.

Fact is distinguished from aspect, mere appearance.[28] The horses are usually gored, often in a visceral spectacle, and American or British or otherwise squeamish spectators have demanded that they wear a padding which restrains their entrails as they race about the ring. But this objection is not a true one since it is based on aspect and not fact. As objectionable as the appearance of the butchered horses is, the horses' condition is not alleviated by the padding, but only their appearance. The horses are not in pain since pain comes later, about a half hour after the wound; "there is no proportional relation in pain to the horrible aspect of the wound" (9). When with experience one comes to "appreciate values," then s/he will "prefer to see the horses with no protection worn so that all wounds may be seen and death given rather than suffering caused by something designed to allow the horses to suffer while their suffering is spared the spectator" (12).

Aspect is differentiated from fact in the Faulkner parody (179-82). What the newspaperman takes at first to be a cruel and perverse violation of one young man by another becomes in fact a happily accommodated homosexuality, though the henna "wow" at the end unsettles the denouement. The misfortune of "those unfortunate people" may be an "aspect" that belongs to the Old Lady or even to

---

[28] For "aspect" [*Ansehen*] in Heidegger see *An Introduction to Metaphysics* 102f.; for several aspects of "appearance" (*Erscheinung*) see *Being and Time* H. 29-31, for "semblance" [*Schein*] H. 222 and *Nietzsche*, Vol. I 213ff.

Faulkner rather than a "fact" of the people themselves. Though the author is a traditionalist in his impatience with mere appearance, his penchant for proposing unorthodox distinctions and categories and finding the truth to be occasionally or somehow false place him nearer to Heidegger's thought than to Plato's.

We intimated earlier that this book pretends to "fact," that is, presents the aspect of fact, while it really, essentially, aspires to art and poetics if not philosophy or ontology. Now we see that the *aspect* of fact is never what this work pretends to, but is precisely what it works to overturn, expose. The "fact" is what is under review here, review and revision. We are taught to "see" a difference in actual fact and aspect, mock-fact here, as the mock-naturalist and the mock-historians present it.

Toros Celebre, for example, "is a book, now out of print in Spain, … which chronicles, alphabetically by the names the breeders gave them, the manner of dying and feats of some three hundred and twenty-two pages of celebrated bulls" (110), with the occasional inclusion of a bull unremarkable in the long run but timely, that is, topical and of commercial appeal in the short. This timeliness—as belonging to the exigencies of the moment which passes away—of not only a few bulls but also of the book itself, now out of print, is the point of distinction in chapter one between the author's former journalistic motivations and his purer artistic purpose (2). The difference is in the end one of degree. This work continually points out its own timeliness, for example in remarks such as "Saleri may have retired by the time this is published" (201); in the addition at the end of photographs, which fasten on one moment of an event which is all motion; and of topical information, the "Reactions" and "Estimate" and "Dates." We note also that every transaction in the bullring from the unforgiven horse-traders' to the most artistic matador's is (like the journalist's) motivated in part by economic interests, usually a compromising factor.

But timeliness in this work, for which timeliness is an issue, becomes a distinction of aspect as compared to fact and distinguishes
facts in the ordinary sense from the author's revised fact—what actually happens: fact which is preserved or preservable by art. What
marks the latter is its "exceptional" character, in the case of bulls their
exceptional bravery, at its best the quality the Spanish call "nobility"
(113). This is no incidental "fact," but a special one since "the bravery
of the bull is the primal root of the whole Spanish bullfight," and the
whole Spanish bullfight is the fact being written about in *Death in
the Afternoon*. *Toros Celebre* goes to the root of the problem of the
bullfight then, and in a factual, i.e., objective, way, presenting three
hundred twenty-two pages of facts about the bravest bulls in their
bravery: their deeds and dying. Yet *Toros Celebre* reduces fact to
aspect. The alphabetical arrangement of the facts allows the reader
to choose at random Hechicero, the Wizard who sent at least seven
picadors to the hospital and killed seven horses (signifying exceptional bravery: "It is only by his conduct against the pic that the
bravery of a bull can be judged and appreciated," 113) or Vibora, the
Viper, who jumped out of the ring and gored a carpenter (an event
notable probably for its current notoriety). Facts about brave bulls
defying punishment in the ring are mixed indifferently with "facts"
about bulls out of control charging into the stands or off the streets
scattering random destruction.

This presentation of fact as general information robs the exceptional facts of their power to produce the real emotion. Two examples: "… the bull, pursuing the boy, climbed the stairs to the first
floor, where, according to the book, he caused great destruction. He
probably did." The remark "He probably did" speculates about what
actually happened as an aside, outside the writing. This writing is not
"producing" what-happened. "Destruction" umpty-umps the "actual."
The narrative itself obstructs the view. More important, this "destruction" in a list of destructions loses its ability to articulate destruction.
There is no "seeing" in this "factual" account, and there can be no
knowing response. In another case a bull "jumped the barrera and

got into the grandstand, and, driving through the spectators, *the book says*, produced *the imagined* disorder and damage" (111, emphasis mine). The same insensitivity to the actual marks the histories cited later to attest to the validity of claims that the bulls and the matadors and the bullfights were grander in the past (239-44).

Facts are what the author wants to write about, to make endure. In his vernacular "facts" are disclosed and validated in a direct seeing. But he writes, "I have seen two carpenters gored myself and have never written a line about it." Direct seeing alone did not make these events exceptional. We assume that they did not produce the emotion that actual facts produce. We recall the "fact" of the bullfight, at its best the noble bull, the matador of genius and artistry. But only rarely—twice in fifty bullfights for the author—does the spectacle give the emotion that facts produce. The difference in the author's experience was a difference in the killing itself (it had been done properly and artistically), which is a difference in completeness, wholeness, in purity and intensity. The bullring with its order, ritual, had provided a focus and a heightened emotional atmosphere for the spectacle and for the exceptional when it occurred. It was this focus that made it possible for the author to "study" violent death here as he could not in life outside the ring, in "timeliness." What "actually happens," fact, does not *appear* in the unexceptional. Facts as everyday happenings or as general information, are like words themselves which the author says "from loose using have lost their edge" (71). The differences that articulate what happens in fact and in writing get buried or suborned by the ordinary, the timely, the mercenary.[29]

Another dimension to the problem may be noted. The difference in aspect and fact is the difference in mere appearance and appearing, but it is not a moral or an absolute difference. The author describes

---

[29]Compare the priority—and the deficiency—of the everyday in Heidegger. Everyday Dasein as falling, thrown fugitive from authenticity provides the primary human understanding to and through which Being "calls" (*Being and Time* 225ff). And Being is no being; calling is voiceless (see *What Is Called Thinking?* 128ff.).

a kind of apprenticeship of seeing, which begins with aspect, sensitivity to the appearance of suffering in the horses, and graduates through seeing experiences to a more genuine knowing, letting suffering appear as it is. The difference in aspect and fact is a difference in intensity in what-happens and a difference in the seeing emotion; and difference is a difference of "enough" ("...writes truly enough"), a difference of degree. In the last chapter we find that *everything* that happens seems capable of appearing essentially and integrally and could endure in a work of art. The problem is, as here, the lack of "enough" book to address it all.

Seeing has an esthetic character. Learning to see and to know is a developing of taste. But though the author gives an explicit esthetic character to seeing, comparing the appreciation of the bullfight and a proper killing to the appreciation of fine wines, music, art, etc., "esthetic" is only one characteristic of this seeing among others. The bullfight is also compared to sports, to war, to sexual intercourse, to commercial enterprises. Practically speaking, every category for cultural life seems applicable; and "practically" is the key, not the practicality of the Galicians and the Catalonians, who take no "intelligent interest in death" (264-66), but the "practical" in the last sentence of the text, "There were a few practical things to be said," the practical in practice, action, the actual.

The naturalist parody in the introduction to "A Natural History of the Dead," both exploits and develops the aspect-fact relation. "That persevering traveller, Mungo Park," pious naturalist, "self-called Humanist" (139), upon one desperate occasion in Africa in a moment of hopelessness caught sight of a tiny, intricately formed flower and took heart, saying to himself that if God had troubled Himself to give attention in such a place to "a thing which appears of so small importance," and which bore no resemblance to Himself, he would certainly, etc. But Mr. Park is not seeing truly, the fact of the flower is ignored and exploited as an appurtenance of a self-portrait, and any principle he espouses is marked for review. Our mock-naturalist narrator launches a similarly naturalistic study of "the dead"—all "observation," all "seeing," all "facts" of the dead readily available under conditions of war. "In war the dead are usually the male of the human species although this does not hold true with animals, ..." (134). After many interesting "facts" about dead animals comes an account of a mission to recuperate the bodies of women killed in a munitions explosion.

> We drove to the scene of the disaster in trucks along poplar-shaded roads, bordered with ditches containing much minute animal life, ... I remember that after we had searched quite thoroughly for the complete dead we collected fragments. Many of these were detached from a heavy, barbed-wire fence which had surrounded the position of the factory and from the still existent portions of which we picked many of these detached bits which illustrated only too well the tremendous energy of high explosive. (135-36)

But the Natural Historian does not fail to appreciate the gifts of nature.

> ... the fact that it had been so immediate and that the dead were in consequence still as little unpleasant as possible to carry and deal with made it quite removed from the usual battlefield experience. The pleasant, though dusty, ride through the beautiful Lombard countryside also was a compensation for the unpleasantness of the duty .... (136)

What this "study" of the dead attempts to exclude is the fact of death and the emotion it entails. The failure to admit death, like the failure to admit the comic role of the horses, above, prevents the explanation of the dead, robs the "facts" about the dead of their trueness, prevents seeing-knowing. Each of the facts surrounding,

for example, the field of dead women, above, is denied its significance—the long hair of the women or "the occasional absence" of it,
their not unpleasant fresh flesh broken up "along no anatomical lines."
Later in another "factual" description of dead soldiers the "fact" of
swollen corpses, of emptied pockets and strewn paper announce and
renounce death. Our response here is a backlash of emotion against
the lack of emotion in the language, elicited here by the bitter parodic
tone of the narrative, and is not an emotional "seeing" of the dead
but an emotional seeing of the sophistry of the naturalist's language,
substituting mere appearance for fact. It is our author's language
that we respond to against the emptiness (the hollow place, above)
of the "history." In a page of natural history the denial and what it
denies would be more subtly suppressed, and the effect would be a
not-seeing.

Then this rejoinder:

> One wonders what that persevering traveller, Mungo
> Park, would have seen on a battlefield in hot weather to
> restore his confidence. There were always poppies in the
> wheat in the end of June and in July, and the mulberry
> trees were in full leaf and one could see the heat waves
> rise from the barrels of the guns where the sun struck
> them through the screens of leaves; the earth was turned
> a bright yellow at the edge of holes where mustard gas
> shells had been and the average broken house is finer
> to see than one that has never been shelled, but few
> travellers would take a good full breath of that early
> summer air and have any such thoughts as Mungo Park
> about those formed in His own image. (138)

This battlefield breathes death, a kind of gaping, asphyxiating
presence of absence. The one-eighth of the fact that appears declares
the rest to our seeing, knowing emotion. The difference in this passage (a sampling of *A Farewell to Arms*) and the naturalist parody

is the secret of the iceberg principle. Most of what is "known" is not "described"; the knowing constraint of explicit language, "truly" written, "magically" (13) sets forth, sets free, the thing-happening, produces the seeing emotion.

This principle explains in part the effect of the language throughout this work, beginning with the title. The text does not acknowledge the disruption that death is working against the simple order of its surface. The text which admits the disturbing "fact" of death, does not admit its effect, allows no conclusion, and so the reader's opposition, repugnance, the emotion that "sounds" it, is given no shape, no stabilizing form, no relief.[30] Death in the text unsettles the textuality, texture, apparent order, of the text. However pacific or remote the enumeration of simple "facts" over whatever number of pages of just information, this continual intrusion of death continually usurps the simplicity of the otherwise mundane. Death like the dangerous bull is near, gets waved up and waved by according to the arrogance and grace of the author.

Thus the aspect-fact difference discloses levels of textuality, from mere appearance, surface, to an actual functioning that disturbs even as it creates that surface. "A Natural History of the Dead," for example, functions to interrupt the seeming linearity of *Death in the Afternoon*, bringing into play certain oppositions to the thematic and stylistic aspects of the text. As we have noted, its style and its theme mock the style and theme of the preceding text, unsettling the reader's sense of ground, dispelling the illusion of reliable (transparent) language, so that afterwards the reader, chastened, changed, continues, but uncertainly.

This loss of stability or solidity is produced again in the thematic of the doctor-lieutenant opposition in the story. This story is Hemingway's *Billy Budd* and pits rule and order against bravery and moral

---

[30] The idea that language functions to relieve this kind of pressure is Kristeva's, though I do not wish to invoke her thematization of the subject, of originary drive, or of the essential function of language.

sensitivity, with the less than satisfying triumph of law. The doctor's position and the lieutenant's cannot be separated along moral or essential lines. On the doctor's side are the Hemingway virtues of practicality, fact over appearance, and the utility of rule; on the lieutenant's side bravery, a seeing for which the distinction between the dead and the living has not been lost, even in wartime, and a disregard for rule that comes from familiarity with administrators (188), for example doctors who ignore suffering on traditional grounds (220). We may say that the doctor plays the lieutenant as the matador the brave bull, using his own strength against him; but tripping and kicking are not arts but tricks, and the doctor violates his own code in spilling the iodine and wounding the soldier. The nature of contest is to bring to light the essential qualities of the contestants. Here as in the bullring, the backdrop against which the contest appears is the fact of death. What death brings to the afternoon, the still-living man brings to the dead-house anomaly, absolute difference, with in this case the edges worn with overuse under conditions of war. For the doctor the difference is nada, but since in this work it is the very difference upon which everything that happens depends for its appearing, the doctor's nada (unlike the waiter's in "A Clean, Well-Lighted Place") is loss of precision, which means loss of seeing. Still it is impossible to accept or to reject either the doctor's position or the lieutenant's. Brenner gives the best postmodern response: "Having presented [a] half-dozen perspectives, Hemingway dares us to choose only one as the correct one" (75). The opponents contesting each other are the fact appearing in its happening here, without resolution or conclusion.

The instability of language is recapitulated in the author's express treatment of words per se. Words are not facts and they have no essence. The same word carries different meanings for different people according to their different experience and predisposition. To Jean Cocteau the word "decadence" means his friend and protege Radiguet's unfortunate inclination toward "les femmes." "So you see, madame, we must be careful chucking the term decadence about since it cannot mean the same to all who read it" (71). Words do not mean; they accommodate meaning. "[Love] is a word that fills with meaning as a bladder with air and the meaning goes out of it as quickly" (122).

Words are separate from inherent concepts (the notion of the arbitrariness of the sign) and may lose their power to recall them with precision. "Madame, all our words from loose using have lost their edge but your inherent concepts are most sound" (71). Precision would mean not correct usage ("*Old lady*: I must learn to use these terms correctly," when the author explains the meaning of "horseshit," 95) and not horseshit, i.e., "unsoundness in an abstract conversation or, indeed, any overmetaphysical tendency in speech." A word to be precise would convey or precipitate a true seeing:

> *Old lady*: You mean?
> Not exactly, but something of the sort.
> *Old lady*: You mean he——?
> Precisely.... (71)

Words or not-words, according to the iceberg principle, when their edges are sharp, call (and recall) to mind exactly—truly, purely— what happens; evoke, re-evoke, the true emotion. The function of words, as of the work of art, is to provoke the appearing of something, a seeing. Words made the author's small son "see it" when he closed his eyes, above, so that the author "[wished] for the thousandth time in [his] life that [he] could wipe out words that [he'd] said" (228). But words can function to evoke seeing only if one has already seen the thing that the words recall.

> I will not describe the different ways of using the cape, [etc.] ... because a description in words cannot enable you to identify them before you have seen them as a photograph can. (176)

(The passage is ironic; it describes and imitates the butterfly quite, directing the reader to the photograph at the end which "shows clearly what it is"; but it is all movement, manner, pacing, danger, of which the photograph freezes one instant.)

Words are temporal. They call things from past or present experience into appearance. This moment (if we invoke temporality) of "seeing" is the point of ontic-ontological difference in Heidegger (*différance* in Derrida). To speak of delay or asynchronism would be to force the moment into the conception of time as a sequence of now's. In Heidegger these points of difference in time are overpassed, set aside as secondary representation; in primordial temporality there are no such points.

We examine temporality in Hemingway's description of the work of language (art). Things that happen produce a seeing emotion (2). The seeing responds to the happening which comes first—not first in time but first in command. The emotion which is being produced is a seeing, but in life the seeing is haphazard, contingent, timely. In the bullring, in art, the matador-artist directly faces and addresses the thing (the matador brings death itself into the ring, the author brings the entire bullfight into his work), not in order to command or vanquish it but in order to bring it to appearance, set it forth. Words and works of art follow upon or respond to things that happen and preserve their happening. Or, to correct the sequence, the emotion that responds to things that actually happen is the unarticulated seeing that can be invoked by words, language, art, in a purifying, formalizing seeing. Words are not things that happen, but they hold and convey such things. Time is the possibility that they may and the manner of movement by which they do so.[31]

As we are beginning to see, in *Death in the Afternoon* no word or "statement" rests in itself, for countering it, silent or explicit, often

---

[31] I have cited Heidegger's definitions of words throughout this book. Hemingway, like each of the other Americans, brings his own precision to his own definition, but the break with representational language and the word's essential openness and active, actual relation to "life" (not to presence, for "life" is permeated by uncanniness, mystery, death) are general characteristics he and the others share with Heidegger.

juxtaposed to it, is always another "statement" to unsettle it. The principle:

> The sun is very important. The theory, practice and spectacle of bullfighting have all been built on the assumption of the presence of the sun and when it does not shine over a third of the bullfight is missing. The Spanish say, "El sol es el mejor torero." The sun is the best bullfighter, and without the sun the best bullfighter is not there. He is like a man without a shadow. (15)

Where is the best bullfighter? There is a chain of bullfighters: the sun, the bullfighter, the shadow. Remove the sun and there is no shadow; that leaves the bullfighter. But "without the sun the best bullfighter is not there." Being there means projecting a shadow; a shadow is a sign of substantial existence, a material (immaterial) validation. Where is the actual, the "real," the "true," in the chain? The man (the bullfighter) standing between the sun (the best bullfighter) and his own shadow appears in this chain to be himself a reflection of the sun, a platonic image. No, this sun, though generally reliable in Spain during the bullfighting season, is essentially unreliable and unpredictable, belongs to nature in Hemingway and is related, I think, to "luck," that constant unconstant variable in every Hemingway equation.

Without the sun "the best bullfighter" is insubstantial, not actual (fact-ual), is only these words then. The sun—something given, not by the bullfighter or the bull or even by the spectacle, nor by history or all of Spain, but just given or not given—provides the possibility for the actuality, the being there, of the best bullfighter (the sign of which appears in the projecting of a shadow). The sun casts the light, the shining, against or in the face of which the bullfighter appears and projects a shadow. The uncertain sun is the possibility, and the insubstantial shadow is the security in a practical sense for the best bullfighter's being there, a fairly precarious foothold. This does not say that there can be no bullfighter without the sun, but that there can be no *best* (exceptional, above) bullfighter. And no best bullfight either, since more than a third of the theory, practice and spectacle of the bullfight depends upon the undependable sun.[32]

This image invites another: a portrait of the artist—the author, with luck and writing "purely enough" (2).

> People in a novel, not skillfully constructed *characters*, must be projected from the writer's assimilated experience, from his knowledge, from his head, from his heart and from all there is of him. If he ever has luck as well as seriousness and gets them out entire they will have more than one dimension and they will last a long time. (191)

If the author's "project" is his shadow as well as his sword, then he projects not only the appearing of what happens but also its validating sign. As we have seen, language or art is not itself a fact; yet it makes fact (things that really happen) appear. Much has been written about the Hemingway style and its uncanny effects. Critics tend to agree that the effect of his language is poetic, lyric—personal, concrete, immediate—and take it to be as intellectually limited as it is extraordinarily affective. I cannot explain the phenomenon of the shadow, but I am tempted in the direction of the shadows in Malcolm Cowley's 1945 essay. Commenting on a passage from "Now I Lay Me":

> Although the events in the foreground are described with superb accuracy and for their own sake, we now perceive what we probably missed at a first reading: that there are shadows in the background and that part of the story takes place in an inner world. (42)

---

[32] Heidegger discusses Plato's image of the sun in *The Republic*, where as the "Good [*Gute*]" it provides to seeing/knowing and to being seen/being known not only their medium but also the conditions of their possibility, including knowers and beings (*Nietzsche*, Vol. IV 167ff.).

Later Cowley quotes the passage from *Green Hills of Africa* in which "a fourth and fifth dimension" are declared for writing if the author is "serious enough and has luck."

> It is more important than anything else he can do. The chances are, of course, that he will fail. But there is a chance that he succeeds.
> It is much more difficult than poetry. It is a prose that has never been written. But it can be written, without tricks and without cheating. With nothing that will go bad afterwards. (47)

Cowley muses,

> ... without understanding his choice of words, I do know that Hemingway's prose at its best gives a sense of depth and of moving forward on different levels that is lacking in even the best of his imitators, as it is in almost all the other novelists of our time.... (47)

And later, concluding:

> Most of us are ... primitive in a sense, for all the machinery that surrounds our lives... ; and Hemingway reminds us unconsciously of the hidden worlds in which we live. (50)

The validating shadow appears in this light to be the emotion of the spectator, that one chance in fifty occurrence, when a serious spectator catches the figure of what happens. But in this work everything is working twice, once in "life" and again in art which brings life into view and preserves it. In the second sense, art (language) is the extraordinary re-producing of the extraordinary event, the insubstantial ground of substantial reality. As Leon Edel, denouncing Hemingway's lack of style, of seriousness, of maturity, of substance, has stated, ironically for my purpose: "He has conjured up an *effect* of Style by a process of evasion, very much as he sets up an aura of emotion—by walking directly away from emotion!" (19).

Nota: The event figured above, sun-bullfighter-shadow, is motivated not by a principle of accommodation but by a principle of repulsion, the man blocking the sun, the shadow emptying the man's substantiality in signifying it. "Statement" is the sign (shadow) of confrontation, often denial, in *Death in the Afternoon*. Thus, as we have seen, this narrative, which appears in the beginning to be a transparent window onto the thoughts and motivations of the author or an accurate representation or replica of the facts that make up a factual reality, the bullfight, soon runs into another kind of narrative in which a new tone, differing, doubtful or negative, draws what had before seemed real into quotation marks. The two (and more) kinds of narrative have been left, placed, in antagonistic juxtaposition. Some of the counter-narrative appears as digression; the author runs off into matters or interests of his own, literary or aesthetic or artistic analogies or speculations, and then draws himself back to the subject, perhaps with apologies (11, "This seems to have gotten away from bullfighting, …"). Since Hemingway readers are more interested in these matters themselves than in the "stupid brutal business" (2) of the bullfight, these interpolations are likely to be taken for the central subject and the bullfight for artifice, a vehicle, perhaps a symbol, and a decoration. The "difference" between the bullfight narrative and the esthetics is superficial. Indeed, this is at one level the interpretation I am making here, but as a preliminary outline against and beyond which (differing) Hemingway's attempt and achievement come into view. Another fundamental issue of difference comes to light too in this primary analogy. The bullfight by the nature of the opposites that it binds together, brutality and beauty, death and esthetics, is a crude and embarrassing art piece. Confrontation and denial inhere in the subject matter. Disparity and disunity, and something more, a kind of gross or indecent affront to the culture's moral and esthetic sensibilities, characterize the project from the outset.

The work we are reading is a study of the nature of art, the artist, and the work of art. It is a "study" as a painting or an etude may be. In the image above, art (language) was the shadow of the bullfighter, the matador addressing the bull; here at two levels we see the figure: first, the text is the shadow of Hemingway addressing a subject, which happens to be, second, an "author" addressing a subject, in both cases the figure of the matador's approach to the bull. Addressing, like seeing, like slaying, indicates opposition, difference. Language and art in Hemingway, not figured but enacted in the tragedy of the bullfight, are the way an author addresses a subject, by all means—mimesis, parody, irony, understatement, overstatement, omission, contradiction, emotional language, unemotional language, literal language, figurative language—to evoke the true emotion. Success, contingent on purity of writing and luck, is all in the effect. In the flash of that emotion appears the figure of what-happens.

The principal thing for Hemingway in his work as a whole, in this work in particular, as in his life, is the underlying fact of death. "All stories, if continued far enough, end in death" (122); death, "the most fundamental" thing. Perhaps the central Hemingway problem is the antagonism between life and art. The bullfight is art in life and life (death) in art. The matador manifests the genius and strengths and virtues that Hemingway honors in characters ("living people," as he claims here) throughout his canon. Art is not a replication of something, but an essential direct grappling with it. In such an event it is impossible to disentangle life and art or even to give precedence to either.[33] Life involves art; life lived artistically is lived most truly,

---

[33]Living is "moving in the picture," as this draft passage struck from "Big Two-Hearted River" presents it:

Nick, seeing how Cezanne would do the stretch of country, stood up. The water was *cold and actual*. He waded across the stream, *moving in the picture*. (Item 274 of Hemingway Collection, p. 96, quoted by Oldsey 47, emphasis his)

And art is, of course, the "cold and actual" in the picture.

intensely. Art involves life, works its work on life itself, right up to the point of death. And as this work shows and gathers into one image, it is at this point, death in the afternoon, that seeing happens. At the climax of the bullfight, against the shock where the blade disappears, appears the figure of man and bull (and spectator) in their several oppositions. Death against the afternoon. Against the opposing nada[34] rises a country, a people, an afternoon—in thousands of particulars the articulation of what-happens.[35]

The shock the sword sends and its disclosure are refigured powerfully, as the frequent allusions of critics attest, in the anecdote about the cowardly matador who made "a simple technical error." The passage also displays the function of language to make things re-appear, endure. The author watched a novillada (a non-professional bullfight) in which the matador Hernandorena, nervous, already ridiculous with his jittery feet, in order to force himself to stay in one place to meet the bull dropped to his knees, a position that would entail the use of a certain technique which Hernandorena had not mastered. When the bull charged, the man did not use the muleta properly to direct it past his body, and the horns caught and threw him. He stood up, looked about for his sword and cloth, and

> I saw the heavy, soiled gray silk of his rented trousers
> open cleanly and deeply to show the thigh bone from the
> hip almost to the knee. He saw it too and looked very
> surprised and put his hand on it while people jumped

---

[34]Steven K. Hoffman gives a Kierkegaard-Heidegger-Buber reading of the nada in Hemingway's short fiction which is appropriate and strong in my view except in its temptation to conclude, to conceptualize, an "existentialist creed" with more reassurance than Hemingway does, for whom the wound always stands agape.

[35]"Projective saying [*entwerfende Sagen*] is poetry .... Actual language at any given moment [*Die jeweilige Sprache*] is the happening of this saying [*Geschehnis jenes Sagens*], in which a people's world historically arises [*aufgeht*] for it and the earth is preserved [*aufbewahrt wird*] as that which remains closed" ("The Origin" 74).

over the barrier and ran toward him to carry him to the
infirmary....

At the bullring the spectators laughed at his nervousness and
in the evening in the cafe no one expressed sympathy after the gor-
ing. But for the author the subject was fundamental, the problem
"depiction":

> ... waking in the night I tried to remember what it was
> that seemed just out of my remembering and that was
> the thing that I had really seen and, finally, remember-
> ing all around it, I got it. When he stood up, his face
> white and dirty and the silk of his breeches opened from
> waist to knee, it was the dirtiness of the rented breeches,
> the dirtiness of his slit underwear and the clean, clean,
> unbearably clean whiteness of the thigh bone that I had
> seen, and it was that which was important. (20)

The prose is invisible. It leads up to and then away from the figure.
But the figure: rising up out of and against the words themselves, the
clean white bone is the shock from which the words fall away, and it
is that which is important.

Brenner compares *Death in the Afternoon* to Walton's *Compleat
Angler*. I offer it, as Cowley (Brasch 223ff.) offered *The Old Man and
the Sea* and with similar reservations, as Hemingway's *Moby Dick*:
in its (mock-) epic intention, in its encyclopedic collection of information; its habit of abrupt departures from and into forms, literary
play; above all, in its theme, the white white bone. The matador's
approach to his subject is cooler than the captain's, emotional but not
mad, deliberate but not scheming, emptied of malice as it is emptied
of meaning. The dreadful intent remains, no longer blasphemous
or perverse except among the ignorant or the insincere, but in its
skeletal and classic purity as absolute anomaly: death in the afternoon. Without origin or end, there appears in the frameless interim

the figure of the project of the artist. And on a lucky day, against the
shining sun, what happens casts a measurable shadow.

Appendix D: Heideggerian Insights

> Projective saying [*Das entwerfende Sagen*] is saying which,
> in preparing the sayable [*in der Bereitung des Sagbaren*],
> simultaneously brings the unsayable as such into a world
> [*das Unsagbare als ein solches zur Welt bringt*]. (Martin
> Heidegger, "The Origin of the Work of Art" 74)

Death in the Afternoon is Hemingway's "The Origin of the Work
of Art." That is, like Heidegger's essay, this work tracks the artwork to
its source, examines the constituents of the work as well as its work (its
working) and the work of spectators/readers/critics to make and keep
the work(ing) possible. Hemingway's author's determination from
the outset to "see" exactly what happens in the work of art, i.e., in the
climactic moment of the bullfight, a resolution which draws him in
concentrated attention to witness the event again and again, yields a
seeing that is more than perception and different from objectification
or analysis. Similarly Heidegger approached the artwork "directly"
to receive the disclosure of "the happening of truth [*das Geschehnis
der Wahrheit*]" in "The Origin of the Work of Art" (70, e.g.).

In the Hemingway work, what seeing sees is the actual fact of
what happens. Words such as "fact" and "real" or "actual" are honed
to a new edge, and the disclosures they make are often analogous
to the postmetaphysical "ideas" of Heidegger (*eidos* as appearing).
For words are working for Hemingway no more simply or "literally"
than they have worked for the other authors in this book, no more
simply or literally than they worked for Heidegger. In *Death in the
Afternoon* the *word* does not merely "give" (Heidegger's generous
word) an object or a meaning or answer; it more often withholds,
distorts, blocks. Hemingway's author "tacks," shall I say, his way to a

definite, extraordinary "meaning" among and against words (genres are words too, voices are), using them against themselves and each other, to transgress, overpass, contradict their explicit or ordinary significations; he maneuvers not randomly or haphazardly but precisely (see above) and forcefully. "What calls for" all this language, i.e., the uncanny, calls for the canniest language (yet without tricks). Words work obliquely, contrarily, privatively—to, in the end, "give." Fundamental here, as in Heidegger's thought, are silence and absence and the unsaid, as prior, primary language. (See Heidegger's examination of discourse in *Being and Time*, Section 34; see the presence of absence in "The Anaximander Fragment," 35f., the naming of the unspoken, 38.)

In what I call his esthetics, above, Hemingway privileges art as traditional esthetics does, but the privilege is reassigned. Art (writing, here) is exceptional language, superior to, say, reportage, by a difference not of kind but of degree, a measure of "enough": enough "purity" of "statement" (these words accrue special definition in the study). Heidegger too privileges art, privileges poetry among the arts. However, the privilege extends throughout what he calls "language," for, "Language itself is poetry in the essential sense [*Die Sprache selbst ist Dichtung im wesentlichen Sinne*]," he writes ("The Origin" 74). But "language itself" is not considered as "an expression and an activity of man [*Ausdruck und Tätigkeit des Menschen*]" ("Language" 208), and the *speaking* of language is not a human appropriation of language but the appropriation of the human *by* language. Still Heidegger and Hemingway agree that poetry and ordinary language are essentially the same, with a difference of "enough": "Poetry proper [*Eigentliche Dichtung*] is never merely a higher mode (*melos*) of everyday language [*Alltagssprache*]. It is rather the reverse: everyday language is a forgotten and therefore used-up poem [*ein vergessenes und darum vernutztes Gedicht*], from which there hardly resounds a call any longer [*kaum noch ein Rufen erklingt*]" (208).[36] I should add that for

---

[36] The problem is not only in forgetting but in using language, as the "most dangerous of possessions [*der Güter Gefährlichstes*]" (Heidegger quotes Hölderlin, "Hölderlin and the Essence" 273ff.), dangerous according to Heidegger because while it

Heidegger (as well as Hemingway) the difference between poetry and everyday language is not the difference between poetry and prose: "The opposite of what is purely spoken [*rein Gesprochenen*], the opposite of the poem, is not prose. Pure prose is never 'prosaic' [*Reine Prosa ist nie 'prosaisch'*]. It is as poetic and hence as rare [*selten*] as poetry" (208).

The "call" of language (the "of" working twice), and especially of the work of art, "gives" being in its Being. That "giving" is "depicted" (Hemingway's word) in *Death in the Afternoon* with particular subtlety and power: everything coming together in climactic emotion—matador, bull, spectacle, spectators. The thrust of the matador's sword into the bull carrying the eye of the spectator along the blade into: death. The emotion. The appearing of the "figure": all the participants manifest in the unity of their opposition—*phusis*, *eidos*: being and seeing happening. And the double exposure: the artist projecting the subject of art via art, and via that project another violent defiance of Nothing; there appearing in the bright conjunction of these oppositions the opponents in their differences: artist, worthy subject, audience, and artwork(ing), to "give": the emotion, the figure—the appearing (not presence but presencing) of an "actual" thing "really" happening (Hemingway 2).

Note the participation of the audience. For Hemingway as for Heidegger the audience or reader or critic shares responsibility for the work(ing) of art. Hemingway's author teaches and chides, insults and pleads with spectators and readers to move them to expect, demand, appreciate, and reward great art. Heidegger goes farther: he attributes as much createdness to the preservation of art as to the creation of it.

---

grants to entities the possibility of existence, it grants also the danger of the loss of existence. That is, language can express both "what is purest and what is most concealed [*das Reinste und das Verborgenste*], and likewise what is complex and ordinary [*das Verworrene und Gemeine*]," but it does not announce itself as one or the other, one often appears as the other (and in fact it is necessary that language become ordinary, lose some of its efficacy, in order that it work as human language). Thus language in its capability of "saying" both "the pure and the ordinary" endangers what it enables, i.e., existence, and itself as well (275).

Farther yet, in Heidegger "createdness [*Geschaffensein*]" inheres in art itself, and creators and preservers belong to this createdness (not the reverse). Hemingway articulates no such "art," but in his esthetics the more-than-human "emotion" which pervades and emanates from all the participants seems to be the ground of the happening of art as well as the stuff of its happening and the notice of its validation; and this "emotion" ("ecstasy" 206-07) corresponds with Heidegger's "art" at least insofar as it is the origin of the work of art as what "lets ... the creator and the preserver, originate, each in his own nature [*läßt ... Schaffende und Bewahrende, in seinem Wesen entspringen*]" ("The Origin" 71). Heidegger's "letting originate" has cut itself off from any first cause or maker and depends upon a nonpresent (and nonabsent) "it gives," whereas Hemingway's "emotion" is a word reappropriated without being uprooted from its traditional meaning. That is, in a systematic but unorthodox way Hemingway describes something we have no word for; it includes or involves what we have called "emotion," but it transgresses the limits of the word's ordinary meaning. Is the word losing its sharp edges, according to Hemingway's explicit critique of language? Or is it expanding or bursting or evolving? In any case what the word makes us see is something like Heidegger's "art" even though Heidegger does not use the word "emotion" (or other terminology for what we take for human characteristics, such as "intellect" or "mind") to discuss it. If we wamt to surmise how the ordinary notion of emotion is involved in Heidegger's "art" [*Kunst*] we might construct a schematic of Dasein's structures, including especially mood (*Befindlichkeit, die Stimmung, das Bestimmtsein*), or we might make a sketch of the *there* [*des Da*]" as the Open [*das Offene*] where beings rise into appearance), and devise close comparative readings of, e.g., *Being and Time, An Introduction*, and "The Origin" for the happening of truth in language or in the work of art. The exercise would be reductive, however; it would lose the ground Heidegger gained when he abandoned rational analytic terminology, and it would interrupt my purpose here.

To continue the general comparison, then: in the poetics of both Heidegger and Hemingway the work of creating is always unique and the work of preserving is equally essential to the work(ing) of art. (Compare Hemingway 99-100, 162-64, e.g., with Heidegger's "The Origin" 66ff.) "It is only for such preserving that the work yields itself in its createdness as actual, i.e., now: present in the manner of a work [*gibt sich das Werk in seinem Geschaffensein als das wirkliche, d.h. jetzt: werkhaft anwesende*]" ("The Origin" 66).

The reader of *Death in the Afternoon* does not read with impunity. Certain annoyances frustrate the reading, irritants such as erratic style or subject matter not yet brought to rest, a tendency to digression, repetition, contradiction, etc. The discomfiture points toward what is disturbing in the work: its very subject matter—the fact of violent death—and its continuous reiteration. There are two Heideggerian resonances.

First, the "fact" of death. This "fact," Hemingway's author tells us, is "the most fundamental" subject for a writer, and it is its ultimacy, its outreaching itself, that brings about the finest "seeing." Death or oblivion, in contrast or in reaction to which one may see what-happens—and most purely in a work of art—is fundamental too in the thinking of Heidegger. For example, Dasein's Being-towards-death [*Sein zum Tode*] provides the possibility that Dasein may "see" its own individuated, authentic potentiality-for-Being-a-whole (*Being and Time* H. 260-67).[37] Or, just as primordially, Dasein's Being-in-the-world is discussed as a "falling" fleeing in the face of the "nothing

---

[37] "The 'nothing' [*Das Nichts*] with which anxiety brings us face to face, unveils the nullity [*die Nichtigkeit*] by which Dasein, in its very basis [*seinem Grunde*], is defined; and this basis itself is as thrownness into death [*Geworfenheit in den Tod*]" (*Being and Time* H. 308). Being-towards-death is "the null basis of its own nullity [*der nichtige Grund seiner Nichtigkeit*]." "The nullity by which Dasein's Being is dominated primordially through and through [*ursprünglich durchherrschende Nichtigkeit*], is revealed to Dasein itself in authentic Being-towards-death [*eigentlichen Sein zum Tode*]" (H. 306).

[*Nichts*]" and "nowhere [*nirgends*]" of the world, the Being "not-at-home [*un-zuhause*]," (*Being and Time* H. 186-89, "An Introduction" 158). It is against nothingness as horizon that beings arise into Being: appearing, presencing (see the discussion of *phusis*, *eidos*, and *aletheia* throughout the Heideggerian canon). In *An Introduction* Heidegger characterizes apprehension (*noein*) as "a de-cision [*Ent-scheidung*] ...*for* being *against* nothing and thus a struggle *with* appearance" (167-68). Truth itself is *aletheia*, "Being-uncovering [*Entdeckendsein*]" (*Being and Time* Section 44 and every work thereafter), a "wresting" of being from nonbeing (*An Introduction*; see final statement 201ff.). And the work of art is one "way in which truth occurs [*Wahrheit west*]" ("The Origin" 61-2). "The working of the work [*Die Wirkung des Werkes*] ... lies in a change, happening [*geschehenden Wandel*] from out of the work, of the unconcealedness of what is [*Unverborgenheit des Seienden*], and this means: of Being [*des Seins*]" (72).

The second Heideggerian resonance with what is disturbing in the Hemingway text is the disturbance itself; that is, with the very first words of the title, *Death in the Afternoon* opens up the conflict between not-being and being (death and the afternoon), or it brings the conflict into view and holds it there without resolution. As I note above, there are innumerable deaths in the afternoon throughout the work. At one point my reading deadends when I find I cannot or will not proceed (p. 148), leaving the problem at hand as the work leaves it: unresolved. I—readers, the "spectators" in this case—am moved (disturbed) to "see" essentially—that is, to see what-happens *in its happening*. In "The Origin" Heidegger describes the work(ing) of art as "an instigating [*Anstiftung*] of ... striving [*Streit*]" ("Origin" 49) between not-being and being (earth and world), a strife that remains a strife. One telling passage shows how the work of art opens the strife and maintains it: "In the tragedy ["the linguistic work"] nothing is staged or displayed theatrically [*wird nichts auf- und vorgeführt*], but the battle of the new gods against the old is being fought. The linguistic work [*das Sprachwerk*], originating in the speech of the people [*im Sagen des Volkes aufsteht*], does not refer [*redet*] to this battle; it transforms the people's saying so that now every living word [*wesentlich Wort*] fights the battle and puts up for decision [*zur Entscheidung stellt*] what is holy and what unholy, what great and what small, what brave and what cowardly, what lofty and what flighty, what master and what slave" (43).

Hemingway's primary affinity with Heidegger is in what is primary in the work of both: the emphasis on the necessity of death as the possibility or the actuality of seeing and of "being," or, what amounts to the same for both, of seeing being (the ontological difference). Death is not cause for morbidity in Heidegger, though it is the basis of existential anxiety. "As the outermost possibility [*äußerste Möglichkeit*] of mortal *Dasein*, death is not the end of the possible [*Ende des Möglichen*] but the highest keeping (the gathering sheltering) of the mystery of calling disclosure [*das höchste Ge-birg (das versammelnde Bergen) des Geheimnisses der rufenden Entbergung*]" ("Moira" 101). In Hemingway too it is the occasion for everything that counts: seeing without flinching, or courage; love; glamour.

> All violence [*Gewalt-tätigkeit*] shatters against *one* thing. That is death. It is an end beyond all consummation, a limit beyond all limits [*Er über-endet alle Vollendung, er über-grenzt alle Grenzen*]....It is not only when he comes to die, but always and essentially [*ständig und wesenhaft*] that man is without issue [*ohne Ausweg*] in the face of death. Insofar as man *is*, he stands in the issuelessness of death. Thus his being-there is the happening of strangeness [*die geschehende Un-heimlichkeit selbst*]. (*An Introduction to Metaphysics* 158)

Who Gets *Lost in the Funhouse*

The following essay is a Heideggerian reading of John Barth's *Lost in the Funhouse*. In Appendix E, I point out explicitly some of Heidegger's insights that I am finding among Barth's insights here.

Any story, any section of story, will do. This one:

> There's no point in going farther; this isn't getting any-body anywhere; they haven't even come to the funhouse yet. Ambrose is off the track, in some new or old part of the place that's not supposed to be used; he strayed into it by some one-in-a-million chance, like the time the roller-coaster car left the tracks in the nineteen-teens against all the laws of physics and sailed over the board-walk in the dark. And they can't locate him because they don't know where to look. Even the designer and opera-tor have forgotten this other part, that winds around on itself like a whelk shell. That winds around the right part like the snakes on Mercury's caduceus…. (John Barth, *Lost in the Funhouse*, 83)

Now the trick is to get hold of it, hold on. Try it. Identify the character(s), the voice(s), the plot(s), theme(s)—identify fact, fiction, implications, significance if any, truth if. The story moves under your hand, changes. It's Proteus you're onto.

Ambrose in the funhouse? No, he's lying on the sand with that physically whelming presence he thinks is Magda, pretending to watch that impostor Peter show off his diving, muscles—form. The timing's wrong. The funhouse is later. The narrator, then, anticipating his story? Oh yes, and mirroring it, both of them wandering roundly off the track. The narrator's plan and his character's plot wandering off into the wrong time, out of place, astray. The characters' characters (author's, narrator's, characters') blur into each other; there's no focus; space is as imploded as time. The voice (author's, narrator's, characters') attenuates to one multidistinguishable whine. Point of view? Who's to see?

> When I understood that Proteus somewhere on the beach became Menelaus holding the Old Man of the Sea, Menelaus ceased. Then I understood further how Proteus thus also was as such no more, being as possibly Menelaus's attempt to hold him, the tale of that vain attempt, the voice that tells it. (167)

Climactic confrontation. Turning point. Turning, turning, turning point. The rest is a story of diminishing returns.

> Ajax is dead, Agamemnon, all my friends, but I can't die, worse luck; Menelaus's carcass is long wormed, yet his voice yarns on through everything, to itself. Not my voice, I am this voice, no more, the rest has changed, rechanged, gone. The voice too, even that changes, becomes hoarser, loses its magnetism, grows scratchy, incoherent, blank. (167)

The last word? Hold-on.

One more interpretation.

In my discussion of John Barth's *Lost in the Funhouse*[1] I shall treat his "series" of stories as a novel: because a unity, a wholeness, is intended, according to the "Author's Note," because a single work is achieved, as I hope to demonstrate, and because, as Barth remarked in a "conversation" referring to "book-length fiction" written today, "it's got to be called something or other."[2] Besides, the form this novel takes (selected stories) is not new to the genre. The moderns broke up whatever unity the form had previously assumed: Anderson (*Winesburg, Ohio*), Williams (*In the American Grain*), and Faulkner (*Go Down, Moses*), for example, used collected stories in a technique of fracture, collage, collation, conflation. I shall call Barth's work a novel, but not to place it in the tradition of the moderns. If its form was predicted, legitimized, in the first half of the century, its themes and its attitudes toward them were not. Postmoderns lost something of the moderns' sense of shame, of shock, of loss, grief. The moderns' reactionary reaction to revolutions and world wars, to radical disorientation, first devolved to a milder, less passionate, because existentialist or nihilistic, dis-ease. The emphasis turned from events themselves to interpretations of them. We seemed to have passed another crisis. The fever abated a bit, spirit revived. This turning point is the "ground-situation" for *Lost in the Funhouse*. The novel discloses the impasse to which Western thought has brought itself, predicts the necessity of a turning if there is to be a going on, and even points out some possible directions. I would classify the work as a comic tragedy. It evokes an effect very much like that of Wallace Stevens' "The Comedian as the Letter C," in which a quotidian Real eventually simply preempts all philosophical speculation about

---

[1] *Lost in the Funhouse: Fiction for Print, Tape, Live Voice* (New York: Doubleday, 1968). An early version of this essay was published in *Arizona Quarterly* 44: 4 (Winter 1989): 80-97.
Republished in *Contemporary Literary Criticism* (CLC), ed. Chris Giroux, 89 (Winter 1989).

[2] *A Conversation with John Barth*, ed. Frank Gado, *The Idol*, special issue, ed. Robert A. Hahn and Jean Howard, 49: 2 (Fall 1972): 34.

the nature of reality. Barth's novel brings us to the end of an era with the logical demise of a metaphysical paradigm.

Critics have addressed the issues I shall address, for example the problems of a human identity crisis and of the exhaustion of literature, of the author, of authority and motivation, of culture and art; they have noted the technique and thematic of artifice and ultimacy turned against themselves. My study is new only in the weight and concentration I give to a single fundamental Heideggerian insight and to its illumination of each story and of the work as a whole. My purpose is to trace the Cartesian-Kantian subject-object paradigm[3] through the novel, exploring Barth's exploration of the implications and ramifications of that entrenched metaphysics.

The novel has at least three fundamental themes, which develop all at once all the time. They are the "progress" of literature, of language, and of a metaphysical assumption. The "progress" of each and

---

[3] For Heidegger's discussion of Descartes's demonstration and Kant's appropriation of subjectivity, see passages in *Being and Time* such as H. 23-5, 45f., 94-101, 116, 179, 319-21. For indications of his impatience with the notion of the "subjective [*subjektiv*]" see e.g. H. 109, 119, 229, 278, 361. The problem is that the interpretation of the Being of the "subject" derives from the interpretation of the Being of the thing (overlooking the already presupposed structures of the world and Dasein), rendering a subject-object confrontation rather than a relation of Being-in-the-world.

> In saying "I", I have in view the entity which in each case I am as an 'I-am-in-a-world' [*das Seiende, das je ich bin als: 'Ich-bin-in-einer-Welt'*]. Kant did not see the phenomenon of the world, and was consistent enough to keep the 'representations' apart from the *a priori* content of the 'I think' [*die 'Vorstellungen' vom apriorischen Gehalt des 'Ich denke' fernzuhalten*]. But as a consequence the "I" was again forced back [*zurückgedrängt*] to an *isolated* subject [*ein isoliertes Subjekt*], accompanying representations in a way which is ontologically quite indefinite [*in ontologisch völlig unbestimmter Weise*]" (368).

The historical interpretation of the "thing" (reality, being: what Heidegger in *Being and Time* calls the "present-at-hand" [*Vorhandenes*] is given, e.g., in "The Origin," *Poetry, Language, Thought,*" ed. J. Glenn Gray (New York: Harper & Row, 1971): 23-31 and in "The Thing" 174-77.

all proceeds (but not chronologically, not logically) through the novel and almost reaches its ultimate logical achievement, that is, the end. As I have noted above, no matter which theme one tries to grasp, one finds one's taken hold of all three. They are different aspects of one phenomenon, but it is the metaphysics that is responsible for the rest, in my view, and I shall try to untangle that thread from the weave without raveling the whole.

If this series of stories is a novel, as I take it to be, then who is the protagonist? If I generalize, conflate the characters central to all these stories, the protagonist is an author, telling a story, perhaps to himself. He is the subjective self, given Kant's revision of Descartes's philosophical schematic. The subjective self is cut off from the Other—the substantial, the real; isolated but not sufficiently insulated; without immediate access to the real, but with mediated access somehow sufficient to impress him unequivocally with its solidity, its mass, its validity, this impression sufficient to put into question the validity, reality, of the impalpable self.[4] Given the metaphysical point of view and its development in the novel, protagonists as subjective selves must experience (if subjective selves can bring themselves to presume the experience of experience) a "little *crise d'identité*" (36).

If this series of stories is a novel, how can we delineate the plot? "Once upon a time there was a story that began once upon a time there was a ..." (1-2). Follow the Moebius strip to the end. To the beginning, then, the source ("Autobiography" 35). Then just follow. Identify the principle: repetition? replication? reduplication? reproduction? continuation? Determine the design: circle? cycle? spiral? mirror? maze? what-all? Address the question: endlessly?

The metaphysical schematic is given in "Night Sea Journey." (Never identified explicitly as such, it is the journey of sperm flooding upstream toward an ovum.) It is the perilous journey motif, a voyage

---

[4]This characterization of the problem is appropriate to Barth's novel but not to Heidegger's reasoning or his language. See footnotes 3 and 7.

of sorts, this time a self-protagonist struggling alongside the innumerable others, blindly no one knows whenceforth or why toward
no one knows what. The self is helpless witness to pointless bravery
pointlessly overwhelmed, and pointlessly he is himself singled out
for survival. This journey is not the traditional episodic tale of adventure: temptations and fearsome opposition to be courageously
ignored, avoided, escaped, endured, or fought, routed, vanquished.
This journey consists of a vague, vast turmoil of washing-about, -
along, -under. Death is arbitrary and abrupt on all sides, a constantly
visibly real threat, but except for the early death of a particular com-
rade, a seer of sorts or a good guesser, there are no episodes, events.
What there are are abstract speculations. Instead of fires, teeth, and
cannon, our "hero" contends against an absurd absence-of-answer-
to-his-questions. The *what* about him is terrible—take his word
for it—but the unbearable last straw is simply the lack of concrete
whenceforths, whitherwards, whys.

If character and plot are submerged in situation, what surfaces
are theories—shocking, irreverent, perverse theories. Perhaps the
Maker created us accidentally, carelessly, stupidly, maliciously. Perhaps he regrets his error and would correct it; perhaps he is our
enemy, destroyer! Perhaps he himself is nothing like ourselves, can't
swim. Perhaps there are many Makers, other seas; perhaps Makers
are swimming in their own Makers' floods, seas in seas in seas. In
short, perhaps the universe is nothing like ourselves, is oblivious or
hostile to us. Its design is inscrutable; we are mere effects to its cause.

The object of the journey is grounds for speculation too, of course.
A *shore* would mean the end of swimming—and what else are swim-
mers for? Our self's friend imagines an Other, a She, awaiting the
sole survivor, different from him and complementary, both death
and resurrection, end and beginning again. Our self-protagonist
cannot conclude. The journey and the problem of the journey are
absurd. Our self-protagonist concludes: obscene (the recurrence
of this word throughout the novel subtly reiterates the indictment).
Schopenhauer-like, he brings his will to bear against the surging flood.

"No," he wills to will—how else can he oppose the senseless slaughter? But miserable lucky he—caught up in warmy rhythmic waves, he's carried off beyond himself to Love! Love! Love![5]

The metaphysical conclusion isn't metaphysical: life is physical. Pit his will against the matter (matter) if he will, will-he, nill-he, he will be lifted up and surged about by forces forcefuller than his. The Cartesian schematic has provided a dualism—matter and the thinking self—but something has gone wrong with the equilibrium: the *res* looks stouter than the *cogito*.[6] The self struggles to survive his way—by way of his attempt to see, to justify, to rationalize, to turn into story. The She—that "vasty presence"—draws him or drowns him as She pleases, overwhelming even his will. The self's judgment on the case: guilty; death penalty. But this self is not up to the task. He "wills" his negative will to posterity. "Hate love!" The injunction echoes through the novel. And throughout the novel the subjective self—the thinker, the writer, the artist—shrinks in validity and vitality in proportion as he withdraws from the milieu, "real life" going-on.

It is in a Cartesian-Kantian context that the real, the other, opposes and invalidates the self. In this context stories, which objectify the self, subjectify the world; the verification of the self is the dissolution of the real. The sum of the two processes is the difference—zero. Remove the Cartesian-Kantian framework and the justification for the fatalistic theme dissolves.[7]

---

[5]The spermatozoan's negative will is Schopenhaueren; the impotence or the futility of willing in the face of the physics of sexuality indicates that the novel's metaphysics submits "will" to fatal objectivity. The opposition is not Nietzschean will to power, the spermatozoan's will against the egg's; for the sperm wills *not* to will and "Love" is absolute but willless power. Will in Heidegger, as well as so-called drives, urges, and addictions, belongs to Dasein's character as Care (*Being and Time* 238ff.), implicated here only as the novel systematically subordinates it to objectivity.

[6]See the over-weight of the *res corpora* in *Being and Time* 123, 127, as Descartes fails to clarify (1) the ontological foundations of both structures or (2) his argument as it regards "*substantia*."

[7]Heidegger has more patience with the notion of the self than with the notion of the subject, but he appropriates the term to his own uses, first, as the "they-self [*Man-selbst*]" and, second, as an authentic "I" (*Being and Time* 317ff.). The "factically

And that we should and that it may is perhaps what this work suggests should happen.

The Cartesian theme is treated directly in "Petition." The subjective self is coupled to the objective body in a Siamese twin arrangement, the self on the body's back, both ways (61). The subject-object, spirit-body union of contraries amounts to one entity, of course. But union does not guarantee unity. This unit incorporates self-division.[8] All the differences are significant, fundamental. The subjective self can understand but cannot speak; the other is vocal with nothing to say. The self is conscientious (reasonably so), the other sly. The self is a solitary thinker, a dreamer; the other lives practically, gregariously, in the "real world." The self is unemotional, detached, the other moody, irrational. The self tends toward the analytical, the other to synthesis. The self recognizes the duality he shares with his brother and is amenable to compromise; the other denies the division, attempts to repress, repudiate, the self. The self has a refined nature, finds pleasure in the conception and contemplation of abstract ideas, art; the other is filthily physical, clumsy, practical (and makeshift at that), gluttonous, lecherous, and so on (62-3).

The brothers compete for control of their life. In childhood their "antipathies …[smolder]" (64), in adolescence burst into flame. They each impede the activity of, embarrass, the other. The crisis comes when they fall in love with the pretty contortionist Thalia. The solitary, analytical self with his natural disinclination to copulation (66) finds

---

existing Self [*faktisch existierenden Selbst*]" is what Heidegger calls Care (472), the fundamental character of Dasein. (But note also that Care, or the Self, as thrown, is free, that "*Care itself, in its very essence, is permeated with nullity through and through* [*Die Sorge selbst ist in ihrem Wesen durch und durch von Nichtigkeit durchsetzt*]" (331). What I refer to as "self" throughout my reading can be compared with this overlooked Dasein as Being-in-the-world, overlooked when Being in general is interpreted as Being-present-at-hand, objectivity.

[8] Against Descartes's metaphysics, which splits the human down the middle, set Heidegger's revision, which gathers up Dasein, always both ontic and ontological; always altogether involved in mood as well as understanding and thrown into facticity.

repugnant the coarse, lascivious zest that characterizes his brother's loveship. Which brother Thalia loves is the question. Even when the self becomes convinced that Thalia has a twin too, is two Thalias, the prospect is no less bleak; for if there are two Thalias, one is *inside* the other (fascinating psychological suggestion), and a sorting out of lovers is out of the question. Both brothers are confident that they are Thalia's primary interest, but the self's confidence wanes; he doubts; his doubts grow; the uncertainty becomes unbearable: Thalia must choose one brother or the other. Thus the petition to the visiting Oriental potentate to sever the connection between his brother and himself even though it will mean the death of one of them. "Death itself I would embrace like a lover," he writes, "if I might share the grave with no other company. To be one: paradise! To be two: bliss! But to be both and neither is unspeakable" (71).

And the process of withdrawal or cutting-off, of shrinkage (and wastage), of retreat to the interior, is just the process this novel follows. Before our very eyes both the theme and the text trace a wasting corpus; the self and the language that expresses it diminish to moribund-if-not-dead shadows of themselves. The subjective self, thinker/writer/artist, is "not up to life" (186). He evades or circumvents confrontation with life, consigns his own subjective experience of the reality about him and in him to idea, consigns idea to fiction, fiction to the status of the illusory, arbitrary irreal. Thus to oblivion.[9] A matter of time.

Another exegetical clue is offered in the "Petition" story. The contrast drawn between the twins-at-odds, above, and a set of twins in the mystic East more amicably joined heart-to-heart (though even in the East, love is problematic to the design) serves to define the novel's

---

[9] Echo: Heidegger's disparaging reference to religious or biological interpretations of conscience, dependent upon the "ontologically dogmatic guiding thesis that what *is* ... must be *present-at-hand*, and that what does not let itself be Objectively demonstrated as *present-at-hand*, just *is not* at all [*was ist, ... muß vorhanden sein; was sich nicht als vorhanden objektiv nachweisen läßt, ist überhaupt nicht*]" (*Being and Time* 320).

perspective on the subject-object polarity-duality. The problem is a matter of construction, of design. The nature of the universe is not the problem of the novel: the nature of interpretations that attempt to deal with the nature of the universe is the problem. " 'When will I reach my goal through its cloaks of story?' " Menelaus cries. " 'How many veils to naked Helen?' " (144). Attaining naked Helen is not the ground-situation of *Lost in the Funhouse*.[10] The postmodern problem of penetrating how-many-veils is.

The Menelaus-Proteus metaphor has been alluded to above. In the story "Menelaid" Menelaus' salvation lies in holding on to Proteus, no matter what form he takes. But in the ultimate encounter, when Proteus speaks to him in his own voice, Menelaus loses all sense of identity, any point of reference. The certainty that Menelaus grasps is uncertainty. Whether he is a form of Proteus' conceit or Proteus his can never again be ascertained. Undeceived, he understands the nature of things at last: deception. " ' "He continues to hold on, but can no longer take the world seriously.... all subsequent history is Proteus, making shift to slip me ..." ' " (166).[11]

---

[10] Though, of course, "the subject of [novels], ultimately, is life," as Barth remarks in "The Literature of Exhaustion," *Atlantic* 220 (Aug. 1967): 33.

[11] Heidegger gives the history of the distinction between Being and Appearance in *An Introduction to Metaphysics* 98ff., esp. 102, 109f.: "Because being and appearance belong together [*Sein und Schein zusammengehören*] and, belonging together, are always side by side, the one changing unceasingly into the other [and entangling: *den Wechsel ... und damit die ständige Verwirrung*]; because in this change they present the possibility of error and confusion [*Verirrung und Verwechslung*], the main effort of thought at the beginning of philosophy ... was necessarily to rescue being from its plight of being submerged in appearance [*die Not des Seins im Schein zu bändigen*], to differentiate being from appearance [*das Sein gegen den Schein zu unterscheiden*] .... Because of this relation between being, unconcealment, appearance, and nonbeing [*Sein, Unverborgenheit, Schein und Nichtsein*], the man who holds [*sich hält*] to being as it opens round him ... must bring being to stand, he must endure it [*aushalten*] in appearance and against appearance, and he must wrest both appearance and being from the abyss of nonbeing [*muß Schein und Sein zugleich dem Abgrund des Nichtseins entreißen*]" (109, 110).

In fact, all subsequent history is not subsequent. As "Frame-Tale" tells and "Echo" echoes: the ending is contained in the beginning. From Oedipus' pursuit (self-knowledge) through Tiresias' prophecies (that Oedipus' pursuit is Narcissus'; that the objectified self is no object, and the catch to the catch is the loss) to Echo's ambiguous misrepresentations of the same: all history is this series of stories. "Thus we linger forever on the autognostic verge—not you and I, but Narcissus, Tiresias, Echo.... Is Narcissus addressing Tiresias, Tiresias Narcissus? Have both expired?" (103)

The self submitted to subjectivity, protagonist of the novel, is represented by the character Ambrose in three stories, "Ambrose His Mark," "Water-Message," and "Lost in the Funhouse." In the first story Ambrose's identity is established—as a self who has no established identity. Thus his identity as author is foreshadowed. He is deprived (through simple negligence) of the usual personal and social ceremonies of identification—a name, baptism; his paternity is uncertain, especially in the view of his father; the portent of his birthmark (a disoriented purple bee near one eye) is ambiguous.

In the second story Ambrose struggles to come to terms with the world of signs, significance. After a certain afternoon's dramatic proliferation of linguistic and semiotic perplexities, discomfited if not defeated, he finds among the seaweed washed up by the tide a bottle containing a message:"TO WHOM IT MAY CONCERN" (Blank) "YOURS TRULY" (56). A little Anonymiad. Life is suddenly charged with significance.

In the third story Ambrose attempts to make to make a pass at to make a move toward Magda, whose figure is surprisingly well-developed for her age; but his preoccupation with his own feelings, his own self-aggrandizing fictions, prevents any success. He wanders off alone in the funhouse, *"wherein he lingers yet."* The author of the story, who has been narrating the story in an excruciatingly self-conscious manner, progressively withdraws from and finally abandons his story.

The pattern of withdrawal can be followed in the changing point of view in the three-story segment. The first story is narrated in first person (an unlikely *Tristram Shandy* point of view since it is an account of events surrounding Ambrose's birth and infancy up to the time when he is eventually given a name). The second story is narrated from a third person point of view, a distancing technique—but not from self-consciousness:"The more closely an author identifies with the narrator, literally or metaphorically, the less advisable it is, as a rule, to use the first-person narrative viewpoint" (77). The point of view of the third story is removed one more remove, narrated by "an author" outright. What's more, the story slips out of the author's hand again and again until finally both the character Ambrose and the plot of the story get lost in the funhouse; neither is heard of again in the novel.

The Protean dilemma is refigured in this central metaphor of the novel, Ambrose's disappearance into the labyrinthine corridors of the funhouse. All day, like Menelaus in his turn, Ambrose has been grappling with reality, his self-consciousness cutting him off again and again from any effective move toward Magda. The climactic moment occurs when he stands before the endlessly replicating mirrors in the funhouse, as Menelaus came face to face with Proteus:

> Stepping from the treacherous passage at last into the mirror-maze, he saw once again, more clearly than ever, how readily he deceived himself into supposing he was a person. (93)

Ambrose's irony is like Menelaus' too—that his most radical revelation, the one that illuminates everything forever afterwards, the vision he sees "more clearly than ever," emanates from a series of distorting reflections of himself.

At this point Ambrose finds his nametag, which he dropped when he first entered the funhouse. He doesn't associate the name

AMBROSE with himself at all, but with "the famous lightship" and with a certain dessert his grandfather favored (94).[12] After Menelaus on the beach, Ambrose loses his sense of identity.

So does the author of "Lost in the Funhouse," distancing and then removing himself from his story. First he involves himself more and more consciously with himself as author, with the writing of stories, with the problems of authorship and the nature of fiction, the problems of language and the nature of language. And for "problems" read "loss." As noted above, there is a law of diminishing returns at work in the novel. As the self enlarges its domain, consciousness, reality loses its; and vice versa. Here the principle is given in a comic exposé. The sensitive, imaginative artist-type is satirized as a self-deluded pretender, his fictions as excuses, evasions, refuges against an overwhelming reality. As he loses hold of even his fictions, his story empties of content, reduces to its bare structure, design. It can't be long till silence.

The problem is recapitulated in the mock-epic "Anonymiad." Besides recalling all the preceding stories' motifs and all the protean themes, this story in particular traces the *reductio ad absurdum* of the metaphysical paradigm. The story begins, of course, in the middle. "Of course" because all these tales about telling tales profess to do the same, to plunge in where they find themselves: *in medias*

---

[12]Edgar H. Knapp ("Found in the Barthhouse: Novelist as Savior," *Critical Essays on Barth*, ed. Joseph J. Waldmeir [Boston: G. K. Hall, 1980]: 183-89) suggests that these displacements of the self signify "mythic overtones," evoking "the Ambrose Lightship, beacon to lost seafarers, and ... *ambrosia* (the bee-belabored stuff of immortality)" (184); they invite, Knapp continues, a reading of Ambrose as mock-savior, his "heroic suffering [adventures in the funhouse], death [disappearance], and [possibly at least, Knapp cautions] resurrection" buying time, as the story does by its "imaginative design," buying perhaps some fun as well and a fresh perspective for the other characters and for us; buying time, fun, and perspective most essentially, Knapp concludes, for Barth as author (188-89). Perhaps. But I submit that Ambrose's identification of his own name with these mythic symbols hints the very self-aggrandizing self-apotheosizing tendency (narcissism plus genuine intellectual deadend) that marks and mocks the subject and the artist conceptualized as separate from the world in all of these stories.

res. The yarn's been being spun since the beginning (see "Frame-Tale"). The ground-situation is a state of fallen-off (see the Moderns for details, laments). Where muses were are amphorae of souring spirits. For Agamemnon's hearty herohood find nameless, themeless, almost-lifeless minstrel. Instead of fecund Helen to inspire, reward, the stalwart(s), see mild milkmaid Merope. In short, for Truth read Fiction; and for Epic, last-gasp stop-gap.

The last lost word, the *Anonymiad*, is of course the history of the race entire: the portrait of the artist. His grateful fall into Experience, first forced stop and last on his voyage over the wine-dark sea (mirror and sequel to "Night-Sea Journey"'s journey) is, like Adam's, Descartes's, and ours, "a flowered, goated, rockbound isle" where he is thrown ashore and abandoned, to his vast relief. Like Adam's? Who's to say? Like Descartes's (and Kant's) and therefore ours we know: the isolated subject (exactly what our "Petition"-twin desired).

What cast him out, set him forth? Aegisthus', Clytemnestra's, Merope's and his own weak heart's ambiguous ambitions; in his own case, the vain conceit that there was in Fact an Other to be gained to make him whole: sad, sere Experience. Never mind what matter(s) he had in mind; the rock's the thing, the Cartesian limit: elemental encounter with absolute reality. If the ground-situation for this novel is the postmodern turning-point, Barth's vehicle-situation is this story in its protean forms, figured most boldly here with the minstrel isolated on a deserted island, the subjective self set off against the *Ding an sich*.

First he dreams a woman. (There are no "real" women here. Merope is a name he will forget [though something lingers], Helen a name he names the goat [romantic hope either way]. He dreams her in a story with optional endings, his favorite one an option he's forfeited, the fact of Merope. His lyre lost, he discovers his voice, his realm, his happiness: his imagination.

After the first some years of singing, he discovers writing. It's that that saves him. He vacillates twixt joy and deep despair; it's fits and

starts with him (another motif that rhythms the novel). History en-
sues: a series of beginnings. The first six eras (muses corresponding)
are joyful in the main. With the invention of writing he imagines
readers, improvises a system of disseminating his works (amphorae),
discovers fiction. The doubts his fancy falls into—that readers never
receive, can't decipher, his works—his fancy assuages with assurance
that Zeus, Poseidon, say, get them, get them. And even barring that
verification he's confident of the fact, the being, of his works, therefore himself, for they are objectified in the universe. "[S]omewhere
outside myself my enciphered spirit drifted, realer than the gods, its
significance as objective and undecoded as the stars'" (194). The self
is no safe depository for anything of significance, gives no guarantee
of existence, carries no weight on an absolute scale. But outside the
self in the "real" universe, in ink, on parchment, in an amphora, set
safely (i.e., physically) adrift on the sea, the *cogito* confides itself to the
res; the object can be objectively verified (isn't that, too, tautology?).

At any rate, our minstrel comes to his seventh and eighth epochs.
He "[has] begun to run out of world and material," has already published, since he came to write, "effusions of religious narrative, ribald
tale-cycles, verse-dramas, comedies of manners, and what-all" (194).
Now he manages to rouse himself to write a round of realistic, then
romantic, on to fantastic, comic fiction. But he's aging, waning, out
of "new [things] to say, new [ways] to say the old" (195). He loses
inspiration altogether, interest then, then memory, identity.

Then Something happens. Word comes. Never mind from whom
if anyone. "[A] new notion" (196). A sign, signifying: another: a
writer—possibly, of course, himself, possibly another: a reader. The
old boy is on his feet again. One jug remains, one goat (-skin then)
and time for one more masterpiece, piece: this *Anonymiad*, "written
from [his] only valid point of view, first person anonymous" (199).
He works the work, expending his last muster. He sets his one thing
more once more afloat. There it washes, a mayhap undecipherable
symbol signifying fiction, submitted to the Real. Last reflection of
"Night-Sea Journey": the flood has dimmed, the surge subsided to a

gentle, rocking wash. The sperm of urgent negative resolve has turned tale, the tale confided to the ebbing tide. No determined defiance of predestination here, but a tentative gesture, one last grateful gamble on any destination at all. The night-sea journey spawned a fiction. The fiction is at last cast upon the waters. How fertile fiction is the sequel must show.

Is this novel a dark apocalypse? Well, yes, the subject(s)-object(s), the plot(s), the stated theme(s), the language tied to the metaphysics, talk themselves into an ending, the end. The novel articulates the postmodern ground-situation. A burgeoning present and no system of seeing or interpreting to account for it, no language to express it; everything sayable already said, said in all the possible ways to say it. The metaphysical paradigm in shreds, used-up, and language caught in a cause-effect cycle with it, part and parcel of it now, trapped with it in its doom. Nothing to do but make clown suits out of both, mock them once for all, have done with them forever. It's only a matter of time now, not much time.

And yet, as we have seen, this novel teems with robust energy, life going on. The ironies and contradictions between the themes stated and enacted and the wit, the joyful play with which the moribund-if-not-dead is exposed and debunked (the style, as Michael Hinden identifies it, "self-exhausting and yet comically triumphant"[13]), the provocation of LIFE, evokes a counter thrust of counter themes, indicating though not articulating the case of a vigorous universe, of a fallible human condition, laughable but not absurd. The situation, at least in the novel, cannot be taken to be as negative or as nihilistic as Tony Tanner and Jac Tharpe have assessed it until these counter elements have been counted, as critics are attempting to do in both philosophical and psychoanalytical contexts.[14]

---

[13] "*Lost in the Funhouse*: Barth's Use of the Recent Past," *Twentieth Century Literature*; rpt. in *Critical Essays on John Barth*, ed. Joseph Waldmeir, *Critical Essays on American Literature*, gen. ed. James Nagel (Boston: G. K. Hall, 1980) 191.

[14] Tanner, *City of Words: American Fiction 1950-1970* (London: Jonathan Cape, 1971) 253-59. In *John Barth, The Comic Sublimity of Paradox* (Carbondale: Southern

One element that subverts the apocalyptic tenor is the irony in the wit and in the energy of the wit that sets against all dire projections of doom a quotidian stability.[15] To the ground-situation, above, the vehicle-situation (shade of Scheherezade's, 116) is the novel itself. The soul of the novel is its wit, which Tharpe and others have characterized as Rabelaisian, an exuberant exhibition of life, as any passage will serve to show. In spite of the ostensible gloom, the novel insinuates an effect of reassurance.[16]

The irony is found, for example, in "Life Story" where the problem of the author (the protagonist) unable to differentiate himself from his protagonist, his life from his fiction—the old Proteus-Funhouse dilemma—is reduplicated out of the story into the author's author's study and by the logic of the reduplication into our own living rooms (middle-class, educated, 20th century living rooms). The improbable effect, however, is that it is not our reality that disappears into the fiction so that we dissolve before our own eyes; it is the *ideas* of reality and fiction that dissolve, resolve into each other. The most significant implication of the work is that philosophy has gone astray, that perhaps it is not life that is absurd, but a way of "reading" it, a way of reading reading it.

Illinois UP 1974), Jac Tharpe discusses Barth's *farce splendide*, the attempt to "Outdo the universe with laughter and enthusiasm, realizing that in fact the universe seems out to get you and, with despair and death as methods, will get you" (114).

[15] Alan Wilde offers a study of irony, the ironic stance developing from Kierkegaard through the moderns to what he calls the postmodern "horizons of assent." Wilde's thinking shares many of the Heideggerian assumptions that enable my reading of this text. His rereading of postmodernists' treatment of the quotidian is helpful here, not to explain what it means but to detect in it an unconceptualized potentiality, a sense of expectation traditionally reserved for the extraordinary. *Horizons of Assent; Modernism, Postmodernism, and the Ironic Imagination* (Baltimore: Johns Hopkins, 1981).

[16] In *Passionate Virtuosity: The Fiction of John Barth* (Urbana: U of Illinois, 1983) Charles B. Harris calls the same element "passionate virtuosity" (Barth's phrase), the artist's irreducible impulse "to construct meaning" from nothing through language (8). According to Harris, Barth enters onto a new schematization that attempts to reach past schema, the old schema at any rate.

Another element at play and at odds with doom is the motif of plans, designs, open options. Of course, this element indicates uncertainty, instability, as clearly as freedom or hopeful possibilities. Since plans, designs, and options almost always prove to be extraneous to actual performance in this novel, we cannot construe the motif as a sign of hope, of rescue. We are merely tempted. The story "Title," e.g., not only presents the case that literature—and man—is moribund-if-anything, but it confronts the problem of fatalism directly and sketches several options available to us yet. "Title" is a *Waiting for Godot* meditation and response. The story and, therefore, whatever consciousness it objectifies are merest skeletal remains. Lost are the "novel, literature, art, humanism, humanity, the self itself" (108), claims (what remains of) the narrator. All that isn't finished is the story. The ghost traces of characters wait for the end, only their conversation delaying it. The conversation consists of "her" interruptions (to, she mocks, the Progress of Literature ... to its demise), if "she" is indeed the source of interruption, if indeed, that is, "she" "is." She is all that remains of Scheherezade: the possibility of an interruption. It is uncertain whether the conversation is dialogue or monologue.

The "Title" problem is Ambrose's problem in "Water-Message": the "message" in both cases is the medium: form, sign, design, intent, refiguring the old minstrel's problem in "Anonymiad": nothing left to say nor any way to say it. Something (memory perhaps) of the form remains: beginning (middle) and waiting-for-an-end. What remains of content is the all but empty blank. But "Hold onto yourself" (109). There are three, no four, alternatives to ringing down the curtain: (1) "rejuvenation: having become an exhausted parody of itself, perhaps a form ... may rise neoprimitively from its own ashes" (109); (2) replacement of the "moribund what-have-yous" by the "vigorous new," the end of one thing the beginning of another (109); (3) his own recommendation (and Borges'[17]), a stop-gap expedient: "turn ultimacy against itself to make something new and valid, the essence

---

[17] According to Barth, "The Literature of Exhaustion" 31-32.

whereof would be the impossibility of making something new" (109). The fourth possibility (Beckett's): "Self-extinction. Silence" (110).

In the almost-empty blank, to which language in this story is reduced thematically, Barth replies to Beckett (and Proteus-style, in Beckett's voice):

> [T]o write this allegedly ultimate story is a form of artistic fill in the blank, or an artistic form of same, if you like.... The storyteller's alternatives, as far as I can see, are a series of last words ... or actual blank. And I mean literally fill in the blank.... The fact is, the narrator has narrated himself into a corner, a state of affairs more tsk-tsk than boo-hoo, and because his position is absurd he calls the world absurd. That some writers lack lead in their pencils does not make writing obsolete. (111-12)

Barth's plan for the Rerouting of Literature, like his plans for the stories in this novel, gets rewritten many times. For our purpose here there are two points to reiterate: the author blames authors' "accursed self-consciousness" for the condition of literature, and in order to rescue the corpus from certain oblivion he reverses the priority that history and this novel have given to reality over subjectivity:[18]

> [T]he fact is that people still lead lives, mean and bleak and brief as they are, ..., and people have characters and motives that we divine more or less inaccurately from their appearance, speech, behavior, and the rest ... and they do these things in more or less conventionally dramatic fashion ... and what goes on between them

---

[18] Barth neither recognizes nor represents the thought of Heidegger; However, operating in a subject-object framework and giving some preference to the subjective, giving moreover the sense that something vital is inexpressible but not suppressible in the language of objectivity, Heidegger would probably say that he errs on the right side. Cf. *Being and Time* 250ff.

is still not only the most interesting but the most important thing in the bloody murderous world .... And
that my dear is what writers have got to find ways to
write about ... or ... their, that is to say our, accursed
self-consciousness will lead them... [Fill in the blank].
(113)

In this story, where Barth seems to write directly about what he
is trying to do in this work,[19] are found the articulation of a state
of mind and an era, Barth's in both cases, exhaustion of possibilities
in both cases, and also a series of sets of schemes to avert the catastrophe imminent. We can choose between an exhausted logic and
inexhaustible life, but if we choose life we must abandon or redefine
our logic. Barth seems to opt for abandoning our logic and redefining
as we go on.

Barth's diagnosis of and prognosis for the state of literature and
man agrees in many respects with Alain Robbe-Grillet's views in *For
A New Novel*, especially in the essay "Nature, Humanism, Tragedy,"
written at about the same time as *Lost in the Funhouse*.[20] Robbe-
Grillet claims and demonstrates that the late-moderns, absurdists,
e.g., Beckett, are not de-humanist or in-humanist to depict the ab-
surdity and prophesy the disappearance of man; it is, Robbe-Grillet
claims, precisely their essential, uncompromised humanism that has
led them rationally to tragic resolutions. For his own part, he believes
that the metaphysical paradigm is in error and has rendered literature
and philosophy unnecessarily anthropomorphic and anthropomor-
phism unnecessarily tragic. He recommends that we face the fact
of an empty, impersonal universe, abandon tragedy. The future and
language are for exploring in.

---

[19]For what he wrote later about his intention here see "More Troll than Cabbage,
Introduction for Tape-and-Live Voice Performances From the Series *Lost in the
Funhouse*," *The Friday Book: Essays and Other Nonfiction* (New York: Perigee, 1984)
77-79.
[20]Trans. Richard Howard (New York: Grove Press, Inc., 1965): 49-76.

But it may be a delusion to think that one can think of man "in" a universe unrelated to him, given his proclivities as we define them—sensory, intellectual, emotional—since this thought (as well as every sensing/thinking/feeling) sets up or depends upon relationship already.[21] Besides, the Other maintains the advantage. Man continues to define human-ness as weakness, dullness, diversion, error. Though Barth agrees with Robbe-Grillet that the paradigm is wrong, the correction he indicates is essentially different. He does not opt for further objectification of Kantian objectivity. He shows that the paradigm has been played out to the end. The next turn is not delineated. But the turning is not a turning from "subjectivity"; it turns instead from "objectivity," that idea which cancels out the heart's desires. It is ideas that have reached a deadend. In "How to Make a Universe,"[22] Barth's "first proper public lecture," delivered in 1960 well before he began to write this novel, Barth said:

> [A]s soon as Being is *conceived of*—that is, as soon as it's represented as a concept (opposed to not-Being) and therefore made problematical—the problem can't be solved. Even to say "Being simply *is*" is to impose upon Reality the human conceptions of noun, verb, and adverb, the human logic of grammar and syntax, and thus to falsify it, since there are no categories in Nature's warpless, woofless web. (22)

Barth does not escape the Cartesian-Kantian schematic, but he suspends its nihilistic force; or he suspends above or inside it something enigmatically human.

In his now-familiar "The Literature of Exhaustion," written during the *Lost in the Funhouse* period, Barth congratulates postmodern authors who manage yet "to speak eloquently and memorably to our

---

[21] Compare Heidegger's schematic of relationships, beginning with Dasein as Being-in-the-world.

[22] *The Friday Book* 13-25.

still-human hearts and conditions, as the great artists have always done" (30). Thirteen years later in a twin essay, "The Literature of Replenishment," he again describes literary masterpieces as works "not only artistically admirable but humanly wise, lovable, literally marvelous" (71).[23] Something unthematized among the vestiges of the traditionally "human" offers perhaps the "ground of being" in this novel, perhaps the clue to the unaccountable "significance" that the language manifests, a this-ness that outwits, outlasts, the subverting/subverted notions that inform the language literally.

It is at this point that Heidegger's post-philosophy nonconceptual thinking assists the reading of Barth and of the postmodern situation. The rational paradigm which since Descartes has separated and since Kant has increasingly alienated the human as subject from a world of things in themselves neglects or denies and suppresses: human being, always already ontically/ontologically in-the-world, the world always already engaged as it is drawn into history by and in that relationship. My point here is that *Lost in the Funhouse*, which does not propose to propose a new paradigm, explores the inadequacy of the current one, and that the "argument" of the novel is compatible in many essential respects with Heidegger's argument against the Cartesian-Kantian dichotomy, especially in *Being and Time*. For reasons such as these, I expect, William V. Spanos, in "A Preface" to a collection of essays published in 1976 to initiate and stimulate Heideggerian studies among Anglo-American literary scholars, listed this novel among postmodern works which without direct communication with Heideggerian thinking parallel it.[24] Barth's thematization and

---

[23] *Atlantic* 245 (Jan. 1980): 65-71. In his Friday-pieces Barth reiterates the theme; for example, the "real concerns" of "real artists" are "the passions of the human breast and the possibilities of human language" ("Historical Fiction, Fictitious History, and Chesapeake Bay Blue Crabs, or, About Aboutness," 191) or, quoting from this essay in his introduction to "Tales Within Tales Within Tales": "the proper subject of literature" is " 'human life, its happiness and its misery' " (218).

[24] "Martin Heidegger and the Question of Literature: A Preface," *Martin Heidegger and the Question of Literature*, ed. William V. Spanos (Bloomington: Indiana UP, 1979) xii.

demonstration of language as a medium exhausted conceptually but powerful essentially to evoke "meaning" which has no conceptual reference follows the deconstructionist route through exhaustion or totalization to provoke an unaccountable radical revitalization of language.

In an era distinguished for its increasingly neurotic language-consciousness, Barth writes an expose of the phenomenon. He strips language to its vitals: in "Lost in the Funhouse" he unfrocks the operator behind fiction, busy with his funhouse machinations; but both here and in "Autobiography" he shows that the story has a being of its own. In "Title" Barth reduces language to syntax. But still the story's story persists! These are not hoarse, dulled, diminished echoes. They are *stories* of hoarse, dulled, diminished echoes. This is not the "book ... of a man who cannot really find any sanction for writing either in world or self, yet feels that it is his one distinguishing ability, the one activity which gives him any sense of self," as Tanner claims (254). These are telling explorations as well as fascinating stories. Exposing the operations behind, beneath, and in authors and stories and language, they discover by demonstration that the operations can not account for the effects, that stories persist quite healthily regardless of "content" or "form."[25] Something of language transcends and includes systems that explain it.

"Ambrose His Mark" is a tour de force on the nature and significance of signs.[26] The primary disclosure—here as in the novel as a whole—is that language itself is not the thing. "This is what they mean by '[ ],'" Ambrose occasionally suddenly understands. The "this" is the thing. Language is meaningless, sound only, structure only, until one "gets" the "this" it "means." Language does not imitate;

---

[25] Harris, summarizing and assessing Barth scholarship to date, suggests that Barth's wit or his voice or his style, and all of these entangled, await critical investigation; this novel works not a meaning but an effect, which is to upset the idiom of traditional literary criticism.

[26] The chapter deserves a separate Heideggerian analysis; cf. e.g. *Being and Time* 120f., 160f. (significance); Sect. 17, 107f. (signs); Sect. 34, 203f. (discourse).

it points. Or, as Heidegger had it, language does not represent; it gives. In "How to Make a Universe" (22-3) Barth compares the artist to a Zen master: "He does not describe reality; he points to it. He gives you a little piece of it."

Appendix E: Heideggerian Insights

> Why should we [not] … [make] sure that in starting our analysis we have not given *too low* an assessment of Dasein's Being, regarding it as an innocuous subject endowed with personal consciousness, somehow or other occurring [*als harmloses, irgendwie vorkommendes Subjekt, ausgestattet mit personalem Bewußtsein*]? (Martin Heidegger, *Being and Time* 323)

Lost in the Funhouse presents itself as the argument with proofs that John Barth is the consummate postmodern, but I include him here for two reasons: (1) his work, the "novel" itself, refutes the argument and carries the proofs off to its own subversive purpose, and (2) it does so by a function of language that escapes the postmodern situation in spite of the fact that there is no place to go.

To conceptualize has been the Western way to "see." If that way is deficient, ineffectual, or detrimental, then to conceptualize the problem is to stand still or to regress. Barth points beyond conceptualization insofar as he evokes a spirit witty and perverse enough to survive, even to subvert, an exhausted tradition of forms and concepts. But everything beyond that point is inarticulate.

I read *Lost in the Funhouse* for the first time just after I had read *Being and Time* for the first time. Same hi/story. Barth put the words, *turned* the words, (in)to music: American music. The world in which Barth's stories operate is the world Heidegger deposed (after Nietzsche exposed it) in *Being and Time*, the Cartesian-Kantian subject-object, cause-effect, true-false, real-romantic, schematic of polarities that circle upon each other, eventually collapse upon each other, as Nietzsche and Heidegger taught us to think, and as I make it my primary business to point out in Barth's novel. Here the apocalyptic thematic is rendered in the voice of the comedian—voice and little more than voice, since language per se is emptied and minimized (unless the notions of emptying and minimizing are parodied and exposed for frauds). Once the point is made, the novel can be said to resonate with Heidegger's thinking only in some extraliteral ultrathematic "way."

But though for Barth the articulable world is a shambles, saying so calls for exquisite design, elaborate mazemaking, fine art, finer technique, working the problem out to the end. What comes to an end is not the will or the power to say, and not something to say, but the conjunction of these. It would not be possible to say what the novel "has" to say in the language of the novel. Therefore the novel says what it has to say outside its language, and the interpretive language that could recoup it is even now in the forging. It could be a still-unfinished Heideggerian "way."

> Here again we are faced with the Being-present-at-hand-together of some such spiritual Thing along with a corporeal Thing [*einem Zusammen-vorhanden-sein eines so beschaffenen Geistdinges mit einem Körperding*], while the Being of the entity thus compounded remains more obscure than ever. (Martin Heidegger, *Being and Time* 82-3)

Language As Disclosure

In the light that Heidegger's thinking casts onto works of literature, I have tried to "see" what a handful of modernist American authors were seeing and saying about the nature of language. The point was not to compare the views of the authors with Heidegger's, nor to verify their views by his or vice versa, nor even to define or sketch out a modernist position on the subject, though something of that does appear. The attempt was to exercise for myself that freedom, with its rigorous demands, enabled and empowered by Heidegger's thinking, to follow after, in a sense, to re-collect what is appearing in or by way of the modernist works. The experiment has brought a sense of genuine encounter, through the mediation of Heidegger and the five pieces, with *what the works brought to the encounter.*

A "Heideggerian reading" has taken an attitude toward its subject: this one has set itself to questioning the nature of language. All of the readings above have so placed themselves, ordered themselves, have entered and followed through the works according to that interrogation.

If I survey my study as a whole in order to surmise something about the modernists or about lines of kinship that can be drawn with the early Heidegger, it is not to bring the work to a conclusion. I have followed some Heideggerian paths as they opened up certain literary works, and have come to a point where finer branching may occur.

The works of the literary authors as I have read them give to language in general, and to works of art a essential language, some responsibility for "originating" "reality"—i.e., whatever exists, whatever happens. In each case this point of origin occurs when/where in one strange way or another language arises in opposition to whatever is not language—massiness, doing, the abyss, death, empty silence. Gone is the possibility of an ideal or an objective world-in-itself; nor is the world subjective. Though human language seems to be operative in the continuous originating of a world, its adversary, a chaotic or massy waste of not-world—freedom, groundlessness—is equally contestant and generative. I return once more in brief review.

Williams was an outspoken critic of the tradition. As in *Paterson* he would call for the burning down of libraries, so in *In the American Grain* his representative Poe recognizes the necessity of destroying everything: in order to begin again. Thus though *IAG* formally appropriates the literary tradition, it does not revive and reinvigorate it; in the terminology of this work, "recognition" of the tradition "annihilates" it.

In this work the notion of origin changes from its rational conceptualization as the point of temporal or motive or causal beginning, a point fixed and referential, to in this case not a notion at all but a fact: ground as actual place. But fact and place too lose definition; ground is "massiness": the undifferentiated, the chaotic (comparable, perhaps, to James' "magnificent waste"), the stuff of physicality and sexuality and spirituality admixed ("genius"), a generative, continuously regenerative esthetic-moral potentiality.

This originating ground may be missed or ignored or lost; the *genius* of the New World is even yet disappearing under European domination. The discovery or recovery of the genius of a place requires that a people pay attention, that they look at and see what is offering itself all about them. Such "recognition" would not be an act of intellectual objectification or of objective taking-measure, but a spiritual, emotional, intellectual submitting-to, immersing-in ("touching," "marrying"), the effect of which would be to "release" things into their own "emergence." (Refusals, such as ignoring or denying, refuse existence itself.) Thus Rasles frees the Indian into his own existence, and thus such men as Boone, Burr, and Houston cultivate what survives of the lusty genius of the New World; thus also Poe releases his method, himself, and his period, as Williams releases all of these, along with the genius of his own place and time—and the genius of his own: method.

That is, the path from ground to existence, from beginning to end, is not teleological but spontaneous, not linear but reciprocal. Not only is the ground's genius released into existence by the poet, but the poet's genius is released by the ground. The self or the poet is not merely a channel or conduit by which the ground has its say; s/he is another self-asserting genius. A third factor too, oppositional and unoriginal, enters into and issues from this process of emergence: the historical locality, the period: "the mass of impedimenta which is the world." That is, the local and contingent, which resists and obstructs (or supports and assists) the emergence of the original and the authentic, enters into existence also as it shapes (and distorts) the genius and the method that emerge.

This "method of composition" by which the poet sets forth his ground, his locality, and his self neither forms these things nor contains nor represents them. Like James' presentation of language as a formative, ordering human movement over against chaos, Williams' method of composition occurs only in and according to an active opposition. The self-declaring, which is never finalized or totalized, proves the existence and potency of the self as, and as long as, it maintains itself in active opposition to the (existing, potent) driving and opposing forces. One difference is that in the James story the opponents in the conflict, form against disaster, interpenetrate more freely, conjoin or admix more imperceptibly. The most intense, deliberate opposition in the James story, the governess against Quint, conceals the most total surrender. Total victory of language over potentiality achieves total defeat—i.e., the collapse of the story. In

Williams too the success of the method means maintaining a precarious balance, but the self-supporting self-assertion seems to hold itself more definitively apart, and the assertion seems to be more essentially assertiveness; the potentiality which realizes itself in potency in both works tends further in *IAG* toward will to power. Williams' work is a dense assemblage of "fresh" entities and notions in new relationships: origin, culture, history, language, the work of art—and in all of these arises a new sense of what it means to "be."

If Williams' and James' element is subjectivity, Faulkner's is objectivity, but scrutiny "annihilates" (in Williams' sense) the generalizations in each case. Objectivity is not Faulkner's objective; such a word would be a high, thin sound unrelated to the blood and flesh and terror that he presents as Addie's *truth*: "doing." And it is Addie who makes the case against words in Faulkner's story: i.e., their element is not earth, but ether. Their function is not to present or to represent life, but to evade it, "correct" (erase) it. Life and language are separate and different, in her view. The effect of the irrelevance and ineffectuality of words is to separate and alienate the users of words not only from life ("doing") but also from each other, since it is words that work among people a mediation, communication, community. Language is dysfunctional in Addie's world because its origin, its purpose, its use, and its effect have lost their connection to blood and earth. (The notion is something like Williams' sense of lusty, massy, original relatedness to ground. The difference seems to be that the smell of blood is stronger in Faulkner, though less blood is spilled in his story.) What words indicate are "gaps in peoples' [*sic*] lacks" (166); they mark the empty spaces which "doing" does not inhabit: "love," "sin."

But "dysfunction" is dysfunction only when "function" is operating to mark the difference. Addie's bitter proclamations about language are part and parcel of a broader presentation of language—including her own practice of it. The most radical element in Addie's language theory is her analysis of the function of words: words hold and carry, bring to presence. And they hold and carry and bring to presence not meanings or concepts but actual people and things, and more.

Addie is Faulkner's governess in at least one respect, i.e., she sees clearly and with self-certainty "truths" which the story itself enlarges and renders ambiguous. First, Addie's denunciation of words is "carried" to the reader *by way of her words.* Second, we find, as we find in James' story, that meanings are communicated which are different from or opposite to the literal meanings of the words that carry them—Cora "gets" (understands) Addie's reticence, ambiguity, or even silence, for example, and Addie "gets" the resentment (compare *ressentiment*) underneath Cora's truisms.

And so in spite of her protests to the contrary, language functions for Addie, directly or not, to "mean" (bring to presence) living "doing." In fact, we discovered in the dictum of her father an ambiguity principle, an elasticity and openness that allowed words to accommodate living, changing "doing." The freedom that belongs to unfixed, unstable language allows language to move and change as unfixed, unstable "doing" changes.

As in the James story language moving against disaster founds a social order, so language functions in the Faulkner story as the point of origin where living "doing" (or not-living not-"doing") enters into reality. As in James' story the governess is a fallen (weak, blind, self-deluded) governor, implicating history, so in Faulkner's South the Bundrens are morally shabby, deliberately ignorant; they choose false words, suppress and deny knowledge available to them in their own unarticulated understanding and in Darl's extraordinary vision. And both stories intimate genuine danger. At Bly disaster is the "proof" of the governess's method; for the Bundrens, turning toward such "truths" as they suspect would mean turning toward something in or underneath those truths which is dreadful. They turn away—as false words allow them to do.

Faulkner has achieved what Williams required of American authors. In his work his time and place, which have shaped and distorted his genius, are set forth in and as that opposition. Meanwhile an originary vision emerges through the impedimenta, asserts and supports itself, its ground, its "doing."

The James novella emphasizes language from the outset as the narrator purports to offer to the reader his own transcript of the governess's story rendered to him by Douglas, who received it from the governess herself in her own handwriting. Story itself is the problem of the story. The problem is form, whose character as containment is given rein to seek itself out. The content of the story, or what it seeks to contain, is "evil" or "love." That is, by means of her story the governess attempts to clarify and justify (manage, control) the experience she claims to relate. Indeed the story *is* a relat*ing*: is the governess's attempt to forge relationship between her experience and herself, or between herself and the master and other figures in the story; is, equally and pointedly, the attempt of each narrator in the chain to establish authority and credibility and justification: from governess, Douglas, and the narrator to the canny James himself.

The narrative is about things suppressed, locked up, breaking out. Not only is the story's hi/story a case in point, but inside the story there works a network of such phenomena. What are "contained" in the story—the past, the dead—are not past, dead, but are presenc*ing*, liv*ing*—beckoning from the future. The central passage of the story, in my view, suggests a border between everything drawn or drawing into language and "forbidden ground" (355)—a border where language is stopped by or opens upon a questioning, a questioning of the past and the present, of the dead and the living, of occurrence and recurrence. At the end, the story itself crosses the border. At this point, where Miles' "supreme surrender of the name" (402) brings the story hurtling from the pinnacle of its power, the reader is thrust past the limit of language, beyond the *literal* itself. At this point we see that the literal *is* not something, but it *does* something.

What does the *literal* do? Letters (the master's, the headmaster's, the governess's, e.g.) work to point beyond themselves to something more or other than the meaning they "literally" convey—they indicate; they evoke; they call to view. Originally, or ultimately, letters work to found and to maintain or to subvert and to violate the human "world": Bly, fiction. Traditional representational language (religious, literary, and psychological) appears in the story as secondariness, delusion, evasion, romance. However, as the world loses material solidity or epistemological certainty, "seeing" achieves a new kind of purchase on reality. More flawed than ever, weaker in composition and in character, self-indulgent and self-deceptive, "seeing" yet assumes the responsibility for the world—not to interpret it, but to negotiate the particulars of its relations.

James fashions his story in the face of (i.e., opposing) received ideas on the one hand and "life" on the other. The dreadful threatens in spite of the form/ula/s that should placate it. Statements all but grasp a matter before they disappear into it, when the matter appears (breaks out) on its own. Language works—in reverse. It works (evokes, provokes) by so clearly, so disastrously, *not*-working (to express, to represent). Its figures, forms, and structures do not mime or represent its operation—they enact it. Form forms—in a tightrope performance just one step short of abyss.

Hemingway's bullfighting handbook—his esthetics, in my reading—"sets forth" the work of art, i.e., language in its essential function. Language is the site and the "method," not of the cultivation of a culture (Williams) and not of the founding of a social or human order (Faulkner and James), but of the rising into appearance of what actually happens. The strength of this work is that in it the marvelous is brought into view—the appearing of what-is (-happens) upon the horizon of what-is-not (death). The ground of this appearing is the seeing emotion of a spectator. The occasion or agency is the work of art (demonstrated in the bullfight). As in the Williams work, the nature of seeing is not physical or intellectual; these aspects of perception and cognition are ignored or subsumed in what Hemingway treats as emotion. Morality (Williams' sharpened sense of original relationship to the earth), discounted or opposed outright, gives way to a rigorous demand for "purity" of seeing, of feeling, of writing—the power of which would be to produce a work of art in which Hemingway's modified "truth" could continue to happen.

For Williams the method of composition is the method by which things are released into emergence and held in existence, but the nature of the method is potent self-assertion. In Hemingway, though relationship brings what happens into appearance, sets it forth (human emotion is the very place where things appear, the very stuff of their appearing), yet what appears seems to belong to itself, not to the self-assertion of the author. Language in Hemingway, the work of art (the bullfight) in which the emotion "sees" the appearing of what happens, is nearer to Addie's depiction of words bringing something actual (a "doing") to presence. Like Addie and like Williams' persona, Hemingway's author demands of language a relation to living "doing."

But though the essential function of language is to provide the possibility and the occasion for seeing, there are corollary functions as well. We recall that in James the language principle, the impulse and the intent to order, negotiates its way among and against the chaotic, both contrary forces contributing to the tenuous equilibrium that "skirts" disaster. In Hemingway we find similarly that language may function to displace, evade, hide, suppress; to escape, postpone, buffer. In Faulkner such evasions amounted to lies and delusions, but here they are the tactics and techniques for evading danger and death as well as for approaching and daring them (the closer to death the closer to life). But just as Faulkner's ambiguity principle allows an always changing "doing" to inhabit language, omitting a function of concept or meaning, so Hemingway's language, working according to a principle of opposition, mediates not another mediator (concept, meaning) but "things that actually happen."

In Hemingway the point where "what happens" appears is something like James' border. Its force is the absolute nihil of oblivion. Against the Nothing, Being appears. Hemingway's border reaches to the core of existence, to the ontological difference (being versus not-being). James' border reaches to the unplumbable irrational at the core of the psyche—"love," "evil." In fact, James referred to his use of the ghosts in the story as a "process of *adumbration*" by which he tried to evoke "that sense of the depths of the sinister . . . . Portentous evil. . . ."

In spite of the radical powers of language these works disclose, in Hemingway's handbook—on language, art; not bullfighting—the work of art is not essentially different from ordinary language; its distinction is that it intensifies and clarifies the opposition between itself (the institutionalized, formalized ceremony of the bullfight, for example) and death, intensifies and clarifies, then, the appearing of what happens. The notion is something like Addie's and like Vardaman's: language provides a place for actualization.

Hemingway's method of composition, like Williams', depends upon opposition, antagonism. Language here opposes not only death, but other language; i.e., ineffectual language works against ineffectual language in this work to evoke, to force, the appearing of what-happens. For language sometimes functions as death does, as a negative horizon against which things that actually happen appear in their happening. Surprisingly, the "emotion" of Hemingway's author-spectator seems less virile than the "love" of Williams' "method"; but the power of Hemingway's figure that flares against the shock of the matador's sword gives a sense of rising appearing as uncanny as anything in literature, enacts while it asserts the essential function of language as disclosure.

The difference between Barth and the modernists is clear and, in my view, chastening. We find the same confrontations between language and what there is to say, between language and silence; the same dilemma when language is used up and disfranchised in an objective universe. But these confrontations occur not between a seemingly naked humanness and a "terrible" or gross or chaotic other; they occur between subjectivity and objectivity. These contenders have regained the status of idea, concept, and they are exposed or manipulated with precision; they are not set forth as dangerous and unpredictable opponents with the urgency that the eminence of disaster and death engenders.

The novel impresses first with the aptness, the currency, of its intellectual analysis. Barth follows the conceptual path of thinkers since Nietzsche—follows concepts to their end, or their beginning, and shows what they have come to show: a false fit. Concepts lead away from life, eventually negate it, nihilate it. The dilemma is genuine, but not in Barth's novel, where eventually it is delightful. The power of this work to move us and to make us see (whatever that has come to mean) is in the force of its energy, its joy, *jouissance*, which counters its seeming assertions of emptiness, impoverishment, deadend. Life escapes the dilemma by declaring itself (as the moderns had asserted, above) through the interstices, rising in antagonistic rebellion against falseness, nothing. Not-language overthrows language, in and by means of language.

Which is the expressed intention of the work. By means of language (traditional concepts, here) the novel maneuvers its tautological circle. Yet the point of view seems to issue from a point outside the circle. The concepts and the circle are intellectual; the point of view is human. And language seems still to be working, as Williams had it, to set forth what it does not thematize: a "self," a place, a period.

As we have seen, the modernists delivered up to the postmodernists the quasi-Nietzschean starting point. Their stories ignore, expose, or oppose the Cartesian-Kantian paradigm, in which objectivity as truth threatens the validity of the subjectivity that gave it legitimacy in the first place. An authoritative perspective is deliberately set up inside subjectivity itself, all things, including what we have called objectivity, appearing, then, colored through and through with human involvement, even while their "reality" is struck with penetrating clarity. The perspective is caught in Heidegger's tautological circle. The problem of the circle is ignored or it is not a problem;

seeing continues to proceed from, call it, point of view. There is no sense of loss, but the sense of "objectivity" is compromised.

The authors have redefined such notions as truth (Williams' "original," Faulkner's "doing," Hemingway's "things that actually happen"); essentiality (no longer single or pure or conceptual); temporality (not that the past is present as memory or history, but that memory and history become futural modes of presencing; the difference implicates a revision of spatiality as well); presence (not objective identity, but the appearing of things in human experience; further, absence is no longer the antithesis of presence, but it underlies presence as potentiality or it pervades or even displaces presence); and causality (in Williams the notion of originating as rising, emergence from ground which rises, emerges, too, in what it grounds; in Faulkner and James "saying" as the point of originating, in Hemingway the work of art as it hazards death). As humanness becomes involved in what was formerly objectivity, and the "real," the material, the fact, becomes engaged with humanness, the traditional conceptualization of the human as a confederation of body and spirit or mind undergoes a redistribution in which both components remain but are no longer dissociable.

We find in these works at least three ontological levels, which we may carry into Heidegger's neighborhood for comparison. (1) We find an articulable human understanding, a world—primarily and for the most part a secondary world of received representations of the world, which could be compared and contrasted with Heidegger's everyday falling Dasein or the "they" in *Being and Time*. (2) We find a subconscious level of unarticulated and unappropriated knowledge, for which there is no single corresponding structure in Heidegger's Dasein, though what we attribute to the subconscious shows up, or remains concealed, in Dasein otherwise. For example, ordinary everyday Dasein primarily and for the most part avoids "the task of genuinely understanding" (213) by fleeing into the "publicness" of the "they" (see "Idle Talk," "Curiosity," and "Ambiguity," Sections 35-37). Meanwhile, "mystery" (the concealing of what is concealed) as such holds sway throughout man's Da-sein" ("On the Essence of Truth" 132-33).[1] Untruth is prior to and proper to the essence of truth (132). Truth, uncoveredness, must be "wrested" or "snatched" from beings, is "always, as it were, a kind of *robbery*" (*Being and Time* 265). (3) Finally, outside (and also inside) these two kinds of being lies absolute freedom—chaos, abyss, death of "being," of existence. Against the horizon of chaos or death, of not-being, the emergence or appearing of things occurs in these works in something of the "fresh" (Williams), genuine (Faulkner), stark (Hemingway), silent or invisible (James, Barth) arising that Heidegger attributes to the Greek *phusis, aletheia*. But the difference between being and not-being does not separate the two. The difference that prevents the achievement of totality, identity, provides temporality or movement to this unity of antagonists. Compare Heidegger's descriptions of temporalization (*Being and Time* and *Time and Being*), of identity and difference (*Identity and Difference*),[2] of the earth-world strife ("The Origin"), etc. This point may be the Nietzsche-Heidegger (-Freud) difference that distinguishes modern literature. What was called madness or evil or nihilism is now violating the integrity and the order of the forms constructed to limit or oppose it. What "is" (including what "is said") is contaminated with the "not."

All of the Americans inveigh against losses, resistible ignorance and impotence, impinging darkness; they all describe dilemma, comparable with Heidegger's (Hölderlin's) time of need. Heidegger expresses some hope, but less expectation, that Being will manifest itself in a primordial way even as it unfolds as the technological domination of all that is.[3] The Americans all make a case for diminishment, and yet at the same time, without clear or determined objectives their works vigorously affirm a clarity and a purposiveness. They commence from no beginning but from just where they are,

---

[1] *Basic Writings* 113-41.

[2] Trans. Joan Stambaugh (New York: Harper and Row, 1969).

[3] See the essays contained in *The Question Concerning Technology and Other Essays*, trans. William Lovitt (New York: Garland Publishing, 1977).

a new making-way toward a doubtful destiny. The dread nature of the ground and the way and the end is freedom, the dread task for human freedom: responsibility.

As to their issue (either way), most of these readings, if my particular Heideggerian approach were extracted from them, could be (mis)taken to concern and produce the "effects" that Derridean readings often concern and produce. Note that Williams' "method" in Chapter 2 describes Derrida's in *Spurs* (especially as the "operation" of "oppositional articulation" summarized by Stefano Agosti in the Introduction,"Coup upon Coup, 25). The difference is that Williams' turn against the tradition is a turn to the ground under his feet, submerging and emerging, his hands dirty or bloody, his essays too, not from"handling" the *textual* but from "touching," "marrying," the *actual* ("presence" would be as dismissable as, e.g., the "history" he "annihilates," and on the same grounds).

Or compare James' "literality," above, with Derrida's *Dissemination* "textuality" or with the *éperon* in *Spurs*. Compare my version of James' ghost story, getting around hallucination or projected subjectivity Heidegger's way, with Derrida's deconstructive rendering (rending) of Schapiro (and a bit of Heidegger) in "Restitutions,"[4] and contrast what gets left over in each case: a coming to terms, to the terminal, to more or less determination—the more in James, the less in Derrida. Or compare if you can Derrida's treatment of form, of the frame; of the *ergon* and the *parergon* in especially "*Parergon*"[5] with my little foray into the between in the James chapter. The essential difference in every case is the difference of essentiality. For James, as we noted, "to 'put' things [compare "effects," "style"] is very exactly and responsibly and interminably to do them."

---

[4]"Restitutions of the Truth in Pointing [*pointure*]," *The Truth in Painting*, trans. Geoff Bennington and Ian McLeod (Chicago: U of Chicago, 1987) 255-382.
[5] *The Truth in Painting* 15-147.

In Faulkner "words" are as disconnected from and incommensurate with "life," as "orphaned, and separated at birth from the assistance of [their] father," as Derrida's "writing."[6] Words are arbitrary and unnecessary, and, further, using them cheats, cripples, blinds. But there are true words in Faulkner's story: connected and commensurate not with their faithful authors but with the "deeds" that engendered them: the terrible blood boiling along the land. And language is working, not only like chisels and levers but also as a place to put things (three times Addie puts something different into her father's adage), and a place to meet the painful shapes of things (Darl), or to discover the shapes for the first time or to decide them (Vardaman).

For Hemingway the "fact" disclosed in the work of art (and language per se) is no more undecidability than it is truth, but it is the undimmed event of the deciding, of the contestants in their contesting. Compare the textual complexities, conflicts and play, in *Dissemination*,[7] and the essential blockage at the point of every determination. The question of seeing what really happens is essential with Hemingway (though "essence" is renewed), is not intellectual, not esoteric; it restores the gaping wound in the necessity (happening) of its contradiction. Barth's work differs from the others, ends where Derrida's works end: pointing beyond themselves. Or I could say that Barth's *words* work as Derrida's do, to count the ways they do not mean, while their *style* provokes: "life."

Perhaps Derrida has already provided a response, a warning against the kind of work I have attempted here:

> "Every time that, in order to hook writing precipitously
> up with some reassuring outside or in order to make
> a hasty break with idealism, one might be brought to
> ignore certain recent theoretical attainments ... [here he

---

[6] "Signature Event Context," *Margins* 316.

[7] Trans. Barbara Johnson (Chicago: U of Chicago, 1981) 1-171.

describes the course of his work so far], one would all the more surely regress into idealism, with all of what, as we have just pointed out, cannot but link up with it, singularly in the figures of empiricism and formalism" ("Outwork" 43-44).[8]

If I consider this passage to be adversarial to my project here (though it was not, of course, written with any such intention), I provoke myself to restate my fundamental position, which I worked to define in the beginning. First, I do not recognize or appropriate Derrida's "writing" in this work, but Heidegger's language as disclosure. Second, the world and the human and things that are drawn into relation, and the nothing and death that pervade these with their "not," are not "reassuring" except in their nearness and mineness, and any project that excludes these has stepped into an illusory position. Without sacrificing the necessities of the strange, the other, the infinitely complex, the variable, indeed applying special intensity and rigor in addressing them, I have tried to traverse the terrain of the literary works. I have read under the "spur" of Derrida's opposition (perhaps his work has radicalized—sharpened and toughened—my reading of Heidegger and the modernists), but I believe I have read primarily and for the most part after the vision and along the way of Heidegger.

---

[8]*Dissemination* 1-171.

www.ingramcontent.com/pod-product-compliance
Lightning Source LLC
Chambersburg PA
CBHW071956040426
42447CB00009B/1352